The Betrayal of Anne Frank

ALSO BY ROSEMARY SULLIVAN

Stalin's Daughter: The Extraordinary and Tumultuous Life of Svetlana Alliluyeva
(winner of the 2016 Plutarch Prize and the RBC Charles Taylor Prize and finalist for the PEN America/Jacqueline Bograd Weld Award for Biography and the National Book Critics Circle Award, among other honors)

Villa Air-Bel: World War II, Escape, and a House in Marseille

Labyrinth of Desire: Women, Passion, and Romantic Obsession

Cuba: Grace Under Pressure

Memory-Making: Selected Essays of Rosemary Sullivan

The Red Shoes: Margaret Atwood Starting Out

Shadow Maker: The Life of Gwendolyn MacEwen

By Heart: Elizabeth Smart, a Life

The Guthrie Road

The Garden Master: The Poetry of Theodore Roethke

The Betrayal of Anne Frank

A Cold Case Investigation

Rosemary Sullivan

HARPER LARGE PRINT
An Imprint of HarperCollins*Publishers*

HarperCollins books may be purchased for educational, business, or sales promotional use. For information, please e-mail the Special Markets Department at SPsales@harpercollins.com or in Canada at HCOrder@harpercollins.com.

FIRST HARPER LARGE PRINT EDITION

ISBN: 978-0-06-306300-6

Library of Congress Cataloging-in-Publication Data is available upon request.

22 23 24 25 26 LSC 10 9 8 7 6 5 4 3 2 1

Contents

Preface
Memorial Day and the Memory of Unfreedom

I landed at Amsterdam's Schiphol Airport on Friday, May 3, 2019, and took a taxi to an address on Spuistraat, in the very center of Amsterdam. A woman from the Dutch Foundation for Literature was there to greet me and show me around the apartment I was to occupy for the next month. I'd come to Amsterdam to write a book about the cold case investigation into who betrayed Anne Frank and the other residents in the secret Annex on August 4, 1944, a mystery that had never been solved.

Most of us know the basic outline of the "Anne Frank story": that the Jewish teenager hid with her parents, her sister, and some family friends in an attic in Amsterdam for more than two years during the Nazi occupation of the Netherlands in World War II.

The group was eventually betrayed and sent to concentration camps, and only Otto Frank, Anne's father, survived. We know all of this largely because of the remarkable diary Anne left behind that August day when the Nazis came to take them away.

Part of the cultural narrative in the Netherlands, the Anne Frank story had always resonated strongly with the Dutch filmmaker Thijs Bayens, who in 2016 invited his friend the journalist Pieter van Twisk to join him in the project, which started out as a documentary but soon included a book. Momentum built slowly, but by 2018, there were at least twenty-two people working directly on the case, with numerous professional consultants offering their expertise. The investigation began with the challenge of identifying the betrayer, but it soon expanded. The Cold Case Team, as they came to be called, wanted to understand what happens to a population under enemy occupation when ordinary life is threaded with fear.

The day after I arrived, Saturday, May 4, was National Remembrance Day, when the Dutch remember the atrocities of World War II and commemorate the costly victory. Thijs Bayens had invited me to join him and his son Joachim in the silent procession through the streets of Amsterdam that marks the beginning of the memorial ceremonies.

We were perhaps two hundred people, though the crowd grew as we walked through the city. We listened briefly to the Roma orchestra playing in front of the opera house and then continued through the Jewish Quarter, passing the monumental Portuguese Synagogue, the Jewish Historical Museum, and the Hermitage, where memorial plaques were scattered over the ground. We turned left and followed the Amstel River, walking over the white, wooden "Magere Brug" (Skinny Bridge), which the Nazis had barricaded with barbed wire on February 12, 1941, to seal off the Jewish Quarter. (It had been opened again after a few days under pressure from the municipality.) We continued through the city's center until we arrived at "de Dam" (Dam Square). It was packed with about twenty-five thousand people who'd come to see the king and queen and to hear the mayor of Amsterdam, Femke Halsema, address the crowd. She said:

> *To write a note or call; to make your voice heard, or not; to embrace your lover; cross the street, or not; to come here tonight, to the Dam on May 4, or not. Each time, hundreds of times per day, we choose, without thinking, without constraint. . . . What does it do to a person to lose all freedom? To be occupied? When the space around your shrinks?*

Our freedom was preceded by pain and great sorrow. . . . That is why we pass on the memory of unfreedom, as if the war were yesterday. That is why we commemorate . . . this year, next year, and all the years after that.[1]

The next day, after I'd settled in, Thijs and I met for dinner. We talked about politics in Europe, particularly about growing xenophobia and anti-immigrant sentiments. Then I asked him why he had decided to undertake this cold case investigation. He said that as a filmmaker, you bring your own life into your work. He'd grown up in Amsterdam in the 1970s, when the city was well known all over the world for its idiosyncratic, free-spirited character. There were squatters, artist villages, peace demonstrations. Then you felt free and showed it. But all that has changed. In the Netherlands, in Europe, in North America, we are watching an inundation of racism and fear.

Months back, he'd been on the Prinsengracht and gotten stuck in a long line of visitors to the Anne Frank House. As he watched the crowd, it occurred to him that the Frank family and the others hiding in the attic had just been ordinary people in an ordinary neighborhood full of acquaintances and colleagues, neighbors and retailers, uncles and aunts. It was that simple. And then the creeping machinations of fascism had set in. Slowly but surely, human relationships had come under pressure and people had turned on one another.

Thijs left the crowd in front of the Anne Frank House and made a decision: he would begin a public conversation. Amsterdam was no longer a bastion of individualism. Where there was once tolerance, now there is distrust. At what point do we give up on one another? Whom do we stand up for? And for whom do we not stand up? The betrayal of Anne Frank would be the way into that conversation. Thijs told me that there is a sixty-foot-high mural in the north of Amsterdam that overlooks almost the entire city. It is a portrait of Anne with a quote from her diary: “Let me be myself.” “I think she’s talking to us,” he said.

Thijs wanted to show me something. We strolled to the nearby Torensluis, one of the widest bridges in Amsterdam, crossing over the Singel canal. Looming in front of me was a large sculpture on a marble plinth. Thijs said this was the nineteenth-century author Eduard Douwes Dekker, considered to be one of the Netherlands’ greatest authors. He was famous for his novel denouncing the abuses of colonialism in the Dutch East Indies. When Thijs added that the sculpture had been made by his father, Hans Bayens, I was taken aback. A number of his father’s sculptures are scattered through Amsterdam, Utrecht, Zwolle, and other cities.

Thijs explained that his father had rarely spoken of the war. It had been too traumatic. His mother said that years after the war ended, his father would often wake in the midst of a nightmare, his hands reaching toward the window, screaming that bombers were flying overhead.

Thijs never met his grandparents; both died before he was born. But he'd heard stories. What had left the greatest impression on him was his discovery that their house had been a *doorgangshuis* (transit place), used by the resistance to hide Jews. There were always a number of Jews hiding in their basement, some for weeks at a time, while the resistance looked for more permanent addresses where they could go underground.

When he started the Anne Frank project, Thijs spoke to his father's best friend to ask him what he remembered about the war. The friend told him to interview ninety-three-year-old Joop Goudsmit, who had stayed with Thijs's grandparents throughout the war. Goudsmit had become part of the Bayens family and was able to describe the house, the room in the basement where he had hidden, the banned radio concealed under the floorboards in the closet, and the number of Jews who had come through. He said that the risks the

Bayenses had taken, including contacts with forgers of identity cards, had been extreme.

It's baffling to think that Thijs's father never told him about that, but it was typical. After the war, so many claimed, falsely, to have been involved with the resistance that those who took the real risks, such as Thijs's grandparents, often preferred to remain silent. But the war had shaped Thijs's family, and he recognized that the search for what had led to the raid on the secret Annex would enable him to enter the labyrinth of his own family history. Anne Frank's is an iconic story, but it is also a terrifyingly familiar one, repeated hundreds of thousands of times throughout Europe. Thijs said he also saw it as a warning. "This must never be allowed to happen again," he said.

Part I

The Background Story

1
The Raid and the Green Policeman

On August 4, 1944, a thirty-three-year-old German SS officer, Karl Josef Silberbauer, a sergeant in the Sicherheitsdienst (SD) Referat IV B4, known colloquially as the "Jew-hunting unit," was sitting in his office on Euterpestraat in Amsterdam when the phone rang. He'd bseen about to go out for a bite to eat but answered anyway, something he'd later regret. It was his superior officer, Lieutenant Julius Dettmann, also a German, who said he'd just received a phone call claiming that there were Jews hiding in a warehouse complex at Prinsengracht 263 in central Amsterdam. Dettmann did not tell Silberbauer who'd placed the call, but it clearly was someone reliable and well known to the intelligence service of the SS. There had been too many instances of anonymous tips that had proved to be useless or outdated; by the time the Jew-hunting unit arrived, the Jews had moved on. That Dettmann acted directly after the call meant he trusted the source and knew the tip was well worth investigating.

Dettmann phoned Dutch Detective Sergeant Abraham Kaper at the Bureau of Jewish Affairs and ordered him to send several of his men to the Prinsengracht address with Silberbauer. Kaper pulled two Dutch policemen, Gezinus Gringhuis and Willem Grootendorst of the IV B4 unit, into the hunt, along with a third detective.

There are many variations in the accounts of what happened before and after Silberbauer and his men arrived at Prinsengracht 263. The only thing that's absolutely certain is that they found eight people in hiding: Otto Frank, his wife, Edith, and their two daughters, Anne and Margot; Frank's colleague and friend Hermann van Pels, his wife, Auguste, and son, Peter; and the dentist Fritz Pfeffer. The Dutch had a term for hiding: *onderduiken* (diving under).* They'd been diving under for two years and thirty days.

To be imprisoned, even unjustly, is one thing. But it

---

* There were between twenty-five thousand and twenty-seven thousand Jews in hiding in the Netherlands, one-third of whom would eventually be betrayed.

is entirely another to be in hiding. How is it possible to cope for twenty-five months with total incarceration—not to be able to look out a window for fear of being seen; never to walk outside or breathe fresh air; having to remain silent for hours on end so that the workers in the warehouse below would not hear you? The fear had to be extreme to keep to that discipline. Most people would have gone mad.

During those long hours of each workday, whispering an occasional word and tiptoeing while the employees moved below them, what did they do? They studied; they wrote. Otto Frank read history and novels; his favorites were the novels of Charles Dickens. The children studied English, French, and mathematics. Both Anne and Margot kept diaries. They were preparing for life after the war. They still believed in civilization and the future, while outside the Nazis with their accomplices and informants were hunting them.

By the summer of 1944, optimism had spread through the secret Annex. On the wall Otto had pinned a map of Europe and was following the news on the BBC and the Radio Oranje reports of the Dutch government in exile in London. The Germans had confiscated all radios to prevent the Dutch population from listening to foreign news, but Otto had managed to salvage a radio when they had gone into hiding and was now tracking the progress of the Allied forces through the nightly broadcasts. Two months earlier, on June 4, the Allies had captured Rome, followed two days later by D-Day, the largest amphibious invasion in history. By the end of June, the Americans were bogged down in Normandy, but on July 25 they launched Operation Cobra and the German resistance in northwest France collapsed. In the east, the Russians were moving into Poland. On July 20, members of the high command in Berlin had attempted to assassinate Hitler, which brought jubilation to the people in the Annex.

Suddenly it looked as though the war would be over in a matter of weeks, or maybe a few months. Everyone was making plans for what they would do after the war. Margot and Anne began to talk about going back to school.

And then the unimaginable happened. As Otto stated in an interview almost two decades later, "When the Gestapo came in with their guns, that was the end of everything."[1]

As the sole survivor among the eight, we have only Otto's record of what happened from the perspective of the Annex residents. He recalled the arrest in such vivid detail that it was clearly seared in his mind.

It was, he said, around ten thirty. He was upstairs

giving Peter van Pels an English grammar lesson. In taking dictation, Peter had misspelled the word "double" using two *b*'s. He was pointing this out to the boy when he heard someone's heavy footsteps on the stairs. This was disturbing because at that hour all the residents were very quiet lest they be heard in the offices below. The door opened. A man stood there pointing a gun at them. He was not wearing a police uniform. They raised their hands. They were marched downstairs at gunpoint.[2]

In his recounting of the raid, we get a sense of Otto's profound shock. During trauma, time slows and stretches out, and some details are strangely emphasized. Otto remembers a spelling error; a grammar lesson; a creaking stair; a pointed gun.

He remembers he was teaching Peter. He remembers the word that Peter stumbled on—"double"—with only one *b*. That's the rule. Otto believes in rules, in order, but a dark force is sweeping up his stairs with the intent to kill him and all he holds most precious. Why? Power, hatred, or simply because it can? Even in retrospect, Otto keeps the overwhelming horror at bay, maintaining his self-control because others depend on him. As he looks at the gun in the plainclothes policeman's hand, he thinks: *The Allies are advancing.* Luck, chance, fate, may save them all. But he is wrong. He and his family will be transported in freight cars on the last train to Auschwitz. It is unthinkable, but he also knows the unthinkable can happen.

When Otto and Peter reached the main floor of the Annex, they found everyone else standing with their hands up in the air. There were no hysterics, no weeping, only silence. Everyone is numbed by the shock of what was happening—now, so close to the end.

In the middle of the room Otto noted a man he assumed was from the Grüne Polizei, as the Dutch called the German local police force because of their green uniforms. This, of course, was Silberbauer (who was technically not a member of the Grüne Polizei but an SD officer), who later claimed that neither he nor the plainclothes policemen with him drew their weapons. But Otto's is the more trustworthy account. Like that of most SS members after the war, Silberbauer's testimony was designed only to exonerate himself.

The hiders' quiet composure seemed to anger the Nazi. When he ordered them to collect their things for the trip to Gestapo headquarters on Euterpestraat, Anne picked up her father's briefcase, which held her diary. Otto Frank reported that Silberbauer grabbed the briefcase from Anne, threw her diary with the checkered cover and some loose sheets onto the floor, and filled the briefcase with the last valuables and money that Otto and the others had managed to hold on to, including Fritz Pfeffer's little packet of dental gold. The Germans were losing the war. By now, much of the stolen booty collected for the Reich by the Jew-hunting units was ending up in someone's private pocket.

Ironically, it was Silberbauer's greed that saved Anne Frank's diary. Had Anne held on to the briefcase and been allowed to keep it when they were arrested, her diary would certainly have been taken from her at SD headquarters and destroyed or lost forever.

According to Otto, it was at this moment that Silberbauer noted a gray footlocker with metal stripes beneath the window. The lid displayed the words "Leutnant d. Res. Otto Frank" (Reserve Lieutenant Otto Frank). "Where did you get this chest?" Silberbauer demanded. When Otto told him that he'd served as an officer in World War I, Silberbauer seemed shocked. As Otto reported:

> *The man became exceedingly confused. He stared at me, and finally said:*
>
> *"Then why didn't you report your status?"*
>
> *I bit my lips.*
>
> *"Why man you would have been treated decently! You would have been sent to Theresienstadt."*

I said nothing. Apparently he thought Theresienstadt a rest camp, so I said nothing. I merely looked at him. But he suddenly evaded my eyes, and all at once the perception came to me: Now he is standing at attention. Inwardly, this police sergeant had snapped to attention; if he dared, he might very well raise his hand to his cap in salute.

Then he abruptly turned on his heel and raced upstairs. A moment later he came running down, and then he ran up again, and so he went, up and down, up and down, calling out: "Take your time!"

He shouted these same words to us and to his agents.[3]

In Otto's account it is the Nazi who loses his composure, running up and down like the Mad Hatter, while he and the others retain theirs. Otto has caught the German military cult of obedience in Silberbauer's instinctive response to his officer status, but he may have underestimated Silberbauer's automatic, reflexive racism. Years later, he would say, "Perhaps he [Silberbauer] might have spared us if he'd been alone."[4]

This is doubtful. After he'd delivered the prisoners to the truck waiting to transport them to Gestapo headquarters for interrogation, Silberbauer returned to the building to confront one of the office workers, Miep

Gies. Perhaps he'd spared her from arrest because she, like him, was Austrian, but not before lecturing her, "And weren't you ashamed to help that Jewish trash?"[5]

Karl Silberbauer would later claim that it was years before he learned, by reading it in a newspaper, that among the ten people he'd arrested that day was fifteen-year-old Anne Frank.

When tracked down by an investigative journalist in 1963, Silberbauer said:

> *The people I took from their hiding places, did not leave an impression on me. It would have been different if it had been a man such as general De Gaulle or some major resistance member or other. Such a thing you don't forget. If I wasn't on the clock at the moment my colleague got a call. . . . I would never have come in contact with that Anne Frank. I still remember that I was just about to go out to eat something. And because this whole case blew up after the war, I am the one dealing with the mess. . . . I wonder who is behind all this. Probably that Wiesenthal or someone at the ministry trying to gain the favor of the Jews.*[6]

It is hard to imagine a more despicable, emotionally cauterized response. By now Silberbauer knew very well that "that Anne Frank," whom he'd arrested on August 4, 1944, had died of starvation and typhus in Bergen-Belsen concentration camp. It was as if what mattered was not the dead child—she is incidental, not real, her suffering is insignificant—but that he is the victim. How strange that the bully, unmasked, is always awash in self-pity.

2

The Diary of Anne Frank

The Diary of Anne Frank is one of the most harrowing books we will read if we read it for what it truly is: a thirteen-year-old girl's daily account of life in hiding during the terrifying Nazi occupation of her city. Anne Frank catches every detail of the more than two years of claustrophobic life she spent with her family in the Annex attached to her father's company.

She knows what is out there. Like the other seven people with whom she shares the space, she lives with constant fear, hunger, nightmares of abduction, and the imminent threat of discovery and death. She is not the first to experience this, but she may be one of the first to write about it as it is happening. The other masterpieces we have about the Holocaust—Elie Wiesel's *Night*, Primo Levi's *If This Is a Man*—are all written in retrospect by people who survived. But Anne Frank will not survive.

And this is what makes reading her diary so harrowing. From the beginning, we know the ending, but Anne Frank does not.

Anne Frank received the diary as a gift for her thirteenth birthday on June 12, 1942. Less than a month later, on July 6, her family went into hiding after her sixteen-year-old sister, Margot, was sent a summons to report for *Arbeitseinsatz*, compulsory work duty in Germany. Otto Frank already understood that "work duty" was a euphemism for slave labor.

Longing for an intimate companion, Anne Frank invented a friend named Kitty, to whom she writes with complete and utter candor. She writes in her diary about hope, about the mysteries of her female body, about her passionate adolescent crush on the seventeen-year-old boy whose family shared the Annex with the Franks. Anne is still a child: she cuts out images of movie stars and royals and pastes them onto her bedroom wall. Though she was born in Frankfurt, Germany, having arrived in the Netherlands at the age of four and a half, her primary language is now Dutch, the language in which she writes her diary. Her ambition is to become a writer. She dreams of a future when she will be famous. For the reader, all this is shattering since we know that for her, there will be no future.

The world Anne lives in is unrecognizable to us. In July 1943, the family discovers she needs eyeglasses. Miep Gies, one of the helpers of those in the Annex, offers to take her to an ophthalmologist, but Anne is petrified at the thought of stepping out into the street. When she tries to put on her coat, the family discovers she has outgrown it, and that, along with her paleness, would have easily identified her as a Jew in hiding. She does not get the glasses. By August 1944, she will not have walked outside for twenty-five months.

Open windows could alert people in adjacent businesses that the Annex is occupied. To breathe fresh air, the fourteen-year-old Anne must lean down to suck in the bit of air that comes across the windowsill. In her diary she writes that being cooped up in the small rooms is unbelievably claustrophobic, and the silence the hiders must maintain adds a level of terror that never seems to diminish. She finds herself climbing the stairs, up and down, trapped like a caged creature. The only solution is sleep, and even sleep is interrupted by fear.[1]

But she always rallies. She tells "Kitty" that the way to conquer fear and loneliness is to seek solitude in nature and commune with God—as if, for a moment, sitting in the window of the attic space looking up at the pale sky, she could forget that she cannot leave the Annex. How is it possible that she can be so ebullient, so affirmative, so full of life in the midst of such terrifying repression?

Toward the end of her diary, Anne records a particularly frightening night when thieves break into the warehouse and someone, possibly the police, bangs on the bookcase that camouflages the entrance to the secret Annex.

Anne tells Kitty that she believed she would be killed. When she survived the night, her first impulse was to declare that she would dedicate herself to the things she loved: the Netherlands, the Dutch language, and writing. And she would not be stopped until she fulfilled her purpose.[2]

It's an extraordinary declaration for an adolescent just about to turn fifteen. Anne Frank's last entry in her diary is dated August 1, 1944, three days before she and her family and the others in hiding are arrested. Otto Frank will be the only one of the eight residents of the Annex to return from the camps.

After they were liberated at the end of the war, many survivors found it impossible to put what they'd experienced into words. It took the author Elie Wiesel ten years before he could write *Night*. He asked, "How was one to rehabilitate and transform words betrayed and perverted by the enemy? Hunger—thirst—fear—transport—selection—fire—chimney: these words all have intrinsic meaning, but in those times, they meant something else." How could you write without usurping and profaning the appalling suffering in that "demented and glacial universe where to be inhuman was to be human, where disciplined, educated men in uniform came to kill?"[3]

When Primo Levi submitted his book *If This Is a Man* to Einaudi Publishers in Turin in 1947, both Cesare Pavese, by then immensely famous, and Natalia Ginzburg, whose husband had been murdered by the Germans in Rome, turned it down. Levi tried numerous publishers; all rejected the book. It was too soon, they said. "Italians had other things to worry about . . . than reading of the German death camps. Italians wanted to say, 'It's all over. *Basta!* Enough of this horror!'"[4]

The play *The Diary of Anne Frank* and later the movie build to the climax of Anne's comment in the last pages of her diary:

> *It's a wonder I haven't abandoned all my ideals, they seem so absurd and impossible. Yet I keep*

> *clinging to them, because I still believe, in spite of everything that people are truly good at heart.*[5]

It was impossible for people to face what had happened: murder on an industrial scale; mass graves annihilating all personal memory of the dead. In both play and movie, references to "Germans" were changed to "Nazis," and the Jewish experience was toned down. For example, mention of Yom Kippur was eliminated. This was supposedly done to strengthen the story's secular, universal appeal. The translator of the German edition of the diary, which came out in 1950, blurred "every hostile reference to Germans and German" on the grounds that "a book intended after all for sale in Germany cannot abuse the Germans."[6]

But it is as if the diary is a living document. Its reception changes with what we know or are willing to confront. Beginning in the 1960s, books, films, museums, and monuments were created to memorialize the Holocaust. People were finally ready to face up to the madness that was Nazism and willing to examine the indifference to violence that had allowed fascism to spread like a virus.

More apropos to our understanding now would be Anne's comment toward the end of her diary: "There's a destructive urge in people, the urge to rage, murder and kill. And until all of humanity, without exception, undergoes a metamorphosis, wars will continue to be waged."[7]

You might wonder: What is the point of questioning who betrayed Anne Frank in a war that happened so long ago? The answer is that almost eight decades since the end of the war, we seem to have grown complacent, thinking, as the Dutch once thought, that it cannot happen here. But contemporary society seems to be increasingly susceptible to ideological divisiveness and the lure of authoritarianism, forgetting the simple truth that incipient fascism metastasizes if allowed to go unchecked.

Anne Frank's world makes this clear. What are the real tools of war? Not only physical violence but rhetorical violence. In attempting to determine how Adolf Hitler had taken control, the US Office of Strategic Services commissioned a report in 1943 that explained his strategy: "Never to admit a fault or wrong; never to accept blame; concentrate on one enemy at a time; blame that enemy for everything that goes wrong; take advantage of every opportunity to raise a political whirlwind."[8] Soon hyperbole, extremism, defamation, and slander become commonplace and acceptable vehicles of power.

To look at the transformation of a city such as Amsterdam under occupation is to understand that although there were those who supported the Nazis, whether out of opportunism, self-deception, venality, or cowardice, and those who opposed them, the majority simply tried to keep their heads down.

What happens when people cannot trust the institutions that are supposed to protect them? What happens when the fundamental laws that constitute and protect decent behavior crumble? The Netherlands in 1940 was like a petri dish in which one can examine how people brought up in freedom react to catastrophe when it is brought to their door. It is a question still worth asking today.

3

The Cold Case Team

The office of the Cold Case Team is located in the northern reaches of the city, which requires taking a ferry from Amsterdam Central Station across the IJ River, which connects the main city with Amsterdam-Noord. With its twin clock towers, turrets, and Gothic Renaissance facade, the station is so large that it could easily pass for a royal palace until you enter and see the stores, restaurants, railway tracks, subway entrances, and ferry docks. Walking through it today and stepping onto a boat on the Amstel River, with most of the passengers leaning on their bicycles, feels almost surreal; the freedom of it all is so seductive. But it isn't hard to imagine the goose-stepping Wehrmacht marching through the huge building or, out in the square, men, women, and children being herded down the street by soldiers with truncheons, a sight that devastated Anne Frank as she peered through a narrow slit in the curtains in the front office of Prinsengracht 263.

The team's office, in a newly developed residential area, turned out to be a large room organized into sections for investigators and research and administrative personnel. I was told that by January 2019 the office housed a team of twenty-three people, with an "ops room," timelines on the walls, and highly secure access. A soundproof MuteCube enabled up to four people to confer privately.

One of the walls was filled with photographs of the Nazi hierarchy, their Dutch SD collaborators, and the informants called V-Männen (Men) and V-Frauen (Women)—the *V* stands for *vertrouwens*, or trust—who played a role in the persecution of Jews. Beneath this photo gallery sat a small three-dimensional model of Prinsengracht 263, with the Annex at the back.

On the wall opposite were photos of the residents of the secret Annex: the Frank family, the Van Pels family, and Fritz Pfeffer, and also of the helpers: Johannes Kleiman, Victor Kugler, Bep Voskuijl, and Miep and Jan Gies. The walls of the ops room were covered by maps of wartime Amsterdam and a timeline filled with photos and clippings that represented important events concerning the betrayal.

A three-and-a-half-foot square print of an aerial photo of the Prinsengracht canal taken from an English RAF airplane on August 3, 1944, covered a large part of another wall. It had been shot just twelve hours prior to the arrest of the people in the Annex. In the photo you can clearly distinguish Otto Frank's office and warehouse and the Annex behind it. The people in hiding were still inside. They had no idea that they were spending their last night in what passed for freedom. Thijs told me that looking at the map gave the team an uncanny sense of connection with the hiders, as if time were suspended.

Thijs's partner, Pieter van Twisk, has the cragginess of all bibliophiles, which must come from their thoroughness and obsession with detail; you can be sure that any conclusions he reaches are backed up by proof. Like Thijs, Pieter found that the research the Cold Case Team had undertaken had turned out to be much more personal than he'd originally expected. In the early stages of the project, he was looking for information in the archives of the city of Groningen about a Dutch collaborator named Pieter Schaap. Toward the end of the war, Schaap had been in Groningen hunting down a resistance leader named Schalken. To Pieter the name Schalken sounded vaguely familiar.

Eventually he discovered a document in the Groningen Archives that acknowledged and registered people who had been in the resistance. It confirmed that Schalken had been one of the leaders of the National Fighting Squads (Landelijke Knokploegen; KP), the fighting arm of the resistance. It also indicated that he had been in hiding in the house of Pieter's grandparents. He'd heard the story before in the family but had never taken it seriously.

The document he found listed the name of his grandfather Pieter van Twisk, after whom he'd been named, with text at the bottom of the page:

> *Was this risky and why? Yes, for the duration of his resistance career his was the contact address of the KP, the OD and the LO etc. Several prominent resistance fighters, among them Schalken, found shelter at the family house. The above-mentioned people were wanted by the SD. Earlier he was being useful in the hiding of weapons.*[1]

Schalken was never caught, nor were Pieter's grandparents arrested. Pieter remembered his uncle, who had been a young boy during the war, telling him that he'd looked up to Schalken. Once, during a Nazi raid, the man calmly walked out of the house, stopped, lit a cigarette, and, very relaxed, stepped onto his bike and rode off. None of the Nazi officers suspected that he was the one they were looking for.

Clearly, it's hard to find a family in the Netherlands that does not have a story connecting it to the war.

In the decades after the war, the popular narrative was that most Dutch people had been against the Nazis and many people had been in or supported the resistance. During the postwar period, most European countries clung to this narrative, but reality was much less monochromatic. In the last thirty years, Pieter believes, a more nuanced picture has emerged about the Netherlands and the Holocaust, first among historians and now also among part of the population.

His is the country that gave birth to Baruch Spinoza, the philosopher of liberalism, and had a long history of tolerance that led many Jews to seek refuge there after Hitler's rise to power in 1933. Anti-Semitism there was mild in comparison to that in many other European countries. Yet the Netherlands transported more Jews to their deaths in extermination camps in the east than any other country in Western Europe. Of the 140,000 Jews living in the Netherlands, 107,000 were deported and only 5,500 returned.

Pieter said that one of his motivations for joining the project was that he needed to understand why the numbers in the Netherlands were so high. Is racism like a pathogen in the human psyche and certain circumstances can activate it? In the Resistance Museum (Verzetsmuseum) in Amsterdam, the crudity of Nazi anti-Semitic propaganda was vicious and unrelenting. Posters of murderous "Jewish Bolsheviks" standing over bodies; a bloodied crucifix on the floor; grotesque caricatures of rapacious Jews in bowler hats and suits; terrifying images of Jews as subhuman cultural parasites. How could people believe such propaganda? By studying the society that Anne Frank lived in, Pieter hoped he might come to understand what had happened, the only way never to repeat it.

Having decided to launch an investigation into what led to the raid on the Annex, Thijs and Pieter searched for funding from a variety of sources, including crowdsourcing, the Municipality of Amsterdam, and private investors, as well as publishers. They then set out to build a team of Dutch investigators, historians, and researchers. These included Luc Gerrits, a former homicide detective; major crimes investigator Leo Simais, the head of the Cold Cases and Missing Persons Department of the National Police Corps; several retired detectives; and one investigator from the General Intelligence and Security Service (AIVD).

At the first meeting of the team, on June 30, 2016, Leo introduced the so-called FOT sessions: with your "feet on the table," you start talking, brainstorming, analyzing. Where to start? Leo couldn't have been clearer—with the suspected phone call that the betrayer made to the SD about Jews hiding in a warehouse at Prinsengracht 263. How probable was it that the phone call actually took place? In Amsterdam in 1944, were there any public phone booths left? Had the copper telephone lines not been turned into weaponry? Was the SD phone number publicly known? And so on.

In this preliminary stage of the investigation, it quickly became clear that the Amsterdam police force during the Nazi occupation had played a questionable role. Like every other official body in the Netherlands, the police had had to collaborate to a certain extent with the Nazis during the occupation, but it seemed that a number of them had gone further in helping the Nazis than was strictly necessary.

So Thijs suggested that it would be good to have an independent outsider, someone non-Dutch, on the team. He asked Luc if he could find an FBI agent to lead the cold case. Betrayal is a nonforensic crime, since there are no physical traces, and the Cold Case Team would need to work with cutting-edge methods of information gathering to make headway. Luc turned to Hans Smit, the head of the National Police Corps undercover branch, who had been trained by the FBI. Smit suggested that Thijs call an old colleague from the FBI undercover unit who had only recently retired. "He's the guy you are looking for," Smit said. "His name is Vince Pankoke."

Soon Thijs and Pieter skyped with Vince, who was living in Florida. Both were impressed by the kind and clearly highly professional investigator, who said he was intrigued by the project.

After eight years as a police officer, Vince had spent twenty-seven years as a special agent with the FBI, working undercover on high-profile cases against Colombian drug traffickers.

He had also worked the case against Sky Capital, whose CEO, Ross Mandell, might be considered to be a bit like the fictional character Gordon Gekko in the movie *Wall Street*. To meet Vince, you would never suspect him of having such a past. He still seems to be living undercover, a mild, anonymous man in a guayabera shirt, until you discover his passion for dangerous motorcycle races or his thirst for new challenges.

Vince has an affable nature, talking easily about his family and his German heritage. His father had fought in the US Army in World War II. Even when he was a kid and his father told him stories of the war, it struck him that the soldiers his father was shooting at could have been relatives. It is evident that Vince believes in evil and has seen a lot of it. The Russian author Aleksandr Solzhenitsyn, fresh from the gulags, once said that the world has a certain tolerance level for evil; there will always be evil in the world. But when that tolerance level is surpassed, all morality cracks and human beings become capable of anything.

How, Vince wondered out loud, did German culture—sophisticated, advanced, democratic—submit to totalitarian dictatorship and so disintegrate, so lose its way, that it initiated a war that would eventually kill an estimated 75 million people, Allied and Axis, civilian and military? With his FBI undercover experience, Vince knows that one element is always present: somebody is making money. German industrialists bankrolled Hitler in secret from 1933, and the war proved profitable to them, with Bayer, BMW, Krupp, Daimler, and IG Farben emerging richer than they had gone in. In the occupied Netherlands, Vince understood that the bureaucratic ingenuity the Germans called on to remove all Jews from the country was matched only by the stealth with which they plundered Jewish property.

Like almost every other American, Vince learned about Anne Frank in school. He visited the Anne Frank House when he was well into his career—and was astonished to find that the question "Who betrayed Anne Frank?" has never been decisively answered. He said he loved nothing better than a challenge, and so he signed on to the cold case investigation immediately. But when he was well into the project, he had moments of wondering what he'd gotten himself into: the case was more than seventy-five years old, the betrayer and most of the immediate witnesses were probably dead, and there were so many other complexities. "We couldn't get any tougher circumstances," he said. Still, he couldn't shake the feeling that this was what he needed to do. One of his first steps was to build a team of experts on wartime police matters, Amsterdam history, collaborators, looting Dutch fascists, and the resistance.

Monique Koemans, who works as a criminal analyst for the Dutch government, joined the team in October 2018. Besides obtaining a PhD in criminology, she had also trained as a historian. When she found an email in her mailbox with an invitation to join the Cold Case Team, she didn't hesitate. It's not often that a project calls on her skills as a criminologist as well as historian. She requested a one-year leave from her job.

Monique read Anne Frank's diary more than twenty times when she was young and wrote about Anne Frank at the beginning of her career as a journalist. The case of the betrayal may be old, but she feels that the present is never far from the past.

At least in Amsterdam, remnants of the war are everywhere in the streets—on her way to work she used to pass the offices of *Het Parool*, a national newspaper that was started in 1941 as the resistance newspaper. In The Hague, where she now lives, she says the scars of the war are deep. Walking through Bezuidenhout, a neighborhood in the city where her grandparents lived and where her grandmother barely survived a devastating bombing, she passed the house where her grandfather was in hiding while he worked for a resistance newspaper. Her former neighbor was the son of a Holocaust survivor. He told her that at the end of the war a train full of prisoners coming from Bergen-Belsen concentration camp was left abandoned by the Nazis in the middle of a forest. His mother and grandmother were on that train. They managed to survive by eating berries until Allied troops finally found them. For his mother, leaving Bergen-Belsen at that moment meant that she survived the war. Anne and Margot Frank, who were kept behind in the same concentration camp, did not.

Several other young historians—Christine Hoste, Circe de Bruin, and Anna Foulidis—undertook much of the research work in the city's archives, including at the NIOD Institute for War, Genocide and Holocaust Studies and the Stadsarchief Amsterdam. They pored over thousands of files, took notes and wrote reports, set up appointments, and prepared the interviews. When asked how their research into the Holocaust had impacted them, they said it had been painful to enter that past but at least they had been focused on the Netherlands, for instance, Westerbork transit camp (now a museum), where they interviewed the museum director. Christine said she didn't believe she could have coped with the camps inside Germany and Poland.

Thijs invited his friend Jean Hellwig, a guest professor of public history at the University of Amsterdam, to join the team as project manager. It was a natural follow-up to his earlier project, Warlovechild, which had collected stories, films, and photos about children of Dutch soldiers abandoned after the colonial war in Indonesia between 1945 and 1949.* "With my own eyes I saw the healing potential of finding historical truth," he said. Jean then invited eleven students to help with the search, allowing them to do their university internship with the Cold Case Team.

The final addition to the team was Brendan Rook, a detective who'd served as an infantry officer in the Australian Army and spent more than ten years with the International Criminal Court in The Hague investigating war crimes, crimes against humanity, and genocide around the globe. While Vince was still with the FBI, he'd worked closely with the Dutch National Police Corps, and one of his principal contacts from that time introduced him to Luc Gerrits. Vince mentioned to Luc that he needed someone to bounce his ideas off, a fellow investigator able to isolate and focus

---

*One hundred thirty thousand young Dutchmen were sent to Indonesia to win back the colony, and many of the atrocities of that period are still wrapped in silence. After the colonial war was lost, the soldiers retreated, leaving behind abandoned, fatherless children, who were often despised by the locals because they were half Dutch. The history of the colonial war became tangible when Jean met some of those children, now in their sixties, and also their long-lost fathers and relatives. He, too, is half Dutch, half Indonesian, although of a later generation.

on the facts that might lead to solving the crime. Luc met Brendan in The Hague and, after learning about his investigative background, mentioned the Cold Case Team to him. Brendan was extremely interested and soon arranged for a leave of absence from his work to join the team.

Vince and Brendan are kindred spirits. They share a unique way of seeing things. Whereas the Anne Frank House is a museum where hundreds of visitors line up outside, for them it was a crime scene. They pictured the events of August 4, 1944, and exactly where they took place on that pitiful morning.

Brendan said that each time he visits a crime scene, he discovers new details. Standing in front of the building today, looking at its four floors, its front attic, the windows, he knows one thing for sure: a professional policeman would certainly have deduced the existence of the back Annex, and it wouldn't have taken him long to find the secret entrance.

4
The Stakeholders

In this increasingly complex cold case investigation, Vince was an outsider watching, as it were, from the periphery and having to figure out things that were self-evident to the Dutch. The upside of this was that he could remain dispassionate in the face of developments that drove the others crazy. The first shock to the group was the degree of acrimony among the various stakeholders of the Anne Frank legacy.

Thijs described the first meeting he and Pieter had had with a man he referred to as "from the world of Anne Frank," namely Jan van Kooten, a former head of education and presentations (1983–2004) at the Anne Frank House.[1] Thijs had asked Van Kooten if they could meet to discuss the organizations devoted to the story of the Franks. He wanted to know how the various groups worked and how they collaborated.

On Friday, March 4, 2016, Thijs and Pieter visited the office of the National Committee for May 4 and 5, the Dutch institution responsible for the annual Remembrance Day and Liberation Day celebrations.[2] Van Kooten, currently the director, sat behind his large desk, looking rather intimidating. Thijs and Pieter were somewhat anxious, as it was the first official conversation in which they had to explain their idea: an investigation into what is popularly called "the betrayal of Anne Frank." Their first questiosn was cautious: What do we need to know when we start?

Van Kooten quickly pulled a blank sheet of paper and a marker from a drawer. For just a moment he stared at the paper. Then he started to draw circles and lines. He spoke softly but firmly. The two men could sense that he knew the world he described intimately and that he was choosing his words carefully—very carefully.

The drawing became increasingly complex, and it was clear that the world they were entering was difficult to explain. The essence was this.

There are three versions of Anne Frank's diary:

A. *The original journal.*

B. *Anne's rewriting of the diary in her last months before the raid on the Annex. (In a broadcast on Radio Oranje on March 28, 1944, the Dutch minister of education, art, and science advised people to preserve their diaries so that there would be a chronicle of what the nation had gone through and survived. Anne rewrote her diary with the ambition of having it published.)*[3]

C. *The rewritten diary with adjustments by (or under the supervision of) Otto Frank. This is the version that has been published all over the world.*

There are two Anne Frank foundations, both founded by Otto Frank:

1. *Anne Frank House (AFS)/Anne Frank Stichting (Foundation) in Amsterdam. This was established in 1957 by Otto Frank to save the house and Annex at Prinsengracht 263 from demolition. The main objectives of the foundation are the management of the Anne Frank House and the propagation of the life story and ideals of Anne Frank. The foundation*

develops exhibitions, educational programs, and publications based on Anne's life. It also manages the Anne Frank collection and opens the "hiding place" to the public.

2. *Anne Frank Fonds (AFF) in Basel, Switzerland. This was founded in 1963 by Otto Frank to distribute his daughter's diary and manage the copyright of the Frank family.* * *The Anne Frank Fonds has an educational center in Frankfurt, supports many charities, and is active in the field of books, films, and plays.*

Fair enough. But now things get more complicated. Version A of the diary is owned by the Dutch state. Version B used to be the property of the Anne Frank House in Amsterdam but now belongs to the Anne Frank Fonds in Basel, and in any case the image rights, including images of the text, have always belonged to the Fonds. Version C is also the property of the Anne Frank Fonds.

The two organizations have gone through quite a few lawsuits disputing copyright ownership. Whatever you

---

* Now held by Otto's nephews and nieces, including Buddy and Stephen Elias (the sons of Otto's sister, Leni).

do with the one could therefore have an impact on the other. That was the essence of Van Kooten's graphic.

In the very first phase of the project, Thijs was drinking tea with a friend and explaining his thoughts about the cold case investigation. The friend told him that on one of his visits to the luxurious hotel La Colombe d'Or in the south of France, he'd run into one of the board members of the Anne Frank Fonds (AFF). (The hotel is well known for its art by Pablo Picasso, Henri Matisse, Marc Chagall, and many other famous artists, who left their works on the walls as payment in kind for their stays.) Thijs's friend said that when they were ready, he would set up a telephone call between Thijs and the board member. Thijs waited until he was certain that the project was funded and ready to go forward. When they finally spoke, the AFF board member let Thijs know that he was not very receptive to the project but would nevertheless discuss it with the other board members. That led to an invitation to visit the AFF headquarters, and on Wednesday, September 28, 2018, Thijs, Pieter, and Vince took a one-hour flight to Basel.

The Fonds is located near the old center of Basel in a modern and very unobtrusive office building. The interior is luxurious but not lavish. The meeting took place in a small room with five members of the board of trustees present, including President John D. Goldsmith, Vice President Daniel Fürst, and Secretary Yves Kugelmann. The conversation was jovial and pleasant for an hour or more as sandwiches were passed around. Everyone introduced themselves briefly, and then Thijs, Pieter, and Vince spoke about their research ideas and motivation for taking on the project. Vince remembered that Goldsmith had seemed quite skeptical; he had asked why they had started an investigation and whether there was some new information to justify it.

Vince explained that the purpose of a cold case investigation was to review previously unearthed information in the hope of finding new clues. In this case, earlier investigations had been done with too narrow a focus. New techniques and technologies could bring fresh insights. After that, the board members seemed somewhat less skeptical. The atmosphere was so friendly and pleasant that Vince began to entertain the hope that the board members would pledge their cooperation. That optimism came to an abrupt end when Kugelmann asked if they already had a name for the project.

Thijs replied that the working title was "A Cold Case Diary: Anne Frank." The room immediately became quiet. Kugelmann started to speak. He said that they really objected to that. Why misuse the name Anne Frank for the study? Did they not know that the name Anne Frank was protected and that the AFF owned the trademark rights? The Cold Case Team would not be allowed to use her name. And wasn't it particularly unethical to make money on the back of the poor girl? After all, the betrayal was not about Anne alone, it was about all eight people hiding in the Annex—and it was also about 107,000 other Jews who'd been taken from the Netherlands and were not named Anne Frank. Why did the Netherlands claim Anne, anyway? She was first of all a German girl and a Jewish girl and not a Dutch girl! For that reason, they supported the Anne Frank House in Frankfurt. In fact, for them, it was simply incomprehensible that there was an Anne Frank House in Amsterdam.

Vince, Thijs, and Pieter were dumbfounded. Pieter in particular was outraged. The AFF was reproaching them for trying to make money from the name Anne Frank? The same AFF that has rights to one of the best selling and most profitable books of all time? Anne foremost a German girl? Wasn't she stateless and more or less expelled from her country by a regime that deemed her an *Untermensch*? Did she not write in her diary that it was her greatest wish to become a Dutch national as well as a famous writer? Didn't she write her diary in Dutch? If she had survived the war, she might have had second thoughts about becoming Dutch, but that was clearly her intention.

Kugelmann said he saw opportunities for support and collaboration, but only if the Cold Case Team did not use the name Anne Frank. It could even cooperate with a research group that was already financed by the AFF. Although the atmosphere had clearly cooled, everyone still behaved courteously. Thijs indicated that they had not anticipated that condition as the basis of future cooperation and they needed to think about it.

And then Kugelmann spoke the words Thijs, Vince, and Pieter would not soon forget. He said that the team would never be able to solve the case without the help of the Anne Frank Fonds, insinuating that the Fonds possessed something that was key to solving the mystery. If it did have something, it would likely be in its archives, but it was unclear what specific evidence Kugelmann meant. As the three men were leaving, Goldsmith pulled Vince aside and said, "You know that Otto lied to Wiesenthal about knowing the identity of Silberbauer. Why do you think he did this?" Vince replied that he didn't know yet but was determined to find out. This was the first time the Cold Case Team understood that Otto Frank had held back secrets.

A few weeks later, Thijs had a short phone call with

a board member, who asked if the team had reconsidered using the Anne Frank name in the title of the investigation, the book, or the film. When Thijs replied that they had not, the board member let him know that the AFF was not interested in a collaboration. Later, when the investigation was at full speed, Thijs sent a letter to the AFF inviting the board to visit the team's headquarters, which it politely declined. Also, Vince officially asked for access to the AFF archive in a letter that was answered two months later with a formal request for more details. Though he provided the requested information, silence followed.

And so the Cold Case Team learned lesson number one: the entities devoted to maintaining the legacy of Anne Frank were more mysterious and complex than even Jan's labyrinthine graphic had suggested. And the team had no idea how much, much more complicated everything would become.*

---

* As it turned out, we did not receive permission from the AFF to quote from the letters of Otto Frank, although those we selected had been published in other books.

5

"Let's See What the Man Can Do!"

Otto Frank was born in Frankfurt in 1889. On his mother's side he could trace his ancestral roots in Germany back to the sixteenth century. He'd fought in the First World War, responding to the call "Patriotic Jews, fight for your country!" and had been promoted to lieutenant for his bravery in leading reconnaissance missions. He'd been in the trenches in France during the Battle of the Somme, which had seen 1.5 million casualties. He'd known loneliness, isolation, and fear in war. Perhaps that was why he wrote to his sister in 1917 that love and family must take precedence in a human life.[1]

Those who knew Otto Frank spoke of a man of merry, even jocular, temperament who was lively and full of energy but also private; he kept his own counsel. He'd met his Jewish wife in Germany, and his two daughters had been born there. He was not observant. His attachment to Germany was as strong as his attachment to his Jewish heritage.

Soon after Germany's defeat in 1918, Jews were scapegoated for the country's humiliation. Angry crowds attacked Jews on the streets of Berlin, blaming them for food shortages, for inflation, for the war that Germany itself had started. And a young man in prison in 1924 began writing a book, *Mein Kampf.* He ranted:

> *The discovery of the Jewish virus is one of the greatest revolutions that has taken place in the world. . . . If, with the help of his Marxist creed, the Jew is victorious over the other peoples of the world, his crown will be the funeral wreath of humanity and this planet will, as it did thousands of years ago, move through the ether devoid of men. . . . by defending myself against the Jew, I am fighting the work of the Lord.*[2]

Those who espouse conspiracy theories, with their superlatives, always suggest that the survival of humankind is at stake. And there is always an enemy, here the Bolshevik Jew. In that case it worked.

As soon as Hitler was appointed chancellor in January 1933, the persecution of Jews began. The process was remarkably bureaucratic, systematic, and devious. In March 1933, the SS established Dachau as a camp for political prisoners; by 1938, it was converted into the first World War II concentration camp. Extensive propaganda spread theories of racial hygiene, which claimed Jews were genetically unfit. The firing of Jews from their jobs and the confiscation of Jewish property soon followed.

For Otto Frank, the decree separating Jewish and non-Jewish children in schools, which forced his elder daughter, Margot, to sit apart from her non-Jewish classmates, was the defining moment. He said he would not raise his daughters "like horses with blinkers, ignorant of the social landscape outside their small group."[3] He wanted his daughters to be part of the world, not isolated as inferiors, as pariahs, and by implication, he wanted his country to be part of the world, not isolated by an absurd sense of Aryan superiority.

Otto Frank was forty-four and thoroughly German—friends smiled at his Prussian self-restraint—but he was also prescient. In January 1933, he and his wife were having dinner with German friends when the announcement of Hitler's election win came on the radio. He and Edith looked at each other in horror as the friends remarked, "Let's see what the man can do!"[4]

For those friends, Hitler was the strongman who would bring order and make the country great again after the terrible Depression. They thought they could cope with his "eccentricities."

That night, Otto and Edith discussed how to leave Germany. Otto had been watching the rise of nationalism and knew how dangerous it could be. He asked himself how he would be able to support his family, since flight would mean giving up everything. Where could they go? Much of his extended family had already left Germany. In 1932, his older brother, Herbert, had fled to Paris, where his cousin Jean-Michel Frank had become a talented designer working with artists such as Salvador Dalí. His younger brother, Robert, and Robert's wife, Lottie, had emigrated to England in the summer of 1933 and opened an art dealership in a basement gallery on St. James's Street in London. His sister, Helene, called Leni, and her husband, Erich Elias, lived in Basel, Switzerland, where Erich was a founding member of Opekta, a branch of the Frankfurt company Pomosin Werke, which produced pectin, the gelling agent in jam. In 1933, Otto's mother, Alice Frank, had emigrated to Basel to join her daughter.

When Otto looked at his choices of countries, he saw that England and the United States were out. He told himself that he did not speak English well enough.

How would he earn a living? He knew his siblings would help in whatever way they could, but they were also struggling, and he did not want to burden them even more. He thought that France might work. But then his brother-in-law Erich wrote that his company wanted to expand into the international market and asked Otto to open an Opekta office in Amsterdam.

Otto had spent time in Amsterdam in 1923 setting up a subsidiary branch of his father's bank, Michael Frank & Sons. Unfortunately, the project failed within a year as the family faced bankruptcy, and Otto was forced to return to Germany. But he had liked the city, and the Dutch were known for their tolerance. Hadn't they remained neutral in the First World War? In early August 1933, Otto Frank became a refugee. Packing his country in his suitcase with his shoes, he and his wife and daughters left Germany forever.

Luck was not on Otto's side. To speak of fate implies that some external or superior force was controlling things. Rather, it was chance that would now send Otto and his family this way and that as his capacity for controlling his life was gradually stolen from him.

Otto could not have anticipated it, but by the end of World War II, the Netherlands would have the worst record of Jewish deaths in Western Europe: 73 percent of Jews in the Netherlands died. In Belgium, 40 percent of Jews were killed; in France, 25 percent; in Denmark, .6 percent. In Fascist Italy, only 8 percent of Jews were killed.[5] The estimate of Jews in hiding in the Netherlands varies between twenty-five thousand and twenty-seven thousand. One-third were betrayed due in part to the Nazis' sophisticated system of financial rewards to tempt police officers and civilians into betraying hidden Jews.

That was one of the issues that had drawn Pieter van Twisk to the cold case investigation in the first place; he wanted to understand why that had happened in such large numbers in the Netherlands. One long-held theory was that the structure of Dutch society, namely, its separation into groups by religion and associated political ideas, had worked against the protection of the Jewish population. The Dutch called this "pillarization." There were four main pillars: Catholics, Protestants, socialists, and liberals. Each pillar (the Dutch word is *verzuiling*) had its own trade unions, banks, hospitals, schools, universities, sports clubs, newspapers, and so on. Such segregation meant that people were tightly knit within their own group and had little or no personal contact with members from other pillars. Yet Pieter said that was too easy an explanation.

Pillarization is too vague and generalized a notion to explain the Netherlands' actions during the war, he said.

The historians Pim Griffioen and Ron Zeller have a more complex explanation. They point out that the Dutch method of civil registration helped the Nazis. Municipal registration cards listed name; birth date; place of birth; nationality; religion; names and birth dates of spouses and children; date of marriage; date a person died; addresses within the municipality where people lived from start date to end date; whether a person had a passport or ID. Officially, religion was listed since religious groups received government funding based on their membership. Jews were identified by the initials *NI*: Netherlands Israelite. Thus, when the Nazis' roundups began in the summer of 1942, Dutch Jews were easy targets. Given the country's geography, flight was not an option. To the east was the long border with Germany; to the south, Belgium was occupied; and to the west and north, the sea was closed to shipping. There was virtually nowhere to go.[6]

It is also true that the experience of the Netherlands during the war was different from that of other countries. The Netherlands was, in effect, a police state. Whereas, for example, Belgium and occupied France were ruled by the Wehrmacht, and Denmark came under the control of the German Navy, the Netherlands was initially under a civilian government led by the Austrian lawyer Arthur Seyss-Inquart, whom Hitler had appointed Reich Commissioner. A power struggle ensued between Seyss-Inquart and the Dutch Nazi Party (Nationalsozialistische Deutsche Arbeiterpartei; NSDAP), which was under the influence of Hermann Göring, the commander in chief of the Luftwaffe, on the one hand, and Police Commander Hanns Albin Rauter, the highest-ranking SS leader, who reported directly to SS Commander Heinrich Himmler, on the other. As Göring's power waned and Himmler's was in the ascendant, Rauter's influence increased. He oversaw the deportations of 107,000 Jews, the repression of the resistance, and retaliation for assaults on Nazis. Initially the death of one Nazi called for the execution of several Dutchmen; the ratio increased over the course of the occupation.

In addition, the Dutch endured brutal repression after any dissent from the Nazi dogma. A national strike organized by the Communist Party in Amsterdam on February 25, 1941, in response to the *Razzias*, or roundups, of Jews is considered to be the first public protest against the Nazis in occupied Europe and the only mass protest against the deportation of Jews to be organized by non-Jews. At least three hundred thousand workers in and around Amsterdam took part.[7] German repression was immediate and brutal. The strike organizers were rounded up and executed. It took a long time for the resistance to recover. "Only in the spring of 1943 did another strike take place, but . . . the protest came much too late for the vast majority of Jews who had already been deported" to the death camps.[8]

Still, there were many different groups and individuals who worked on behalf of the Jews. There were four networks dedicated to the rescue of Jewish children. Henriëtte "Hetty" Voûte, a young biology student, joined one group calling itself the Utrecht Children's Committee. It set about finding hiding places for several hundred young Jewish children who'd been separated from their parents. Hetty cycled around the countryside, literally knocking on doors.[9]

It is impossible to estimate the exact number of people who helped Jews hide, but an approximate number would be at least twenty-eight thousand and probably more—an extraordinary figure, given these people were putting their own and possibly their family's lives on the line, often for strangers.

6
An Interlude of Safety

By December 1933, Otto Frank found his family an apartment at 37 Merwedeplein in the River Quarter of Amsterdam. It was a modest three-bedroom, upper-floor apartment in a complex of row houses built around 1920.* The River Quarter was filled with hundreds of newly arrived Jewish refugees from Nazi Germany. The poorer Dutch Jews envied their middle-class comfort, while the locals warned the newly arrived not to speak German in public lest

* It is now possible to visit the Frank home. In 2004, the apartment was purchased by the Anne Frank House and turned into a retreat for writers. Great care was given to restoring the 1930s style of furnishings, copied from Frank family photos. Above the flap-down mahogany writing desk in Anne's bedroom is a photo of her sitting at its twin.

they be identified as immigrants. Otto thought he'd found a safe refuge for his family. Anne loved the area, calling the Merwedeplein "the Merry." For the first five or six years, the Franks felt at home in Amsterdam, and the children were soon integrated into their schools, spoke Dutch, and found friends. What was happening in Germany was tragic but remote.

In the Netherlands at that time, anti-Semitism was not overt. When it did rear its head, it was usually through verbal assaults. But a different kind of intolerance was growing. As refugees fled from Germany, then Austria and Eastern Europe, anti-refugee sentiment began to build slowly among the Dutch. The refugees came to the Netherlands in three waves: first after Hitler's ascendance to power in 1933; then with the promulgation of the Nuremberg Laws in 1935; and finally, after Kristallnacht, the Night of Broken Glass, in 1938, when Jewish shops were vandalized and an estimated thirty thousand Jews were arrested and six hundred seriously wounded. Accused of inciting the violence, the Jews were fined millions of marks as punishment. When truth could be so distorted, it was time to flee. Between 1933 and 1940, an estimated thirty-three thousand refugees entered the Netherlands.

The Dutch government voted to treat the refugees as "undesirable elements."[1] In 1939, Camp Westerbork was set up to house both legal and illegal Jewish refugees, and private Dutch Jewish organizations were forced to finance it. Located in a remote northeast corner of the country (Queen Wilhelmina had vetoed a more central location that she felt was too close to a royal residence), the camp was made up of crude barracks and small huts. Initially, it was an open camp where people were supposedly being prepared for emigration. Eventually, Westerbork was ready and waiting for the German occupiers to convert it into a transit camp for Jews en route to the concentration camps in the east.

In the midst of all that, Otto Frank managed to establish his Opekta business with a loan from his brother-in-law, Erich Elias. The profits were slim, but by 1938 he formed a second company, Pectacon, specializing in herbs, spices, and seasonings to sell to butchers and other tradespeople, which meant he could carry on business in the winter months, when the fruit used to make jam was scarce. He'd tried to establish a branch in England, traveling to London and Bristol in October 1937, which of course might have meant his family's eventual emigration to England and freedom, but the plan had fallen through.

Looking back at the family's first years in the Netherlands, Otto could say that after the horrors in Germany, they had recovered their freedom and life had been peaceful. In the summers Edith and the children often traveled to the spa city of Aachen just inside the German border, where her family had rented a large town house in 1932. It was there that she and her children stayed for four months while Otto found them the apartment in Amsterdam. Otto also took the children to Basel to visit his mother, Alice, and his sister, Leni, along with the extended family of cousins.

The measure of Otto as a businessman and a person can be seen in his relationship with his staff. It's hard to imagine workers who were asked to sacrifice more in support of their boss and who gave more freely than the four people employed by Otto Frank: Johannes Kleiman, Victor Kugler, Miep Gies, and Bep Voskuijl.

Otto had known Johannes Kleiman since 1923; they'd met when Otto had been attempting to set up a branch of the Michael Frank & Sons bank in Amsterdam. Kleiman had Otto's total confidence. When Jews were forbidden to own businesses in 1941, Otto passed the running of Pectacon to Kleiman to prevent its being confiscated or liquidated by the Germans. It would eventually be renamed Gies & Co. to give it a Dutch pedigree. When Otto and his family went into hiding, Kleiman cooked the books in such a way as to hide the money he always set aside for Otto as the company's true president.

Victor Kugler had served in World War I with the Austro-Hungarian Navy and had been wounded. He had moved to the Netherlands in 1920 and been one of Otto's first employees, joining Opekta in 1933. Kugler shared Otto's politics, telling Otto that he'd left Austria in 1920 because "he was disgusted with the fascism and anti-Semitism he encountered regularly in the Austrian imperial armed forces during the war."[2] He was thirty-three years old and married to a woman in serious ill health. Miep Gies described him as "a husky, good-looking man, dark haired and precise. He was always serious, never joked . . . always quite formal and polite."[3] What she didn't know was that he'd had a complicated childhood, born to an unwed mother in a small town where being labeled illegitimate was painful, which may have accounted for his reserve.

Miep Gies, born in 1909, was also Austrian. Food shortages were so extreme in Austria after World War I that many children, including Miep, suffered from severe malnutrition. As her condition worsened, her parents enrolled her in a program through which starving children were sent to the Netherlands to recover. The children traveled alone by train, an identification card with their name hung around their necks. Miep remembered the train stopping in pitch darkness in the Dutch town of Leiden. A man took her by the hand, and they walked away from the station out of the town. Suddenly there was a house. A door opened; a woman greeted her with warm milk. Children stared. She was taken to bed and immediately fell asleep. She formed a deep bond with the Nieuwenburg family, with whom she stayed for five years. During a visit to Vienna when she was sixteen, she asked her birth parents to consent to her remaining with her adoptive Dutch family.[4] Such a personal history gave her a profound compassion for refugees.

Miep was hired by Otto in 1933, when she was twenty-four. She once described Otto as a man of few words, with high principles and an ironic sense of humor.[5] Her soon-to-be husband, Jan Gies, worked for the Social Services Authority and, beginning in 1943, was active in the National Support Fund (Nationaal Steun Fonds; NSF), the resistance organization in charge of providing funds to all the other branches of the resistance, with much of the money coming from the Dutch government in exile in London.[6] It was dangerous work. She said, "More than twenty thousand Dutch people helped to hide Jews and others in need of hiding during those years. I willingly did what I could to help. My husband did as well. It was not enough."[7] Miep and her husband became close friends of the Franks, dining with them most weeks.

Elisabeth "Bep" Voskuijl was eighteen when she was hired by Opekta in the early summer of 1937. Ten years younger than Miep, she seemed painfully shy, but she had extraordinary courage. She spoke eloquently of her boss: Otto was "affectionate, unsparing with himself and keenly sensitive . . . a soft word always made far more impression than any shouting."[8] Her father, Johannes, joined the company as warehouse manager. A committed anti-Nazi, it was he who built the bookcase that camouflaged the entrance to the secret Annex.

Those five people would hide Otto's family, save his life, and share his tragedies. They were not only employees but friends who had the same clear-eyed perception of the Nazi menace as he had. When he looked back at Amsterdam after the war, Otto would say that it had been an ambiguous place for him. He identified it with friendship unto death. He also identified it with betrayal.

By 1938, Otto's sense of security began to fracture, particularly after Hitler's annexation of Austria. Were the Netherlands really safe? If Austria could be invaded and declared part of Greater Germany, why not the Netherlands? According to Nazi ideology, the Dutch were a Germanic people who spoke a form of High German. That spring Otto traveled to the US Consulate in Rotterdam to apply for a visa to emigrate to the United States. He was not alone. By the beginning of 1939, US consulates in Europe had received a total of three hundred thousand visa applications. The annual quota of visas for German and Austrian citizens was twenty-seven thousand.[9]

If he thought of joining his mother and sister in Switzerland, he soon gave up the idea. Even before the war began, the Swiss had refused to accept Jewish refugees or Jewish immigrants. They did not want to offend Hitler or compromise their neutrality. The only Jews allowed into the country were people such as Palestinian Jews who could prove they were in legal transit to another country. Otto knew that if he tried to cross the border into Switzerland, he and his family would almost certainly be turned back and then would be arrested. Jews were not allowed to leave the Netherlands without visas.

Otto held on to the hope that Germany would respect Dutch neutrality as it had during the First World War. But mostly, he was putting on a brave front. He understood that he and his family were again at risk. His cousin Milly Stanfield in London recalled her correspondence with Otto in the spring of 1940. "I got a letter from him saying how terribly unhappy he was because he was sure Germany was going to attack."[10] He said he could hardly think about what would happen to the children. Milly suggested he send the girls to London; they might be safer there. Otto wrote back that he and Edith couldn't imagine being separated from them, even though Milly was the one person he would have been able to entrust with his daughters' lives.

Likely that was one of the decisions Otto would regret bitterly, but this is mere hindsight. Hitler had attacked Holland; why not England next? And what guaranteed that England would hold out? His children might have been alone in an occupied London, for which he could never have forgiven himself.

In March 1939, Edith's mother, Rosa, arrived from Aachen to take up residence at 37 Merwedeplein. Then, in the summer of 1940, Edith's brothers, Walter and Julius, were finally able to emigrate to the United States and promised to obtain visas for them all. There was again hope of a route to freedom.

7
The Onslaught

It was Friday, May 10, 1940. Miep remembered everyone being crowded around the radio in Otto's office. The mood was one of desolation and shock. The announcer reported that German troops and planes had swooped across the Dutch border at dawn. Some of the troops were said to be dressed in Dutch uniforms, as ambulance crews, or riding bicycles. Was this true? Was it rumor? But when Queen Wilhelmina spoke that morning, urging calm, it was clear that the German invasion was in progress. Three days later the queen fled to England; four days later the Germans bombed and virtually destroyed the core of the port city of Rotterdam, killing an estimated six hundred to nine hundred people, even as the terms of surrender were being negotiated. Adolf Hitler blamed faulty radio communications for not calling off the bombing in time. However, the day after the bombing of Rotterdam, he threatened to bomb Utrecht if the Dutch did not surrender. The Netherlands capitulated on the fifteenth. The whole "war" lasted five days. Expecting the Germans to honor their neutrality, the Dutch had been spectacularly unprepared.

At first the German occupation seemed nearly benign. The Nazis treated the Dutch like their lesser cousins and anticipated that they would be easy converts to the tenets of National Socialism. German orders for Dutch goods created something of an economic boom, and Arthur Seyss-Inquart's velvet-glove approach even meant that some Dutch welcomed the occupation.

But slowly things changed. On January 10, 1941, Decree no. 6/1941 mandated the registration of all Jews. Local authorities set up offices in every community to ensure compliance. Registration had to be in person at the cost of one guilder a head. Cases in which the definition of "Jew" was challenged were to be referred to the generalkommissar's office in The Hague and adjudicated by Dr. Hans Georg Calmeyer, a German lawyer and the head of the Nazi-controlled Internal Administration Department, under whose auspices Jews were registering.

The vast majority of Dutch Jews complied, concluding that their names and addresses already existed in local population registers and in the records of synagogues. Nonregistration carried a prison sentence of up to five years.[1] Furthermore, they had been deceived into believing that registration with the Central Agency for Jewish Emigration (Zentralstelle für Jüdische Auswanderung; JA) would facilitate their emigration to countries outside Europe.

As Miep Gies described it, "From out of their ratholes appeared Dutch Nazis, who were cheering and waving and welcoming."[2] The Dutch Nazi Party (Nationaal-Socialistische Beweging; NSB), established in 1932, had been banned in 1935, but after the occupation it returned in strength. By 1943, it would have 101,000 members. Under Seyss-Inquart's directive, the NSB created a paramilitary arm called the Resilience Department (Weerbaarheidsafdeling; WA), which acted as an auxiliary police force.

By February 1941, hatred of the Jews percolated into the streets and NSB gangs roamed the neighborhoods of Amsterdam, spreading terror. Jews were violently removed from trams and windows were smashed. The owner of Café Alcazar was one of the last to refuse to display the sign "Jews not wanted" and continued to allow Jewish cabaret artists to perform in his venue.

However, on Sunday, February 9, in midafternoon, a group of about fifty WA men attacked the Alcazar, throwing a bicycle through its front window. They were outraged that the owner had permitted a Jewish singer, Clara de Vries, to perform the previous night. They beat up the customers, Jews and non-Jews alike, and smashed the furniture. Preventing the Dutch police from intervening, the Grüne Polizei stood by and enjoyed the vandalism, which soon spread to other cafés.[3]

Seyss-Inquart's velvet-glove approach had seduced the Dutch into thinking that the Germans would be friendly and aloof in their occupation. But that dream ended on February 11, 1941, when a group of about forty Dutch Nazis invaded the Waterlooplein market in the center of Amsterdam, a shopping area run mostly by Jewish shopkeepers, and sang anti-Jewish songs. Breaking into the market storage areas, they armed themselves with heavy objects. A violent confrontation then erupted between the Dutch Nazis and a small commando group of young Jews who had formed to defend themselves. Locals, mostly Communists, responded in solidarity with the Jews. After the fight ended, Hendrik Koot, a WA man, was found unconscious and died three days later. The NSB had found its perfect propaganda tool in the "martyrdom" of Koot.

On February 18, more than two thousand uniformed NSB members marched in Koot's funeral procession through the streets of Amsterdam.

On February 12, 1941, German and Amsterdam police officers closed the access roads and bridges to the Jewish Quarter. No citizens were allowed to enter or leave that part of the city. In a speech to the Dutch section of the NSDAP (the German Nazi Party) at the Concertgebouw on March 12, Commissioner Seyss-Inquart declared, "We will strike the Jews wherever we find them, and anyone who walks alongside them will have to bear the consequences."[4] That June, the Nazis purged the Concertgebouw of all its Jewish musicians. On their final day as members, the orchestra performed Beethoven's Ninth Symphony. When the chorus sang the line *"Alle Menschen werden Brüder"* (All people shall become brothers), it was meant to shame the Nazis. In 1942, the names of Jewish composers carved into the walls of the concert hall were effaced.[5]

The Germans had already created a brilliant template for how to deceive, control, and slowly destroy a community. In 1939, in the newly occupied countries and in the Jewish ghettos, they established Jewish Councils to act as filters between the occupiers and the Jewish community. The Germans imposed directives, and the

Jewish Councils were responsible for implementing them. In the Netherlands the council published its own newspaper, *Het Joodsche Weekblad*, which listed each new anti-Jewish decree out of the eye of the general public. Had the decrees been published in a newspaper of more general circulation, the Germans would have risked an adverse reaction from non-Jews.

At its first meeting on February 13, 1941, the Jewish Council responded to the violent incident that had just occurred in the Jewish Quarter by insisting that all weapons in the hands of Jews be turned over to police. It was as if it was conceding that the Jews bore some responsibility for the violence initiated by the Nazi thugs when in fact they'd simply been defending themselves.[6] The council was clearly acquiescing to German orders, which set a ruinous precedent.

There was much blackmail by the German high command; if the council refused to carry out a measure, the Germans threatened to do it much more brutally. The real force behind the scenes was the Zentralstelle (Central Agency for Jewish Emigration). The name was devious in the extreme, implying that the possibility of emigration for Jews was real. It would seem that at least initially, the leaders of the Jewish Council assumed that the Germans had no intention of removing the entire Jewish community from the Netherlands and that the council's role was to protect those in the most danger. In the early days, even as they received dire warnings about concentration camps in Poland and Germany, Dutch Jews remained convinced that the Germans would never dare to do in the Netherlands what they were doing in Eastern Europe.

When the deportations began, the Zentralstelle created a system of *Sperres*, or exemptions from deportation, and allowed the Jewish Council to make recommendations. Members of the council and their families automatically qualified for *Sperres*, and those who were selected were safe for a time. However, the system was rife with abuse. The line between cooperation and collaboration gradually grew thinner and thinner.[7]

Meanwhile, civic chaos continued in Amsterdam. On February 22, 1941, a Saturday afternoon and therefore the Sabbath, trucks with six hundred heavily armed members of the German Ordnungspolizei entered the sealed-off Jewish Quarter and randomly arrested 427 Jewish men between the ages of twenty and thirty-five.[8] They were sent first to Kamp Schoorl in the Netherlands. Thirty-eight were returned to Amsterdam due to ill health. The remaining 389 were sent to Mauthausen concentration camp in Austria and some eventually to Buchenwald. Only two of them survived.

Three days later, on February 25, in protest against the roundup, Dutch workers staged a massive strike. Joined by three hundred thousand people, the strike lasted two days. Responding ruthlessly, the Nazis called in the Waffen-SS, which had permission to use live ammunition against the striking workers. Nine people were killed and twenty-four seriously wounded. The strike leaders were tracked down, and at least twenty were executed. Men from the Jewish Quarter who had been arrested were photographed with weapons in their hands. The photographs were published in the Dutch press as evidence that the German command was dealing with "an outbreak of terrorism."[9] If any Dutch had harbored illusions about what the German occupation might mean, they now lost them.

But German Jews had no such illusions. Otto Frank knew the Nazi drill: excluding Jews from air-raid shelters; banning Jews from employment; the Aryanization of businesses; the registration of Jews, who were forced to wear yellow stars; the confiscation of wealth and property; mass arrests; transit camps; and finally, the deportations to the east, where it was not clear what awaited them. Otto now put every ounce of his strength into the fight to save his family. He knew he had to secure his business and get out of the Netherlands.

He tried again for emigration to the United States.

His wife's brothers, Julius and Walter Holländer, had searched for almost a year before they had found work. Finally, Walter had gotten a laborer's job at the E. F. Dodge Paper Box Company outside Boston and sent guarantees of support to the Netherlands for his mother, Rosa; Otto; and Edith. Remarkably, Walter's boss, Jacob Hiatt, and a friend signed affidavits of support for Anne and Margot. It should have been a go, but a deposit of $5,000 for each immigrant was required to ensure that they would not become indigent.[10] Neither Otto nor his brothers-in-law had that amount of money.

In April 1941, Otto wrote to his wealthy American friend Nathan Straus, Jr.; the Straus family owned Macy's department store, and he and Nathan had been roommates at Heidelberg University. Though it must have been humiliating, Otto asked Straus for a character reference and the deposit, reminding his friend that he had two daughters and it was mainly for their sake that he was asking for help. Straus contacted the National Refugee Service, offering to provide the affidavits but suggesting that his influence was so strong that no deposit of $5,000 (the equivalent of approximately $91,000 today) should be necessary. By November 1941, with no visas to be had, Straus finally offered to cover all expenses, but it was too late.[11]

An internal memo from Undersecretary of State Breckinridge Long to his colleagues in June 1940 revealed the US policy. The strategy to control immigration (branding refugees as spies, Communists, and negative elements) was to "put every obstacle in the way and require additional evidence" to "postpone and postpone and postpone the granting of the visas."[12] The US consulate in Rotterdam, where Otto had applied for a visa in 1938, had been destroyed during the 1940 bombing of the city, and all applicants needed to reapply since the original documents had been destroyed. Finally, in June 1941, saying that there was a risk of espionage cells, the United States closed most diplomatic embassies and consulates in Nazi-occupied territory. Otto would now have to go to a US consulate in a supposedly "nonbelligerent" country, such as Spain or unoccupied France, where he would apply in person for a visa. But he couldn't leave the Netherlands without an exit permit, which he couldn't get unless he had a visa to enter that other country. The whole system was deliberately roundabout. He was caught in the catch-22 of the bureaucratic nightmare of war.[13]

Otto never wavered in his efforts to save his family. Even as late as October 1941, he was trying for a Cuban visa, a risky and expensive venture that was often simply a swindle. In September, he wrote to a friend that Edith was urging him to leave either by himself or with the children. Perhaps once they were outside the country, he could buy their freedom. He finally did get a Cuban visa on December 1, but ten days later, on December 11, four days after the Japanese attacked Pearl Harbor, Germany and Italy declared war on the United States and the Cuban government canceled the visa.[14]

Otto's last effort was an appeal to the Emigration Section of the Amsterdam Jewish Council on January 20, 1942. In the files of the Anne Frank Stichting in Amsterdam, there are four stenciled forms, one for each member of the family, requesting exit visas. They were never sent.

The Nazis were very efficient in "cleansing" Amsterdam of its Jews. There were eighty thousand Jewish inhabitants in Amsterdam in 1940, about 10 percent of the city's total population. By September 1943, the city would be declared Jew free.

8
Prinsengracht 263

On December 1, 1940, seven months after the German invasion, Otto Frank moved his business to new premises at Prinsengracht 263. Opekta and Pectacon were stabilizing, and sales were satisfactory. He'd chosen a seventeenth-century house facing the canal and around the corner from the Westerkerk, the imposing church where Rembrandt van Rijn is buried. The street was occupied by small businesses, warehouses, and modest commercial factories, sometimes with apartments above.

Number 263 was a typical Amsterdam structure with a warehouse area on the ground floor and offices and storerooms in the three stories above. Like many of the period buildings, it had a four-story annex attached at the rear. The warehouse floor ran the entire length of the building, including under the Annex, with double-door street access to Prinsengracht and courtyard access at the rear. This meant that the Annex, though invisible from the front of the building, could be seen from the back, which abutted on a very large interior courtyard. Dozens of neighbors on the other three sides of the courtyard had a view of the Annex.

About five weeks before the move to the new premises, on October 22, 1940, the Germans passed a law that all industrial and commercial firms owned in whole or in part by Jews had to be registered with the Economic Inspection Agency (Wirtschaftsprüfstelle). Failure to report meant a large fine and five years in prison. Otto knew that it was the first step in the "de-Judification" and expropriation of his companies. He subverted the Germans by having Victor Kugler and Miep's husband, Jan, become managing director and supervisory director of the renamed Pectacon, which was Aryanized as Gies & Co., a thoroughly Dutch name. Had the company remained Jewish, it would have been liquidated under the directive of a German trust company and the money deposited with the Lippmann-Rosenthal bank. But Otto's company was never plundered. It had become Dutch.

The Nazis were ingenious at using subterfuge to maintain the pretense of legality. To gain the trust of

Jews, in early 1941 they took over the long-established Jewish bank Lippmann-Rosenthal and turned it into a loot bank. Jews were forced to hand over their assets and all objects of value. They could keep "wedding rings, silver wristwatches and pocket watches, one set of silverware consisting of a knife, a fork, a soupspoon and a dessertspoon."[1] Statements were issued to clients and in some cases interest was paid, but it was a pseudo-bank. Jewish capital was actually being accumulated to pay for the eventual deportations and the maintenance of forced labor and concentration camps.

The deportations began in the summer of 1942. When selected for deportation, Jews were told to hand over their house keys to the Dutch police, along with a list of house contents. Everything was taken, from furniture to valuable art. The Nazis were good at euphemisms. When art was looted, the official term was *Sicherstellung* (safekeeping).[2]

After the first deportations, a Dutch protest leaflet was circulated by the resistance that explained things clearly:

> *All prior German measures had aimed at isolating the Jews from the rest of the Dutch, to make contact impossible, and to kill our sentiments concerning living side by side and in solidarity. They have*

> *succeeded much better than we know ourselves or are probably willing to admit. The Jews have to be killed in secrecy and we, the witnesses, must remain deaf, blind, and silent. . . . God and history will condemn us and hold us partly responsible for this mass murder if we now remain silent and simply look on.*[3]

None of these developments went unnoticed by Otto Frank. In the beginning, the restrictions seemed eccentric and temporary. Walking to and from work each day, he would find himself not being allowed to take the tram or not even being allowed to sit down at an outdoor café to rest his feet. He would tamp down his anger. But when the BBC reported in June 1942 that seven hundred thousand Jews had perished in Germany and the occupied territories,[4] he understood that what was at stake was not simply segregation but rather impending annihilation. There would be no obtaining visas for his family. He knew that the next step must be to go into hiding.

9
The Hiding

There are two versions of the Frank family's finding refuge in the Annex. According to the German author and radio personality Ernst Schnabel in his 1958 book *The Footsteps of Anne Frank*, Kleiman and Kugler approached Otto and said it was time to think of going into hiding, proposing the Annex behind Prinsengracht 263.[1] Melissa Müller, in her biography of Anne Frank, concurred that Kleiman, as early as the summer of 1941, proposed the empty rooms in the Annex as an ingenious hiding place because no one would ever think of Frank hiding on his own business premises.[2] Bep's son Joop had been told by his mother that Kleiman had suggested the Annex and then Kugler had been included in the plan.[3] But Otto had been thinking of going into hiding as early as

December 1940, and it may be that he rented Prinsengracht 263 with hiding in mind.[4]

Otto would later say that it was he who had approached his employees with the plan of going into hiding: first Kleiman, then Kugler, then Miep, then Bep. Miep confirmed this:

> *The initiative to go into hiding, to find a hiding place, to organize everything for it, came from Otto Frank. He thought it all out . . . and he had already divided certain different tasks for his staff members when he asked them to help him and his family in hiding.*[5]

Whoever was the source of the idea, it created a painful situation for Otto. What an incredible question he was forced to ask: Will you help save me, save my family? The Germans had threatened to imprison any Dutch citizen who helped Jews. It would have been typical of Otto to ask each person himself and to stress that they understood what it would mean if they said yes. How hard to place his employees in such a position! And equally hard to find in himself such complete trust that he could put the fate of his family entirely into their hands.

Miep remembered the morning Otto had asked for her help. He had come to the office wearing a yellow star affixed to his coat. Everyone had pretended it was not there. She recalled his phrasing: "Are you willing to take on the responsibility of taking care of us while we are in hiding?" In a practical sense that would mean shopping for the family, obtaining forged ration cards or buying them on the black market, finding food.

"Of course," she replied.

She added, "There is a look between two people once or twice in a lifetime that cannot be described by words. That look passed between us. . . . I asked no further questions. . . . I felt no curiosity. I had given my word."[6]

Jews were forbidden to take furniture out of their houses or transport household goods through the streets. Johannes Kleiman's brother Willy owned a pest extermination company called Cimex and, knowing of Otto's plan to hide, offered the use of his truck to transport the Franks' possessions—furniture, rugs, canned food, beds, and clothing—to Kleiman's apartment, from which they would be taken to the Annex. Of course, it was done quietly on a Saturday or Sunday evening or late at night, so that it took months to transport everything.[7] Few knew that it was happening, certainly not the Frank children. They were told that the furniture was being sent out for repair, which some visitors thought a ridiculous indulgence in wartime.

On July 5, 1942, an official letter with an ornate Nazi swastika was delivered to the Frank home. It was an order for sixteen-year-old Margot Frank to report for *Arbeitseinsatz*, compulsory work duty in Germany. She was advised to bring a suitcase with winter things. For Miep, conscripting a sixteen-year-old girl for forced labor was a "new abomination the Germans were inflicting on the Jews."[8] In fact, it was a subterfuge. For a Jewish child, the end of the journey would be death. With the assistance of Miep and her husband, Jan, Otto immediately activated his escape plan. The family left for the Annex the next morning.

Five months earlier, on January 29, Edith's mother, who had been living with them, had died of cancer after months of suffering. It was a tragic loss that had cut deeply, but now it was also a relief. How could Rosa Holländer, ill as she was, have gone into hiding? Edith and Otto would certainly not have been able to leave her behind, but if Edith had decided to stay with her mother, they would both have been deported and forced to endure unimaginable horrors. The Germans spoke of the Jewish deportations as "emigration" or "resettlement" and made already deported Dutch Jews write postcards to their families saying positive things about the camps. But people managed to transmit secret messages. A salutation such as "Give my regards to Ellen de Groot," using a common Dutch name, got past the censors. In Dutch, *ellende* means "misery" and *groot* means "great."[9]

Three months before they went into hiding, Otto had rented out the large room on the upper floor of their apartment to Werner Goldschmidt, a German refugee who had come to the Netherlands in 1936. His presence was fortuitous, or perhaps, given Otto's shrewdness, it was part of his plan for hiding his family. When they left their home for the last time, Otto left behind, as though inadvertently, an address on a piece of paper that gave the impression that the family had fled to Switzerland. Soon, thanks in part to Goldschmidt, the rumor spread through the neighborhood that the Franks had managed to escape.

Four other people joined the Frank family. The first to arrive were the Van Pels family of three. Hermann van Pels had been working with Otto from 1938 as an expert in spices. They lived just behind the Franks' apartment in the River Quarter and had become close friends. Otto said he thought that sharing the Annex with the Van Pelses would make life less dreary. Then the dentist Fritz Pfeffer spoke to Miep when she went to him for an appointment and asked her if she knew somewhere safe to hide. She talked to Otto. He must have thought, *This is Miep asking*, so he said that there was not much difference between seven people and eight. But he had to have known that it would increase the risk.[10] Finding food for eight and monitoring all noise would certainly be harder. But most difficult was that the sleeping arrangements would have to be reorganized to accommodate Pfeffer. Otto and Edith must have discussed this. It was impossible for them to allow sixteen-year-old Margot to sleep in a bedroom with an older man. When Pfeffer moved into the Annex on November 16, Margot joined her parents in their room, which left thirteen-year-old Anne sleeping in the same room as Pfeffer.

One cannot imagine Edith or Otto being comfortable with the arrangement, but their lives and their capacity for control had changed so much. The choice confronting Otto was always one between life and death. How could he not save Pfeffer? If Otto ever expressed regret that he'd invited the others, thereby putting his family at greater risk of exposure, there is no record of it.

When it came time to hide the Franks, none of Otto's four employees hesitated. What made it possible for those four people to put their lives on the line and hide Jews? Miep put it best for all of them: it never occurred to her to say no.[11]

In the end at least eight people knew the secret of

the Annex: the four employees; Miep's husband, Jan; Bep's father, Johannes; Kleiman's wife, Johanna; and Kleiman's brother Willy, who became the Annex's repairman. Otto came up with the idea of disguising the door to the Annex by putting a bookcase in front of it, which would be on wheels and therefore movable. Johannes Voskuijl, a masterful carpenter, built the bookcase at his home and, to avoid drawing attention to it, brought it piece by piece to the Annex, where he reassembled it.[12]

Miep and Margot rode their bicycles to the Annex the morning of June 6. Otto, Edith, and Anne soon followed on foot. The long walk from their apartment at 37 Merwedeplein in the River Quarter to Prinsengracht in central Amsterdam was exhausting, particularly because they were wearing multiple layers of clothing. A Jew carrying a suitcase would arouse suspicion. But it was raining fiercely, a consolation since the Nazis would not be out checking for Jews in such weather.

As Miep left the Frank family to settle in, she described closing the door to the Annex behind her:

I couldn't begin to imagine what they must be feeling to have walked away from everything they owned in the world—their home; a lifetime of gath-

ered possessions; Anne's little cat, Moortje. Keepsakes from the past. And friends.

They had simply closed the door of their lives and had vanished from Amsterdam. Mrs. Frank's face said it all. Quickly, I left them.[13]

10

You Were Asked. You Said Yes.

In her diary, Anne Frank offers a poignant description of living, in effect, imprisoned in the Annex. Messages of dread penetrated its walls. Sometimes she could hear jackboots ringing against the pavement in sinister rhythm as German soldiers marched by. Once she described peeking through the curtains in the office after the staff had gone home and seeing Jewish people scuttling past in fear. In the evenings, as the war progressed, RAF planes would fly over the Netherlands on their way to Germany, and the humming sound of their engines and the boom of the antiaircraft guns were frightening.* Often USAF Mustang fighters

* In 1943, an American Halifax bomber was shot down and crashed into the Carlton Hotel, which was being used as a

dumped empty fuel tanks over the city to gain speed and maneuverability. The unexpected noise of unexploded shells and shrapnel falling from the skies and hitting the ground was continual.

On the streets of Amsterdam there was a different kind of fear. Miep described it:

> *Recently the Green Police and SS had been making surprise razzias during the day. This was the best time to catch the most defenseless Jews at home: the old, the sick, small children. Many had taken to the streets so as not to be in their homes if the Germans came for them. They often asked passersby if they'd seen any sign of a roundup or soldiers, and, if so, where.*

It was not hard to see what was going on, but after the brutal German reprisals against the railway strikers, fear pervaded everyone. Most people looked away. They knew they had "to be prudent." However much they wanted to help, they went inside and shut their doors.[1]

German headquarters, and thirteen people were killed. In 1944, an Allied raid on SD headquarters on Euterpestraat destroyed many surrounding houses. By the end of the war, thousands of civilians had been killed in bombings.

One of the most eloquent testimonies of life outside the Annex comes from Miep, but it took her forty-two years of reticence before she could speak of the events, so painful was her sense of loss and failure. According to her son, it was a wound that couldn't heal.

She recalled that in the early days of the occupation, before the Frank family went into hiding, Otto had been forced not only to Aryanize his businesses but also to let his only Jewish employee, Esther, go.

> *I remember Esther said good-bye to us. She had to leave because she was Jewish. Dismissed. Yes, that's the way things were. She did not come back, I think. She did not survive the war. She was still there on my wedding day. . . . She gave me a box with a mirror, comb and brush from her and her family. . . . She could not keep it anymore. . . . It was all so painful, you see. You heard about her dismissal but did not talk about it further. You did not know what was going to happen. You gave into that. Had to accept it. The Germans were the boss, and you were scared—frightened to death.*[2]

Only gradually did the psychology of living under occupation change. When Otto asked the staff for help, their motive to do so was simple: he was their friend, and they had to help. Thus they learned to live in separate worlds, to split themselves into different parts: they were one person in the Annex, another among friends, yet another among officials.[3] As Miep explained, you soon learned what to say, what not to say: "We were no longer keeping silent. We had lost the habit of speech. Do you understand the difference?"[4]

Jan continued to work for the Social Services Authority, but he was soon involved with the NSF resistance group, though after the war ended, he rarely spoke about what he'd done. He did explain his motive when he was asked. What moved a person from passivity to action, he said, was not heroism. It was simpler. You were asked. You said yes. The issue then became whom to trust. "You never really knew who to trust . . . [but] somehow you knew anyway."

> *We knew, for example, those people on the other side of the street, they are good. Why? That is hard for us to say. You see things . . . hear things. You hear people talking, and this is how you figure out the value of certain individuals. That is not a one-hundred percent rule but in general it worked for*

> *me. I was lucky. . . . You had to be very limited in your contacts. Not speak with the whole neighborhood. And then, of course, you needed a bit of luck, as well. But I have been damned careful in talking about anything, because you could never be sure. And I have actually never been wrong about a person, after all.*[5]

Around that time, Miep and Jan were sheltering a Dutch university student, Kuno van der Horst. They were actually subletting their apartment from Kuno's mother, who was living in Hilversum, southeast of Amsterdam. His protection was in return for his mother's hiding a Jewish acquaintance of theirs. They never told Otto Frank about it. It was in another compartment of their lives.

Miep said they found it "logical, "self-evident" that they should help. "You could do something, and you could help these people. They were powerless. . . . That is all—there is nothing more to it."[6]

She added, "Yes . . . you were worried sometimes. You would think: 'How can this go on?' . . . But the care for these people—and really, the compassion for what these people went through—that was stronger. That won out."[7]

Still Miep's fear did not disappear: "I did not try to stop my husband. I was terrified for him, for I do love him. If I had not loved him, perhaps I could not have endured wondering in terror every single day: Will he come home today?"[8]

The eight people in the Annex depended on those outside for physical and moral sustenance. They were always eager to know what was happening in the external world, and Miep, Jan, Bep, and the others knew that they could not sugarcoat the truth. "Seeing their hunger, I told them what I knew," Miep said.

> *About the razzias which were taking place in different parts of town. I told them the newest edict was for Jewish telephones to be disconnected. That prices for false identity papers had gone through the ceiling. . . .*
>
> *Every time I pulled the bookcase aside, I had to set a smile on my face, and disguise the bitter feeling that burned in my heart. I would take a breath, pull the bookcase closed, and put on an air of calm and good cheer that it was otherwise impossible to feel anywhere in Amsterdam anymore. My friends upstairs were not to be upset, not to be privy to any of my anguish.*[9]

Johannes Kleiman would occasionally bring his wife to visit on weekends. After the war, he recalled Anne's desperate curiosity:

> *Of course, we tried to keep in mind how hard it was for the child. . . . She was hungering for the world outside, for life with other children, and when my wife came up Anne would greet her with an almost unpleasant curiosity. She would ask about Corrie, our daughter. She wanted to know what Corrie was doing, what boyfriends she had, what was happening at the hockey club, whether Corrie had fallen in love. And as she asked she would stand there, thin, in her washed-out clothes, her face snow-white, for they all had not been out of doors for so long. My wife would always bring something for her, a pair of sandals or a piece of cloth; but coupons were so scarce and we did not have enough money to buy on the black market. It would have been so nice if we could have brought her a letter from Corrie occasionally, but Corrie was not allowed to know that the Franks weren't abroad, as everyone thought, but were still in Amsterdam. We did not want to burden her with this almost unendurable secret.*[10]

Those outside who were devoted to helping the Franks divided the tasks of gathering food between them. Kleiman arranged with a friend who owned the bakery chain W. J. Siemons to deliver bread to the office two or three times a week. To buy food during the occupation, one needed both money and food coupons, which were meant to ensure that goods were distributed evenly. Jan obtained the coupons at first on the black market and then, by mid-1943, through his underground contacts.[11] When those were not enough, the baker agreed to be paid in cash after the war. Bread to feed eight could be disguised as bread for the employees, who numbered about nine in total. But of course, the employees who were not in on the secret wondered where all the bread was going.

Miep shopped for the people in the Annex as well as for herself and Jan. That meant going to several shops so as not to be conspicuous. Miep even suggested that it was a kind of theater:

> *I would go to all the shops and you would try things out a little with the man in the shop. How far could you go. How much could you ask. . . . To what extent you could show compassion. To what extent you could pretend to be in such a terrible situation.*

Yes, that was like playing in a theatre. At least, that is how I felt about it.[12]

Hermann van Pels sent Miep to Piet Scholte's butcher shop off the Rozengracht, owned by his close friend Scholte. He'd been shrewd enough to insist that Miep accompany him there before the hiding so that the butcher would know her face. It had puzzled her at the time, but now she understood. "Go to this man," she was told. "Give him my list. Say nothing and he'll give you what we want." It worked just as promised, without a word spoken.[13]

Bep was responsible for milk deliveries, which happened daily. Supposedly, the office staff drank a great deal of milk. The milkman asked no questions. But as the food shortages increased—the Germans were sending a lot of Dutch produce back to Germany—Bep would ride her bike out to the farms that surrounded the city to find whatever food she could.

On one occasion on her way back into the city with the few potatoes and vegetables she'd been able to buy, she was stopped by a passing patrol of SS. She made herself understood in German and told the young officer who approached her that she had a large family to feed. He let her go but took half her produce. Then the patrol car caught up with her again, and the officer returned the food.

Bep was sharp enough to know that it was a trap. Instead of heading for the Annex, she went home. The car followed her. She gave the SS her most innocent look and hastened into the house. They drove away.[14]

Bep and Miep became very close to Anne, as is clear from her diary. Both gave in to her entreaties for them to spend the night in the Annex. Bep described the time spent there as "completely and utterly horrifying." Lying on a mattress beside Anne, she could hear the bells of the nearby Westerkerk toll every fifteen minutes, shattering the quiet in the rooms:

> *A beam or a door would creak, then it was something outside on the canal, a gust of wind moving a tree, or a car in the distance coming closer. . . . Each squeak and crack . . . was associated with "I've been betrayed" or "they've heard me now."*[15]

The fear was almost insupportable.

Miep also stayed overnight with her husband. After the blackout frames went up, sealing the Annex like a prison with the locks on the inside, Miep and Jan went to bed in Anne's room. Miep later wrote:

All through the night I heard each ringing of the Westertoren clock. I never slept; I couldn't close my eyes. I heard the sound of a rainstorm begin, the wind come up. The quietness of the place was overwhelming. The fright of these people who were locked up here was so thick I could feel it pressing down on me. It was like a thread of terror pulled taut. It was so terrible it never let me close my eyes.

For the first time I knew what it was like to be a Jew in hiding.[16]

11
A Harrowing Incident

Eight people hiding in a small space for twenty-five months—it was amazing that they lasted so long. As Bep put it, "Eight persons are eight individuals. If each one of them committed a single slip each year, that would be sixteen telltale signs."[1] Sometimes domestic arguments broke out during office hours. Bep would recognize the voices and rush to warn the hiders that they could be heard in the warehouse. Once when her father, who was the warehouse manager, heard voices, he started raging at an employee to cover the noise while Bep raced upstairs to keep the peace; the poor worker had no idea what he'd done.[2] It was all agonizing.

The world had gone insane, but Otto kept a modicum of calm. Miep noted the change: "I noticed a new composure, a new calm about Mr. Frank. Always a nervous man before, he now displayed a veneer of total control, a feeling of safety and calm emanated from him. I could see that he was setting a calm example for the others."[3]

There was need for calm. Up until March 1943, Bep's father took care of everything. He always made sure to dispose of the trash carefully and covered up any signs that there were hiders in the Annex. However, that June he was diagnosed with cancer. He continued to work for a brief time, but, as Anne wrote in her diary, he had surgery on June 15 and was forced to leave work so he could recuperate.

Unable to find a replacement on his own, Kleiman consulted the public employment office, which sent him a man named Willem van Maaren. It was risky bringing a total stranger into the closed world of the secret Annex, and Kleiman would soon regret his decision. Van Maaren was suspiciously inquisitive, and the helpers would come to believe that he was stealing supplies from the warehouse that he then sold on the black market.

The change of warehouse manager was probably the most dangerous threat to the Annex residents since they'd gone into hiding, although there were many other things for the helpers to worry about: obtaining food stamps from the resistance (according to Miep, Jan had to take everyone's identity cards to the resistance organization to prove that he was feeding eight people); finding extra money to buy food; and, as rationing increased, finding food at all.

To make matters worse, businesses all over Amsterdam were being robbed. There were at least three break-in attempts at Prinsengracht 263 between 1943 and 1944. On July 16, 1943, as was his custom, Peter went down to the warehouse before the employees arrived, only to discover that the front doors were open. Thieves had forced both the warehouse and the street doors with a crowbar. Ironically, everyone in the Annex had slept through it all. The robbers had reached the second floor and stolen a small amount of money, blank checks, and, most depressing, food coupons amounting to the Annex's entire allotment of sugar.

On March 1, 1944, Peter again found the front door leading to the offices wide open and discovered that Mr. Kugler's new briefcase and a projector were missing from his office. What was worrisome was that there was no sign of a break-in. The burglar seemed to have had a duplicate key, which meant it must have been one of the warehouse employees. Who could it be?

The most harrowing incident was a break-in a

month later, on April 9, four short months before the Annex was raided and its residents arrested.[4] There had been noises from the warehouse after work hours, and Peter, his father, Fritz, and Otto had headed downstairs. Peter noted that a large panel of the warehouse door was missing. The four entered the warehouse and spied the burglars. Van Pels yelled, "Police!" and the burglars fled. But as the men tried to cover the hole in the door, a swift kick from the outside sent the piece of wood flying. They were shocked at the boldness of the burglars. They tried again, and once more the replacement panel was kicked free. Then a man and a woman shone a flashlight through the hole.

The Annex residents raced upstairs. A little later, they heard a rattling at the bookcase. In her diary Anne wrote that she could not find words to describe the terror of that moment. They heard the footsteps receding, and then everything went quiet. The eight retreated to the top floor, where they spent a sleepless night, waiting for the Gestapo.

The next day, Jan Gies learned what had happened. Martin Sleegers, the local night watchman, who patrolled the area on his bicycle with his dogs, had seen the hole in the door and alerted the police. Sleegers and a policeman named Cornelis den Boef, an active member of the NSB, had searched the entire building, including the alcove containing the entrance to the Annex. It was they who had rattled the bookcase.[5]

As he was returning to the Annex later that day, Jan ran into the greengrocer Hendrik van Hoeve, who delivered their vegetables, and told him there had been a break-in. Van Hoeve replied that he knew; he and his wife had been walking past the building and had noticed the hole in the door. He'd put his flashlight through the hole and believed he'd startled the burglars, who had run off. He said he'd thought about calling the police but decided against it. He added that he had his own suspicions about what was going on in the Annex and didn't want to create trouble.[6] Van Hoeve was as good as telling Jan that he knew about the people in hiding. Kleiman's brother Willy soon came to repair the door.

At the beginning of 1944, a man named Lammert Hartog had been hired as an assistant to the new warehouse manager, Van Maaren. He'd been recommended by Petrus Genot, who worked with Kleiman's brother in his extermination business. Hartog's wife, Lena, who occasionally cleaned the Opekta offices, had also interceded to get her husband the job.

At the end of June, Petrus Genot approached Kleiman's brother and warned him that Hartog's wife had casually asked his wife if it was true that Jews were hiding at Prinsengracht 263. Anna Genot had been aghast. How could Lena be spreading such gossip in these dangerous times? Anna told her to be very careful with such talk. But Lena mentioned the same thing to Bep, who also told her that she shouldn't be so casual with that kind of information.[7]

Terrified, Bep then spoke to Kugler and Kleiman. What should they do? If Hartog, his wife, Lena, and maybe even Van Maaren all suspected that there were Jews in the Annex, somehow the information would leak out. Should they tell Otto? Was it time to try to move the eight to other premises? Maybe Anne and Margot could stay together, but how could they find seven hiding places? Would the Franks even agree to be separated? It was summer. People would be outdoors later. Could eight people be smuggled out of the building without being noticed? In the end they did nothing. It would be one of the painful memories they would have to fold into their experience—the feeling of guilt for withholding the warning from Otto. The Annex was raided two months later. If the helpers had moved everyone, would Otto Frank's family, the Van Pelses, and Fritz Pfeffer have been saved?

12
Anatomy of a Raid

Kleiman remembered the morning of Friday, August 4, 1944, as warm and bright:

> *The sun was shining; we were working in the big office. . . . in the warehouse below us the spice mills were rumbling. When the sun was shining the trees along the canal and the water itself would often cast flecks of light on the ceiling and walls of the office, ripples of light that flickered and danced. It was an odd effect, but we knew then that it was fair outside.*[1]

But it was on that day that the unthinkable happened. An IV B4 unit consisting of a German SD officer and at least three Dutch policemen raided Prinsengracht 263. They'd been informed that Jews were hiding there.

Karl Silberbauer, Otto, the four helpers, and the two warehouse workers all provided slightly different accounts of the raid. Not surprisingly, the accounts changed over the years, which is to be expected. Memory is fluid and inevitably alters over time. Official statements about the Annex raid were gathered from four to nineteen years after the event.

As part of the Arrest Tracking Project, Vince and the Cold Case Team put together a precise timeline of the raid based on witness statements, police reports, press interviews, and private correspondence:

> ***9:00 a.m.:*** *The Opekta/Gies & Co. office staff (Miep, Bep, Kugler, and Kleiman) arrive and start their day.*
>
> ***9:10 a.m.:*** *Miep goes to the Annex and obtains the daily shopping list.*[2]
>
> ***10:00 a.m.:*** *A call comes in to the IV B4 "Jew-hunting unit" located at the SD office, Euterpestraat 99, Amsterdam. The report is that there are Jews hiding in the Annex of a building at Prinsengracht 263. SS Lieutenant Julius Dettmann takes the call and then orders SD officer Karl Silberbauer to go to that address.*

Silberbauer's statements varied as to the number of Jews he was told would be found. In his initial statement[3] to the Dutch authorities and to the Dutch journalist Jules Huf,[4] he merely said, "Jews," not citing a specific number. In his second statement, to Austrian authorities, he said, "six to eight Jews" and then, in his final interview, "eight Jews."[5]

Dettmann contacts the desk officer, Sergeant Abraham Kaper, assigned to IV B4, to send Dutch detectives from the Amsterdam SD to the address.

10:30 a.m.: *Otto is in Peter's room, giving him English lessons.*[6]

10:30–10:55 a.m.: *The Dutch SD raid team pulls up in front of Prinsengracht 263 in a German Army car with Silberbauer. In another version Silberbauer arrives separately by bicycle. The warehouse doors are wide open, and the raid team enters. Willem van Maaren and Lammert Hartog, who are standing inside, see the car pull up. A Dutch plainclothes detective enters and speaks to Van Maaren.*[7] *One Dutch SD man stays in the warehouse, while the remainder go up the steps to the office area.*[8]

10:30–11:00 a.m.: *Miep and Bep are at their desks in the office. Kugler is in his office, and Kleiman may not have been at his desk but is in the office area with*

Miep and Bep. According to Miep, she looks up and a fat man (probably one of the detectives) sticks his head around the door frame and in Dutch shouts at Kleiman, Bep, and her, "Quiet. Stay in your seats."[9] *In a 1974 statement she says a tall, slender man also threatened them with a firearm.*[10] *He then walks toward the back office, where Kugler is working.*[11] *Kleiman says that the first thing he saw was the fat man's head.*[12]

Kugler hears footsteps and sees shadows pass behind the glass in his office door. He opens the door to see SD officer Karl Silberbauer.[13] *They go into Kugler's office, where he is questioned. Kugler claims that there is one German SD (Silberbauer) and three plainclothes Dutch detectives in the raid team.*[14]

Bep and Kleiman maintain that they heard the fat man and one other in Kugler's office. The fat man asks him in German, "Where are the Jews?"[15] *The fat man then comes into their office and plants himself there. Bep will later confirm that there were (at a minimum) three Dutch detectives at the arrest.*

11:15 a.m.: *Bep, Miep, and Kleiman remain in their office. Silberbauer takes his pistol (a Browning) out of his jacket and orders Kugler up the stairs. Several Dutch detectives follow with their guns drawn.*[16]

There are two options as to how they got to the upper floor:

Option one: They make an immediate right out of Kugler's office and then up a semispiral staircase that leads to the room where the bookcase is located. (This is the most likely and logical avenue that Kugler and the raid team would have taken.)

Option two: They go back downstairs, out of the warehouse, and onto the street and reenter the building through one of the exterior doors, which reveals a two-story staircase leading up to the Annex level.*

What they did next is important. Did they go immediately to the bookcase because they had prior information, were they led to it by Kugler at gunpoint, or did they find it on their own after looking around? Which of the scenarios is true determines whether the betrayer was an insider who knew exactly where the bookcase was or simply someone who'd received the information of the presence of Jews secondhand.

Kugler describes the raid team tugging at the bookcase until it tears loose from its fastening.[17] The heavy bookcase moves on a bottom support wheel. Over the

---

* Gertjan Broek of the Anne Frank House believes that the raid team may have utilized this option.

two years since Bep's father built it, this wheel would have left a curved mark in the floor, what law enforcement agencies call a "witness mark." The Jew-hunting units were used to searching houses for ingenious hiding places. Rather than having foreknowledge of the hidden door behind the bookcase, they may simply have noted the marks indicating that the bookcase moved to conceal something.

> ***11:20–11:40 a.m.:*** *The raid team enters the Annex and confronts the occupants. Otto is in Peter's room when an unfamiliar civilian with a pistol enters. He searches their pockets for weapons. Otto and Peter are walked down the stairs to where the Van Pelses are standing with their hands up before another man in civilian clothes with his pistol drawn. They then move down a floor to where Otto's family lives. His wife and daughters and Kugler are standing, likewise with hands up. There is a green-uniformed man with his pistol drawn who turns out to be Silberbauer.*[18]
>
> *Silberbauer takes Otto's briefcase and empties it, scattering papers over the floor, including Anne's diary. He keeps the money and jewelry and Pfeffer's dental gold.*

Once Silberbauer notices Otto's World War I trunk, he asks Otto about his service in the German Army. Otto then tells him that they have been in hiding for twenty-five months. He shows the incredulous Silberbauer the ruler marks on the wall indicating how much his daughters have grown. After this, Silberbauer tells the occupants to take their time packing.[19]

While the Annex occupants are packing, Kugler asks Silberbauer if he can get his lunch. He is hoping to flee the building. He gets as far as the lower storeroom, where the doors are standing open, and is at the point of running into the street when he sees another policeman and turns around.[20]

11:50 a.m.–noon: *While the raid team is still in the Annex, Bep Voskuijl leaves Opekta with Kleiman's wallet. He has told her to go to the drugstore on Leliegracht, whose owner is a friend who will let her call Kleiman's wife.*[21] *Bep runs desperately from the building, expecting to be shot at any moment, and waits at the drugstore for some time before phoning back to the office.*[22]

11:50 a.m.–noon: *Jan Gies arrives at the Opekta office as usual for lunch with Miep. Miep meets him at the* *office door at the top of the step, whispers, "Gestapo," and hands him her purse containing illegal ration cards, money, and his lunch. He knows immediately what is happening. He swiftly leaves the building and goes to his office, which is seven minutes away. There he hides the items.*[23]

12:05 p.m.: *Miep returns to the front office. Another man from the raid team comes through the door and directs Kleiman, who is still sitting with her, to come to Kugler's office. After a period of time, she hears the door of Kugler's office open and Kleiman emerges, followed by Silberbauer. Silberbauer orders Kleiman to give the warehouse keys to Miep, and then both return to Kugler's office and close the door.*[24]

12:20 p.m.: *A few minutes later, the Dutchman who first entered the office with a gun comes back, sits at Bep's desk, and phones the SD office on Euterpestraat requesting that a vehicle be sent.*[25]

12:25 p.m.: *Silberbauer comes into the front office and confronts Miep, taking back the keys that Kleiman gave her a few minutes earlier. Miep recognizes his Viennese accent and says that she, too, is from Vienna. After chastising her for helping Jews, he warns her not to flee because he intends to come* *back and check on her. Shutting the door behind him, he leaves her alone in the office. She is shocked that she is not arrested and assumes it is because of their shared Austrian background.*[26]

12:45 p.m.: *The ten prisoners are moved downstairs.*[27] *Little is said. There are no emotional farewells to the helpers.*

1:00 p.m.: *As the prisoners are walked out of the building, the two warehousemen are standing at the front entrance.*[28] *The eight Annex residents, along with Kugler and Kleiman, are loaded into a closed dark green truck waiting on the Prinsengracht. Miep's husband, Jan, and Kleiman's brother, whom Jan has called, watch from across the canal.*[29] *Silberbauer departs on a bicycle.*[30]

1:15–1:30 p.m.: *The SD truck arrives at HQ Euterpestraat, and the prisoners are escorted into cells and locked up. Questioning begins. Silberbauer asks Otto for the names and addresses of more hidden Jews, but he says he knows nothing. He has been out of circulation for twenty-five months. Kleiman and Kugler refuse to talk about their involvement in the hiding. Neither Otto nor the others are mistreated.*[31]

Kleiman remembered that before they were separated, Otto had remarked to him, "To think that you are sitting here among us, that we are to blame," to which Kleiman had replied, "It was up to me, and I wouldn't have done it differently."[32] After spending four nights in a prison in the city center, the eight were transported to the Westerbork transit camp; Kugler and Kleiman were sent to the Dutch labor camp at Amersfoort.

For the SD sergeant major and his Dutch collaborators, there were Jews hiding at Prinsengracht 263. Hiding, according to the Nazis, was a crime. When they arrested them, Silberbauer and his henchmen knew what their fate would likely be; by that time they were aware of the extermination camps, but they were following orders. Perhaps it's just the human capacity to objectify another individual, abdicating all responsibility for his or her mortal destiny, that makes it possible to kill so easily.

13
Camp Westerbork

The evening of the arrest, Miep entered the Annex with her husband and the warehouse manager, Willem van Maaren. The shadow of SD officer Karl Silberbauer loomed over everything. He'd warned her not to disappear because he intended to return. In an interview years later, Miep recalled the fear she'd felt but said she'd had to visit the Annex to convince herself that the people they'd been hiding for 761 days were really gone: "Drawers were open, things strewn all over the floor. Everywhere objects were overturned."[1] In the midst of the chaos on the floor she saw a familiar object: the red-and-white-checkered diary with the brass lock in which she'd so often seen Anne writing. After Anne had filled its pages with her dense handwritten entries and the occasional photo, she'd asked

Miep to bring her another, but there had been no diaries for sale anywhere in Amsterdam. Instead, Miep had brought her notebooks, and after Anne had filled those, Bep had given her blue sheets of office tracing paper to write on. Miep leaned down, picked up Anne's diary and a couple of notebooks, and took them to her office, where she placed them in an unlocked drawer of her desk. To lock the drawer would have drawn suspicion. It was risky to keep the diary, but she wanted to give it back to Anne when she returned. Fortunately, she did not read it. Had she done so, she would have discovered that Anne had used real names in it. To protect everyone, she would have had to destroy it.[2]

Later that evening, Bep and her boyfriend also visited. She told her younger sister Diny that she'd had to see with her own eyes that the hiders had been taken away.[3] "When, all those years, you've looked after these people and they're suddenly torn away, what is there left to say?"[4]

As was done in the case of all deported Jews, somewhere between August 5 and 10, the Abraham Puls movers, the company that had the contract to collect Jewish possessions, arrived to remove all the hiders' belongings. Locals called it being *gepulst* (pulsed) and sometimes even stood outside to watch. Furniture, linen, food, and personal possessions were collected and sold or sent by rail to Germany and farther east to citizens whose homes had been bombed by the Allies. The stripping of Jewish assets led to widespread corruption. Objects taken from houses often disappeared, and many rogue "pulsers" became wealthy in the process.

Bep and Miep ventured up to the Annex after it was emptied and found that the Puls men had left a huge jumble of papers and books discarded as worthless on the attic floor. Bep recognized the blue sheets of office tracing paper she'd given Anne to write on and rescued a bundle tied with string. It was the revision of her original diary that Anne had been working on during the last ten weeks of the hiding. She had hoped to publish it after the war under the title *The Secret Annex*. She thought it could be a mystery story where you were never sure of the ending until the end.[5]

After four days' incarceration in the detention center at the notorious Weteringschans prison, the eight prisoners were transported by truck to Muiderpoort train station for the eighty-mile trip to Camp Westerbork. Among the prisoners traveling with them were two sisters, Rebekka "Lin" and Marianne "Janny" Brilleslijper, whose resistance work had led to their arrest. Janny noticed the Franks immediately: a very worried father, a nervous mother, and two children wearing sports-type clothes and backpacks.[6] No one was talking, only watching the city houses disappear into the distance as they were removed from civilization. The sisters would be some of the last to see Anne Frank alive.

Thirteen years later, Otto described that trip to the author Ernst Schnabel. His reference to Anne's drinking in the natural world that had been denied her for so long is poignant.

> *We traveled in a regular passenger train. The fact that the door was bolted did not matter very much to us. We were together again, and had been given a little food for the journey. We knew where we were bound but in spite of that it was almost as if we were once again going traveling, or having an outing, and we were actually cheerful. Cheerful, at least, when I compare this journey to our next. In our hearts, of course, we were already anticipating the possibility that we might not remain in Westerbork to the end. We knew about deportation to Poland after all. And we also knew what was happening in Auschwitz, Treblinka, and Majdanek. But then, were not the Russians already deep in Poland? The war was so far advanced that we could begin to place a little hope in luck. As we rode toward Westerbork,*

we were hoping our luck would hold. Anne would not move from the window. Outside it was summer. Meadows, stubble fields, and villages flew by. The telephone wires along the right of way curvetted up and down along the windows. It was like freedom. Can you understand that?[7]

Word traveled through Westerbork whenever a new transport arrived, bringing both hope and despair: hope that it might not be family or relatives who'd been betrayed and whose presence would double one's pain; despair that the transports were still leaving Amsterdam regularly and that, despite the Allied advances, the war had not yet ended.

A woman named Mrs. Rosa "Rootje" de Winter was watching the new arrivals with her fifteen-year-old daughter. Suddenly she shouted, "Judy, see!" Eight people were standing in the long line waiting for the clerks to register their names. Mrs. de Winter noted their pale skin: "You could tell at once that they had been hiding and had not been in the open air for years."[8] One of them was Anne Frank. Her daughter and Anne would become friends in that desolate place.

Arrival was scripted: first the quarantine barracks, where an employee of the Lippmann-Rosenthal bank confiscated any remaining valuables, then assignment to Barrack 67, the punishment barrack for criminals, since hiding was a criminal offense. Three hundred people were living in each barrack. The new arrivals were handed blue uniforms with a red bib and wooden clogs. The men's heads were shaved; the women's hair was cut painfully short.

In her diary, Anne shared that her only vanity was her beautiful hair. But the Germans required hair for power belting and pipe joint packing in U-boats.[9] It was the universe gone mad: the hair of the people whose existence the Nazis were annihilating was used in the manufacture of weapons of war.

Westerbork was located in an area of peat bogs that lent dampness to everything. The camp was not large, about five hundred square meters. It was run in part by German Jewish prisoners called the Order Service (Ordedienst; OD), who served as a kind of police force. They were refugees whom the Dutch had confined in the camp in 1939, when the Netherlands was still neutral. Later, Dutch Jews had joined their numbers. The Germans assured the members of the OD that if they enforced authority within the camp, they themselves would not be transported to "the east." They varied in number between forty and sixty men and reported directly to the camp commanders.[10]

For Anne, ironically, Westerbork provided a kind of

freedom after the incarceration in the Annex. Mrs. de Winter recalled, "Anne was happy; it was as if she were liberated, for now she could see new people and talk to them, and could laugh." She could breathe and feel the sun on her face. "Although we weren't in safety nor at the end of our misery," Mrs. de Winter added.[11]

On August 25, 1944, Paris was liberated. On September 3, Brussels fell, and on the fourth, Antwerp. The Americans were halfway up the Italian peninsula. The war was almost over. But still 1,019 people were transported to Auschwitz beginning Sunday, September 3: three days, two nights, 60 to 75 people per cattle car: 498 women, 442 men, and 79 children, among whom were the Frank family, the Van Pels family, and Fritz Pfeffer.[12] It was the last transport to leave Camp Westerbork for the Auschwitz concentration camp in Poland.

Otto had hoped that luck would be on their side. It wasn't.

14
The Return

Of the eight people who had been hiding in the Annex, only Otto Frank survived. The fact that he was in the camp hospital when the Nazi command evacuated Auschwitz meant that instead of going on a forced march to his death, he was liberated by the Russians. It was January 27, 1945. Two days before, he had been in a lineup awaiting execution when Russian soldiers had approached, sending the SS firing squad running for cover. Otto once said that he retained an image of the Russians in their "snow-white coats" coming over the white landscape; it was his image of freedom.[1]

On February 22, almost a month later, as the former inmates regained their strength, the area near the camp came under siege. Throughout the night, Otto and the others could hear the sound of artillery. The Germans had returned, and the Russians seemed to be losing ground. After surviving so much suffering, it was unthinkable that all could be lost now. But finally, on February 23, several Russian officers collected survivors in the main camp square and a dozen trucks arrived to transport them behind the lines to the safe zone.

They reached Katowice, the capital of Upper Silesia in Poland, where they were housed first in a public building and then in a school in the city center. Otto asked all those he met if they had encountered his wife and daughters among their fellow inmates. He wrote to his mother on March 18 that he wasn't yet ready to tell her what he'd been through, but at least he was alive. He said he was tormented not to have found Edith and the children, but he remained hopeful. He worried constantly about Kugler and Kleiman and whether they had survived the concentration camps. That same day, he wrote to his cousin Milly: he said he felt like a homeless person now; he'd lost everything. He didn't even have a letter or a photo of his children.[2]

On March 22, Otto sat alone at a table in the empty school. Rootje de Winter, whom he'd met at Westerbork, approached him. She said she'd been in the same barracks in Auschwitz as his wife and daughters. On October 30, 1944, Anne and Margot had been selected for transport to Bergen-Belsen, leaving their mother behind. De Winter could not say what had happened to them. She never saw them again.

But she assured Otto that Anne still had her face. This was concentration camp slang for people who had not been destroyed by the inhumanity around them. De Winter said Anne's beauty was now concentrated in her huge eyes, which could still look on others' suffering with pity. Those who lost their faces had long since stopped feeling. "Something protected us, kept us from seeing." But Anne, as De Winter put it, had had no such protection. She "was the one who saw to the last what was going on all around us."[3]

In December, De Winter had fallen ill and been sent to the hospital barrack, where she had encountered Mrs. Frank. She told Otto that Edith was delirious, no longer eating. When she was given food, she hid it under her blanket, saying she was saving it for her husband. Eventually it went rancid.[4] De Winter told him that Edith had died of starvation on January 6, 1945. Otto's heart must have cracked.

On the train to Czernowitz in the Ukraine, at one of the frequent stops, among the hundreds milling on the platform Otto was recognized by a girl who had used to play with Anne on the Merwedeplein in the River Quarter. The girl introduced him to her mother, who immediately asked if he'd encountered her son and husband, who were still missing. Her name was Elfriede "Fritzi" Geiringer.

On March 5, after reaching Czernowitz, Otto boarded a Russian troop train heading for Odessa. It was the only way back to Amsterdam, where he hoped to be reunited with his children. He and Fritzi Geiringer parted as strangers, but eight years later she would become his second wife. Such was the outrageous level of chance controlling their lives.

It took Otto three months to make it back to Amsterdam. On June 3, he arrived at the apartment of Miep and Jan Gies. Miep recalled: "We looked at each other. There were no words. . . . 'Miep,' he said quietly, 'Edith is not coming back. . . . But I have great hope for Anne and Margot.'"[5] The couple invited him to live with them. He accepted.

That night, they told Otto that both Kleiman and Kugler had survived. At Camp Amersfoort Kleiman had suffered a gastric hemorrhage. The Netherlands Red Cross had intervened on humanitarian grounds, and on September 18, he had been freed. Such an appeal could work only for a Dutch citizen and only because the prospect of losing the war made the anxious German command more accommodating. Soon the Germans would be bulldozing the extermination camps to hide the evidence.

Kugler had been shuffled from one labor camp to another. On March 28, 1945, during a forced march to Germany, British Spitfires had attacked the column of about six hundred men just as they were approaching the German border. In the chaos, Kugler had managed to escape with another prisoner, making his way home with the assistance of friendly Dutch farmers. By that time, the Germans were too busy saving themselves in a mass retreat back to the fatherland to be interested in hunting down Dutch escapees.[6]

On Monday, June 4, Otto wrote in the agenda he always kept that he'd returned to Prinsengracht 263. It must have been shockingly painful to see the map on the wall on which he'd tracked the Allied advance; the ruler near the door measuring how much his daughters had grown; the pictures of babies, film stars, and the Dutch royal family that Anne had tacked up in her bedroom. Nothing had changed, yet everything had changed. Five days after his return, he wrote to his mother that he didn't feel like himself yet. It was as if he were moving in a trance, and he wasn't able to keep his balance.[7]

His wife was dead. He'd watched Hermann van Pels walk toward the gas chamber at Auschwitz the previous October. He had no news of his daughters, Peter, Fritz, or Mrs. van Pels. But he still hoped. His daughters might be in the Russian-occupied territory in Germany, from which communication was notoriously slow. Survivors were still returning to the Netherlands.

And then the news came. He received an official letter from a nurse in Rotterdam saying his daughters were dead. But he couldn't simply accept that. He needed it confirmed by an eyewitness. On July 18, with the assistance of the Red Cross, he tracked down twenty-eight-year-old Janny Brilleslijper. He knew she'd been imprisoned with his daughters in Bergen-Belsen. She recalled:

> *In the summer of 1945, a tall, thin, distinguished man stood on the sidewalk. He looked through our window. . . . There stood Otto Frank. He asked if I knew what had happened to his two daughters. I knew, but it was hard to get the words out of my mouth. . . . I had to tell him that his children were no more.*[8]

Around that time, information arrived regarding the fate of the others. Fritz Pfeffer had died on December 20, 1944, in Neuengamme concentration camp in Germany. Although Otto had tried to persuade Peter van Pels to stay behind with him in the infirmary, Peter had believed he would have a better chance on the death march to evacuate Auschwitz, which the Nazis had ordered on January 19 as the Russian Army had approached. He had survived the weeklong march but died in the sick barracks of Mauthausen on May 5, two days before Germany's unconditional surrender.[9] According to an eyewitness who testified before the Red Cross, Nazi soldiers had thrown his mother, Auguste, under a train during a transport to Theresienstadt.[10]

Otto was told that he had been lucky to survive. But what was luck? He had lost everything. He kept sane by trying to rebuild his spice business, which proved to be impossible since spices from Indonesia were no longer available, and by helping to reunite orphaned children with their relatives.

He wrote his mother that he'd visited Jetteke Frijda, Margot's school friend from the Jewish Lyceum, which they'd attended together after Jewish children had been banned from Dutch public schools. Jetteke was all alone. Her father and brother were dead. Her mother was in Switzerland.[11] There was such overwhelming need; sometimes it was too much. Yet he did what he could to help.

"He became my father from there on; he took care of everything," Hanneli Goslar, another orphan, said of Otto Frank.[12] Her parents had been friends of the

Franks in Amsterdam, and she had been one of Anne's closest friends at school. Her mother had died in childbirth in 1942, and her father and maternal grandparents had been murdered in Bergen-Belsen.

She'd met Anne several times in Bergen-Belsen. Believing that her father had been gassed right away, Anne had stood at the barbed-wire fence that separated them and cried, "I don't have any parents anymore." Hanneli had lost contact with Anne when she and her younger sister had been transported to Theresienstadt. They had been on the Red Cross's Palestine list, supposedly available to be used as "trade goods" in exchange for German prisoners of war. They had never reached the camp. Fortunately, their train had been liberated by the Russians en route.[13]

Otto had seen the Goslar sisters' names on a Red Cross list of survivors and searched for them in Maastricht, where Hanneli was in the hospital. Thrilled to see that Otto wasn't dead, the moment she saw him Hanneli blurted out, "Mr. Frank! . . . Your daughter is alive."[14] Then he told her the awful truth. It crossed her mind that had Anne known Otto was alive, she might have found the will to survive.

Otto took the girls under his wing, moving Hanneli to a hospital in Amsterdam and then arranging the necessary papers for her and her sister to travel to Switzerland to live with an uncle, even accompanying them to the airport. He could imagine the gulf of terror that could open for orphans alone.[15]

The last image we have of Anne Frank comes from Hanneli Goslar. She is watching Anne through the barbed-wire fence in Bergen-Belsen. "It wasn't the same Anne. She was a broken girl. I probably was too, but it was so terrible."[16] It was February. It was cold. Anne had thrown off her clothes because she could no longer tolerate the lice. She stood naked except for a blanket covering her shoulders. Her mother and sister were dead. She believed her father was dead, too. She was delirious with typhus. She would be dead within a few days.[17]

Another survivor of Bergen-Belsen, a young girl who knew Anne, commented, "There it took superhuman effort to remain alive. Typhus and debilitation—well, yes. But I feel certain that Anne died of her sister's death. Dying is so frightfully easy for anyone left alone in a concentration camp."[18]

15
The Collaborators

At the end of the war, at least 11 million refugees were on the move. It was expected that a quarter of a million Dutch forced laborers would be returning to the Netherlands, and their numbers would swell with the foreign refugees seeking asylum. The Dutch government in exile in London had been preparing since 1943 to receive six hundred thousand people, among whom would be seventy thousand Jews. Borders would have to be secured and systems devised to scrutinize legitimate returnees, who would need to obtain medical, security, and customs clearance. No one wanted Communists sneaking in and destabilizing the country.[1]

As it turned out, officials had wildly overestimated the number of Jewish returnees. Only 5,200 Jews survived the camps and made their way back to the

Netherlands. Tragically, they were treated badly. The returning Jewish survivors were denied public assistance and told to apply to international Jewish organizations for financial help. After the final deportations from Camp Westerbork in September 1944, about five hundred Jews had been left behind, while over the winter months that number had swelled to 896. Though the camp had at last been liberated by the Canadians on April 12, 1945, those people had been kept imprisoned and forced to share the facility with the roughly ten thousand newly arrested NSB members who'd been their tormentors.[2] Only on June 23 had the Dutch military authorities allowed all former inmates to leave.

Female concentration camp survivors whose heads had been shaved in the camps often found themselves misidentified as collaborators and humiliated. Returning Jews discovered that other people were living in their houses or their homes had been robbed, and some even received tax demands to cover the years they had been in the camps. It was blamed on the postwar chaos, but it was traumatizing.

It should be added that the Dutch authorities were not alone in this. When a US intergovernmental committee commissioned a report on US-run displaced persons (DP) camps, they found Holocaust survivors in horrific conditions, poorly fed, and under armed guard.

The Dutch government in exile annulled Nazi legislation that had removed Jews from commerce. That should have been good news for Otto, but he was now classified as a German national and his businesses fell under the Decree on Hostile Property. He was forced to prove that he had never behaved in an anti-Dutch manner. In February 1947, twenty-one months after he had returned from Auschwitz, he was informed that he was no longer considered "a hostile subject."[3] At least he had had Miep and Jan to house him and friends who had supplied letters of support. As he wrote to his brother Robert, some survivors who couldn't prove they had means of support had been put into camps or not allowed to reenter the country.

Dutch civilians were not more welcoming. They'd had their own suffering. The last winter of the war, called the "Hunger Winter," had been brutal. The Dutch government in exile had ordered the railway workers to go on strike in sympathy with the Allies. In retaliation, the Germans had cut off all food and heating supplies. Over the Hunger Winter, between twenty thousand and twenty-five thousand Dutch people had starved to death. As it retreated, the German Army opened the dikes, flooding 8 percent of the landmass, and its systematic looting meant that the economic destruction in the Netherlands was greater than in any other western country.[4] Many Dutch dismissed the stories of the extermination camps in the east as an exaggeration. The truth, at least at that stage, was that many did not realize that there had been a Holocaust. As Miep Gies put it sadly, "Everyone had been through so much misery that no one had much interest in the suffering of others."[5]

Meanwhile, the Dutch government in exile directed much of its attention to collaborators. Because it expected acts of vengeance against those known to have conspired with the Nazis, it set about identifying the collaborators so they could be prosecuted legally. In 1943, it drew up the Special Justice Act (Besluit Buitengewone Rechtspleging), and then, starting in May 1945, it established a series of tribunals and special courts throughout the country. In the newly liberated Netherlands, the Political Investigation Service (POD) looked into hundreds of thousands of cases.*

Over 150 police departments were set up to collect evidence—letters, photos, witness statements, mem-

*In 1946, the POD was renamed the Political Investigation Department (Politieke Recherche Afdeling; PRA) under the control of the Office of the Public Prosecutor.

bership cards—on collaborators. The death penalty, which had been abolished in the Netherlands in 1870, was reinstated.

Dossiers were compiled and were eventually filed in the Central Archives of Extraordinary Justice (CABR) in The Hague. Housed in the National Archives, they stretch for more than two and a half miles and contain more than 450,000 dossiers. Protected by privacy laws, the files include information on convicted collaborators, people who were wrongly accused, people who were acquitted, victims, and those who acted as witnesses. There can be dozens of files on one person since that individual might have been under investigation by multiple police departments and been prosecuted for multiple crimes. The files contain photographs, NSB membership certificates, psychological reports, bank statements, transcripts of trials, witness statements by fellow collaborators and surviving Jews, and more. Two hundred thousand of the dossiers were sent to the Office of the Public Prosecutor. It was chaos, of course, and, though the numbers are somewhat sketchy, it is estimated that 150,000 Dutch people were arrested. (A small number of German officials were also tried and imprisoned in the Netherlands.) Of the Dutch prisoners, 90,000 were released and placed "conditionally outside prosecution." In all, 14,000 sentences were passed, 145 people were sentenced to death, and in the end 42 were executed.[6]

Some of the most aggressive collaborators among the "Jew hunters" were a group of Dutch Nazis working in the investigative division of the Household Inventory Agency (Abteilung Hausraterfassung), which was charged with tracking down and expropriating Jewish goods and property. One of the four subdivisions, or *Kolonnen*, of the agency was called the Colonne Henneicke, named after its leader, Wim Henneicke. A ruthless man, he'd been an underworld figure who'd previously run an illegal taxi service and exploited his contacts with that world in the service of the column.[7] In October 1942, the Henneicke Column began the work of tracking down Jews in hiding. By the time it was disbanded in October 1943, it had delivered eight thousand to nine thousand Jews to the Nazis.[8]

In his remarkable book *Hitler's Bounty Hunters: The Betrayal of the Jews*, Ad van Liempt provided exhaustive proof of the *Kopgeld*, or head bounty, allotted to the Jew hunters for each person they turned in. Among other evidence, he quoted the testimony of Karel Weeling, a Dutch police officer who'd been assigned to the Zentralstelle für Jüdische Auswanderung in 1943. In a police investigation report in 1948, Weeling stated, "It was common knowledge that the staff of the Colonne Henneicke received a bonus for every Jewish person they brought to the Zentralstelle." Weeling had been present several times when Henneicke had paid his men, always at the end of the month. At least initially, the bounty for a single Jew was 7.50 guilders ($47.50 USD today). Weeling stated, "I saw that the personnel then had to sign a number of receipts. I believe there were three in total. . . . I also saw Henneicke paying out sums varying from 300 to 450 guilders per person. In my opinion these sums were much higher than their salaries."[9]

A member of the column could receive a bonus of between $1,850 and $2,790 (in today's money), which probably explains the "unremitting zeal" of those Dutchmen as they hunted their prey. Each captured Jew meant bounty money. Even more sinister, the money to pay the abductors came from confiscated Jewish property. On December 8, 1944, the Dutch resistance assassinated Henneicke.

16
They Aren't Coming Back

That moment in July 1945 when Otto Frank stood in Miep's office, a letter from a nurse in Rotterdam in his hand, was one that Miep would never escape. In a voice that was "toneless, totally crushed," Otto said, "Miep. Margot and Anne are not coming back."

> *We stayed there like that, both struck by lightning, burnt thoroughly through our hearts, our eyes fixed on each other's. Then Mr. Frank walked towards his office and said in that defeated voice, "I'll be in my office."*[1]

Miep went to her desk and opened the drawer containing the small checkered diary and the notebooks and loose sheets that she'd been saving for Anne's return. She carried them into Otto's office and held them out to him. Recognizing the diary, he touched it with the tips of his fingers. She pressed everything into his hands and left.

When Miep and Jan invited Otto to live with them, he said he preferred staying with them because he could talk about his family. In fact, in the early days he rarely spoke of his family. Miep understood that words were not necessary. "He could talk about his family if he wanted to. And if he didn't want to, in silence we all shared the same sorrow and memories."[2]

But then, slowly, he began to break his silence. He started to translate into German snippets of Anne's diary, which he included in letters to his mother in Basel. Some evenings he would come out of his room, diary in hand, and say, "Miep, you should hear this description that Anne wrote here! Who'd have imagined how vivid her imagination was all the while?"[3]

At first, he could read only a few pages a day, overwhelmed as he was by the trauma of loss. But then he began to read excerpts to his friends, and most were impressed, though a few found the material too intimate. In December 1945, he decided he would publish the diary. He knew that Anne had wanted it published, and he was determined to show the world that something positive could come out of all the grief. He gave the typescript he'd created to his friend Werner Cahn, who worked for a Dutch publisher. It made its way to a well-respected historian, Jan Romein, who on April 3, 1946, wrote about it under the title "Kinderstem" [A Child's Voice] for the front page of the newspaper *Het Parool.* Diaries from the war were surfacing all over, but Romein remarked, "I should be very much surprised if there were another as lucid, as intelligent, and at the same time as natural."[4] Soon publishers were calling. The diary came out on June 12, 1947, under the title Anne had picked: *The Secret Annex: Diary Letters from June 14, 1942, to August 1, 1944.* A total of 3,036 copies were sold in the first printing, with a second printing in December 1947 selling 6,830 and a third in 1948 selling 10,500. In the spring of 1952, it was published in the United States and the United Kingdom, with an introduction by Eleanor Roosevelt.

The year 1952 was an important one for Otto Frank. He decided to move to Basel, Switzerland, where he still had family. Staying in Amsterdam had become too painful. The endless barrage of readers of the diary showing up at Prinsengracht 263 wanting to speak with him had begun to overwhelm him. At least when he was in Basel, readers would have to resort to writing him letters, which he conscientiously answered. Interviewed by *Life* magazine years later, he explained that it had come to the point that he could no longer tolerate Amsterdam for more than three days. He'd visit the secret Annex, where nothing had changed.[5]

The next year, on November 10, at the age of sixty-four, Otto married again. His new wife was the woman he'd met at the train stop in Czernowitz in the Ukraine on the journey from Auschwitz eight years earlier.

Elfriede "Fritzi" Geiringer had lived in the same neighborhood in Amsterdam as Otto, but they hadn't known each other. In July 1942, both the Geiringer and the Frank families went into hiding. Fritzi and her daughter, Eva, found refuge in Amsterdam, while her husband and son disappeared into the countryside. Both families were betrayed.

After the liberation Otto visited Fritzi and Eva in their old apartment at Merwedeplein 46. On July 18, 1945, he learned that both his daughters had perished. On August 8, the Red Cross informed Fritzi that her husband, Erich, and her son, Heinz, had been killed.[6]

Between 1947 and 1949, Otto helped Fritzi through the arduous trials of the betrayers of her husband and son. The legal proceedings were devastating for her to attend. Otto was actively seeking the identity of his own family's betrayer, and witnessing the pain and eventual frustration Fritzi went through at the trials, which essentially exonerated the culprits, must have been equally devastating for him.

The relationship between Otto Frank and Fritzi Geiringer provided consolation of an unimaginably tragic dimension, a profound comfort based on their mutual loss. Otto once said that because they both survived concentration camps and both lost spouses and children, they could understand each other. A relationship with someone who didn't share such suffering would have been impossible.[7]

Fritzi's daughter, Eva, gave a moving portrait of the man who became her stepfather:

> *Otto had been living in Merwedeplein with my mother for some time, but they were both haunted by all their memories. . . . Although he was completely driven to ensure Anne's diary was published, and gained the recognition it deserved, the war and loss of his family had placed a terrible strain on Otto's emotional and mental well-being.*[8]

The truth was that Otto needed to be near his existing family. He and Fritzi began the next phase of their lives in Switzerland. In Basel, the couple settled into the home of Otto's sister, Leni, her husband, Erich

Elias, and their two sons. They stayed for almost seven years before moving into their own modest apartment in the Basel suburb of Birsfelden. Nothing, except perhaps Anne's legacy, was now more important to Otto than his connection with his family. Over the years he became very close to Eva, her husband, and their three daughters in London; he and Fritzi visited them as often as they could. And he was close to his mother, who also lived in Basel.

On March 21, 1953, he and Fritzi were in London when his brother Robert phoned to say that their mother had died the previous night of a stroke. Two months later, Robert suffered a heart attack and died on May 23. At the same time, Otto was dealing with the owner of Prinsengracht 263, who wanted to sell the property. At a deep psychological level, losing the building felt as though his history was being effaced. He'd lost his mother, his brother, his past. He wanted to turn the building into something meaningful, a symbolic reminder of what must never happen again.

Working on the book and play of Anne's diary gave him purpose, but at the same time, it must have been very painful for him to relive those years in hiding. He told friends he was feeling fragile and had to be careful of his nerves.[9] In October 1954, he suffered a nervous breakdown and was admitted to hospital, though he soon recovered.[10] He was lucky to have Fritzi's devotion.

Even though it was almost fifteen years since the war had ended, anti-Semitic attacks continued. A German man wrote Otto in 1959, "I'm shocked that you as a father have published such a thing. But that is typical of the Jew. You'd still seek to fill your pockets with the stinking corpse of your daughter. A blessing to humanity that such creatures were extinguished by Hitler."[11] It took courage for Otto to expose himself to that kind of vile filth. In 1959, he and his publishers initiated the first of several lawsuits against those who challenged the authenticity of his daughter's diary. His friend Father John Neiman said, "Stories about the diary being a fake cut [Otto] deeply, and though it cost him a lot personally and financially to fight these people, he did it on behalf of all victims of Nazism."[12] The slanders against the diary never abated in Otto's lifetime. Perhaps it was some consolation that shortly before he died in 1980, the Supreme Court of West Germany ruled that insulting Jews by denying the Holocaust was a criminal offense.[13]

Part II

Cold Case Investigation

17
The Investigation

In April 2017, Vince Pankoke traveled to Amsterdam to meet the Cold Case Team; his only contact with them so far had been via Skype. Thijs Bayens wanted to launch the investigation with a pilot video to determine if there would be any media interest in the project. He proceeded to film Vince as the team created testimonial reconstructions of the investigation with Dutch actors.

Vince used his time with Thijs, Pieter van Twisk, and Jean Hellwig to tour the Amsterdam City Archives; the NIOD Institute for War, Holocaust and Genocide Studies; and the Anne Frank House, which they'd been invited to visit alone in the early morning before the crowds arrived. For Vince, who was already so steeped in Anne's story, contemplating what took place within those walls was a powerful experience. Also important at that stage was his meeting with the scientists at Xomnia, an Amsterdam-based data company that had offered to provide the foundation of the artificial intelligence (AI) program that Microsoft then agreed to develop for the team's research. Everyone knew that AI would change the investigation into the raid; it would enable the team to marshal the millions of details surrounding the case and make connections among people and events that had been overlooked before.

When Vince committed to the endeavor in 2016, he realized that he'd taken on not just a cold case but the ultimate cold case. By their nature cold cases like this one remain unsolved due to a lack of evidence or because evidence was overlooked or misinterpreted. Therefore, the team had to develop a plan blending proven cold case methodology with a historical research model, since they would be working primarily with historical accounts of what had happened. Upon joining the team, Vince reached out to a colleague, the retired behavioral scientist Dr. Roger Depue, the legendary pioneer in the field and later chief of the FBI's Behavioral Science Unit. Over numerous long lunches in Manassas, Virginia, a suburb of Washington, DC, he and Vince discussed how to approach the investigation. Both men knew that Vince was going to get only one chance at solving this case, and he needed to do it right.

As the Cold Case Team was aware from the beginning, there had been only two official police investigations into the betrayal of Anne Frank. The first had been done in 1947–1948 by the PRA and the second in 1963–1964 by the Dutch police. No other official police investigation into the betrayal had ever been undertaken.

But speculation about and sometimes serious investigations into the arrest had never stopped. Over the past several decades, many people had come forward with theories, and to this day, according to an employee of the Anne Frank House, the question most asked by visitors is: Who betrayed Anne Frank?

In 1998, Melissa Müller published *Anne Frank: A Biography*. Based on her research, she decided that Lena Hartog, the wife of Lammert Hartog, the assistant of the warehouse manager, Willem van Maaren, was most likely the betrayer. Four years later, Carol Ann Lee published *The Hidden Life of Otto Frank* and offered the theory that a shady character named Anton "Tonny" Ahlers was the culprit. Of course, both theories could not be correct, and under the pressure of increased public attention, David Barnouw and Gerrold van der Stroom of NIOD decided to investigate the case all over again. They limited their focus to three individuals (Willem van Maaren, Lena Hartog, and Tonny Ahlers) and touched on some other theories only superficially.

In 2015, the biography of the helper Bep Voskuijl was published by her son Joop van Wijk and a young Belgian writer, Jeroen de Bruyn. In their research the two learned about one of Bep's sisters, Nelly, who caused much distress in the Voskuijl family by her involvement with a young Austrian Nazi and later her work in occupied France. The tensions in the family grew so high that she had left the house. Bep's son believed that she might have reported the secret Annex to the German authorities.

In 2017, the Anne Frank House published its own theory of the raid, based on the research of the historian Gertjan Broek. He concluded that although everyone takes for granted that the Annex was betrayed, the SS might have been looking for illegal goods and weapons and found Jews only by chance. That provided a whole new perspective on the case. Each of the theories had to be examined for their credibility.

As lead investigator, Vince continued to visit Amsterdam—in September 2017 for several weeks to explore archives and a number of times in early 2018 to try to locate lost records. By October 2018, he'd established himself in the city full-time. The team opened a small office on the Herengracht and later moved to an expansive office in northern Amsterdam to which Vince traveled by bicycle, which made him feel, he said, almost Dutch.

Vince was well aware of the monumentality of the undertaking and knew he had to define a strategy for organizing the investigation. The first task was to review and question all of the previous findings, statements, and theories, specifically files from the 1947–48 PRA investigation and those from that of the 1963–64 State Department of Criminal Investigation.

Vince was surprised to find that there wasn't a central archive where the investigative files were located. Most of the PRA files were found within various CABR files in the Netherlands National Archives, some copies and others originals with no apparent consistency. The State Department of Criminal Investigation files, which were primarily at NIOD, were organized in a more logical fashion. With both investigations, the team was immediately stalled when told by archive officials that they could not have copies of the files due to the recently enacted European General Data Protection Regulation. That was a shock to Vince, who was used to the liberality of US Freedom of Information Act rules. Illogically, the team was permitted to read and hand transcribe the reports, just not to photocopy them. Luckily, many of the research contacts Thijs and

Pieter had developed shared the copies they had obtained prior to the adoption of the data protection law. A further delay was the fact that all documents had to be translated from Dutch or German so that Vince and the other English-speaking members of the team could read them.

Once Vince and the team had what they thought were all of the available case files (a false assumption, as they would later learn), the next task was to look for new or overlooked evidence. They'd expected that most of the data would be in the Netherlands or Germany, but it turned out that they were wrong there, too. Because of the circumstances, participants, and outcome of World War II, important records and personal accounts (e.g., diaries, witness accounts, military records) were scattered across several continents. Postwar migration, confiscation of records by the Allies, and the establishment of Holocaust-related repositories had resulted in the vast dispersal of records and witness accounts. The team ended up scouring the globe, eventually finding records in Austria, Canada, Germany, Great Britain, Israel, Russia, the United States, and, of course, the Netherlands.

"We consulted twenty-nine archives," Vince explained, "from the Simon Wiesenthal Center in Austria to the Library and Archives Canada to the Federal Archives in Germany and the UK National Archives at Kew." He added, "This was no abstract journey. It was emotionally costly to confront the tragic history these archives preserved."

Vince said he had been encouraged in his work by many cooperative people. "Our calls to institutions or witnesses were usually greeted by a comment that they'd heard or read about our investigation, wanted to assist, and were cheering for us to solve it." The only institution that proved to be unhelpful was the Anne Frank Fonds in Basel, Switzerland. With his map of the relationships among the various stakeholders of the Anne Frank legacy, Jan van Kooten had been right to warn Thijs and Pieter that they would be entering a labyrinth very difficult to negotiate.

In the end, the search for new or overlooked evidence was not confined to the musty basements and vaults of archives and museums; the team went looking for interview subjects.

Of course, there was not much hope of locating direct witnesses, but they were able to find people tangentially related to the Annex raid. Vince particularly recalled the interview with an elderly Holocaust survivor whose parents and sister had gone into hiding in a house on the Prinsengracht and been betrayed a few months before the residents in the Annex. The raid had been the result of information from a notorious female informant, Anna "Ans" van Dijk. One of the policemen on that raid had also participated in the raid on Prinsengracht 263, and it was helpful to learn about the similarities between the two different operations.

Vince said that the team had searched for secondary witnesses who could have had conversations or first-person contact with direct witnesses or suspects, including relatives, friends, and neighbors. They had come up with a list of thirty people. Expanding outward, they constructed a separate list of nearly seventy informational witnesses, as Vince called them, who needed to be interviewed. They were people who conducted research, wrote for a publication, or were experts in a particular field that related to the investigation. That was the mind, training, and methodology of the FBI agent at work.

Once the flow of information and discoveries started, it was time for the team to employ modern law enforcement techniques that had not been available to the investigators at the time the crime was committed, such as behavioral science (profiling), forensic testing, and artificial intelligence, defined as a computer system able to perform such tasks as visual perception, speech recognition, translation between languages, and decision making.

When Vince sat down with the scientists from Xomnia, they suggested that because the team was working on such an old case with missing data, the puzzle of the August 4, 1944, arrest would almost certainly never be complete. Yet at some point the program's algorithms should be able to predict what or who was the likely suspect.

To organize the massive amounts of data collected from documents and interviews, Vince developed a number of investigative initiatives. He called them the Residents Project, the Statements Project, the Media Project, the Mapping Project, and the Arrest Tracking Project.* The initiatives required hundreds of human work-hours, done mostly by a group of dedicated researchers, many of whom were volunteers and students. They ranged from teenagers, such as a student from Italy, who translated Italian press articles, to a retired Dutch professional in her seventies.

In addition to documents and book scans, the speech recognition portion of the Microsoft AI program was able to convert video and audio recordings to text, make them searchable, and translate them into English. As the team had hoped, the program began to show connections among people, addresses, and dates. These

---

* See glossary.

connections—policemen on the same raids, female informants who had worked together—had obviously been there all along but had not been noticed. Now the links began to form a narrative.

Because it was web-based, the AI program could be used anywhere. Pieter described the thrill of working with it at the National Archives: "If for instance, an address of interest came up in one of the files I was examining, I could very quickly cross-reference it within the database. Running the address through the AI would provide me with all relevant documents or other sources in the data store in which this address was mentioned. Sources where it was mentioned the most would appear highest. It could also give me a graphic on how this address connected to other relevant items such as different people who were somehow connected to this address. It could provide a map with all connections between this address and others and would indicate which connections were the most common. It would also provide a timeline when and where this address was most relevant."

Investigative psychologist Bram van der Meer was approached, and he agreed to work with the team. Vince knew him as a criminal profiler and investigative psychologist in the Netherlands, who advised investigative teams throughout Europe and had worked on several cold cases. The team eventually brought him all the data they'd collected about the witnesses, victims, and persons of interest and asked him to examine it from a behavioral perspective. This included information about their backgrounds, family life, social and work life, and especially behavioral responses and decision-making in unusual situations or under specific circumstances.

In the hope of somehow making a miraculous discovery of physical evidence, the team developed a plan for evidence analysis with Detective Carina van Leeuwen, a cold case forensic detective with the National Police Corps. Since the investigation was not officially sanctioned, Vince knew that access to governmental laboratories for testing of physical evidence (e.g., DNA, fingerprint analysis, radiocarbon dating) could be difficult, but he was optimistic. As he put it, in the Netherlands there is probably no unsolved crime closer to the national heart than the betrayal of Anne Frank.

Another of the team's investigative tools was straight out of a millennial's playbook: crowdsourcing. From the day they announced the project and appealed to the public for any information they might possess regarding what had caused the Annex raid, the team received a steady flow of tips. Some even led to new theories that needed to be investigated; others were from people claiming to be the reincarnations of resistance workers or insisting that Anne Frank had survived the war and was living with a new identity somewhere in the world.

The investigation was deeply serious, but there were humorous moments. For instance, at one point Vince was amused to find himself taught a valuable lesson by a teenage student doing a school-sponsored day internship at the Cold Case Team office. He'd asked the student to confirm the addresses and telephone numbers of particular witnesses by checking these in a 1963 telephone book. He went over the names and addresses and explained what he was looking for. Then he asked the young man to repeat the instructions, which he did. "Any questions?" Vince asked. "Just one," said the student. "What's a telephone book?" The lesson: "Never presume."

Based on existing theories, those newly developed by the Cold Case Team, and those received from the public, the team ended up with roughly thirty different possibilities of why the raid occurred. Several of the theories had already been heavily researched, but cold case protocol required making a due diligence review of the material, checking the source of information for accuracy, and carefully evaluating conclusions.

One such scenario came to the team from a Dutch psychiatrist. A patient had told him the story of a youthful memory she'd had in which the arrest of a Jewish couple hiding in Utrecht had ultimately led to the Annex raid. The couple, who knew the Frank family, emerged from hiding every month and traveled to Amsterdam for food. During one of their trips, they were arrested by a well-known Dutch SD detective at the Utrecht train station. While in custody they fell victim to a cruel trick by a V-Frau (informant) named Ans van Dijk, who, posing as a fellow Jewish prisoner, asked them about the location of other Jews in hiding whom she could warn to move on in case the couple gave away their addresses under torture.

The team's interest was piqued partly because of a detail: the couple was known to bring bags of ground spices back from their monthly trips to Amsterdam. Otto's business ground and sold spices. Was there a possible connection? But when the team located reports and confirmed the arrest of the couple, they discovered that it had actually taken place in mid-August 1944, weeks after the Annex raid and with no mention of a female informant. The theory was placed in the "highly unlikely" category.

Vince believed that some theories were like rabbit holes: you went headfirst into the tunnel, which took dips and turns, never seeming to end, and you had no idea where you'd pop up. Yet a good investigator took the plunge anyway. "Such is the way with most investigations," he said. Finally, the list was narrowed down to roughly thirty theories, some of which were then combined because they had common connections or themes. Applying the team's hybrid law enforcement axiom of knowledge, motive, and opportunity to the remaining theories allowed the team to eliminate even more. Simply put, if the investigators couldn't prove that a suspect had ample knowledge to commit the crime, motive to commit it, and the opportunity to do so, he or she would most likely not remain a suspect.

By the fall of 2018, the final investigative team was in place and had started to work full-time. Before then, work had been done on a volunteer basis. By the spring of 2019, the Cold Case Team had reduced the thirty theories to twelve scenarios, including a well-known informant, a local businessman, and a relative of one of the helpers. It would take another year before they landed on the likeliest scenario of all. All in all, the investigation lasted some five years.

18
The Documents Men

Before he went to Amsterdam in the spring of 2017, Vince had already begun research into the cold case at the National Archives in College Park, Maryland. He knew that the National Archives and Records Administration (NARA) holds millions of captured German documents related to the war. As it liberated country after country, the US Army designated a special unit to search for documents that could be exploited for intelligence purposes such as troop strength, weapons depots, and battle plans. The soldiers were told not to overlook burned and bombed-out buildings in the search for such records.

In 1945, the collected documents were crated and shipped to the United States, where they were stored in various military facilities. In the mid-1950s, West

Germany requested their return and the US government agreed, but not before identifying the records that would be of interest to future investigators. Those were microfilmed in an old torpedo factory in Alexandria, Virginia. Named the Alexandria Project, it took more than a decade to complete. By March 1968, the US Army had returned thirty-five shipments of captured war records to Germany.[1]

Most of the records have been available for half a century, though some documents were declassified only in 1999 after legal pressure. However, the collection is so vast that Vince had hopes of discovering useful information others had overlooked. Thinking of the soldiers who had salvaged the documents, he took to calling them "The Documents Men," after the film *The Monuments Men,* about the World War II platoon tasked by President Franklin D. Roosevelt with rescuing art masterpieces from active war zones.

Vince was always surprised that the research room at the National Archives, where microfilm readers were available to the public, was invariably full. Looking at the various screens as he walked past, he could see that some people were viewing US Army documents and others were looking at captured German, Italian, or Japanese records. On a few visits, he observed a World War II veteran asking for assistance at the desk. Based on the man's questions and the collections he was requesting, which dealt with POWs, Vince wondered if he'd been a prisoner in one of the German camps. He thought of his father during the war. Toward the end of his life, Vince Sr. had occasionally talked about a battle in which he'd fired mortar rounds at a German soldier who had been caught in an open field. The soldier had been running toward the shelter of nearby woods but, at some point, he had disappeared in the cloud of dirt and dust kicked up by the explosions. "Of course, at the time I had a kill-or-be-killed attitude," his father had said. "Now I wonder if that guy made it to the woods. I sure hope he did."

For Vince, as for all the other people involved in the cold case investigation, their work wasn't abstract historical research. The evil unleashed by war was self-evident. The people were real, the frustrations and successes palpable. The tragedies were painful.

Vince narrowed his search to documents from the Netherlands. Some of the documents were hardly strategic: there were requests for leave, permission to get married (one such request was from Karl Silberbauer), birthday wishes. But startlingly, there were also files salvaged from the German SD and the Gestapo.

One of the NARA finding guides noted a miscellaneous collection of payment receipts relating to the

Netherlands. Loading the roll of microfilm, Vince saw that they were typed forms with the information filled in either by hand or by typewriter and signed at the bottom. The receipts were organized alphabetically by the last name of the payee. As he scrolled down through the 956 frames, Vince recognized a few last names of policemen who'd actively worked for the SD in Amsterdam. He recalled Ad van Liempt's book, *Hitler's Bounty Hunters*, which described how the members of the Henneicke Column received *Kopgeld*, or payments for Jews they turned over to the SD. The papers in front of him, he suddenly realized, were *Kopgeld* receipts.

Many of the receipts identified the names of the Jews arrested and a payment of 7.5 guilders ($47 today). The payment was called, euphemistically, "expenses" or "investigation." But two of the 956 receipts actually identified the expense as a "head bounty."

Vince searched for the names of the Amsterdam policemen associated with the arrest of the eight residents hiding in the Annex and quickly found several receipts for Detective W. Grootendorst. It was a eureka moment. Vince caught himself saying "Yes!" so loudly that people around him turned and looked.

Then came the letdown. After he entered the basic information from the receipts into a spreadsheet, he discovered that the earliest receipt was dated February 28, 1942, and the last was August 16, 1943. The receipts didn't cover the period of the arrests in the Annex, and it would seem that whatever was paid to Grootendorst was for other deeds.

Until Vince found the 956 *Kopgeld* receipts, which shed light on how the *Kopgeld* system worked, who participated, and who was targeted, fewer than ten such receipts were known to exist. British bombers had conducted a nighttime raid on the SD headquarters on Euterpestraat in Amsterdam on November 26, 1944. It was supposed to be precision bombing, but the damage to the headquarters was light. Sixty-nine Dutch civilians died, and there were only four German casualties. However, the building across the street that held administrative records was totally destroyed. It was assumed that all the documents inside were lost in the bombing.

The Cold Case Team looked in German archives for the missing *Kopgeld* notes dated after mid-August 1943, but found nothing. Thinking that there might be further information elsewhere, Vince contacted Rinsophie Vellinga, a professor of Dutch language and culture at Moscow State University, who volunteered to go to the Russian State Military Archive in case Russian soldiers had captured the documents. The Dutch

Embassy put her in contact with the Jewish Museum and Tolerance Center in Moscow, which helped her get access to the archive. Unfortunately, Rinsophie also came up empty. Still, considering the German obsession with record keeping, the size of the existing archives, and the extent to which information had been scattered and often incorrectly labeled, Vince was hopeful that the missing *Kopgeld* receipts from the summer of 1944, which would include the payments made for arresting the eight residents in the secret Annex, might still turn up.

19
The Other Bookcase

From its very early days, the Cold Case Team managed to collect an enormous number of documents, photos, film material, interviews, and other pieces of information, but the information was scattered, uncategorized, and unfit for archiving. When Monique Koemans joined the team in October 2018, she determined that an electronic filing system was needed for the vast amount of information that had been gathered. She turned to an IT expert to set up a system capable of handling the volume and types of files and designed what came to be called "the Bookcase."

By the end of the investigation, the Bookcase held more than 66 gigabytes of data in the form of more than 7,500 files. Every piece of information was filed under the name of a person of interest; the files included pictures, personal certificates, official documents, transcripts of interviews, the CABR files, scanned diaries, investigation reports, and eventually scenario folders and much more.

Each week Monique gathered the young researchers under her guidance at the evidence board. She'd established three panels: one to identify the research problem to be solved; one to name the individual to do the research; and one to post the job done. Once every two weeks they discussed whether newly gathered information should lead to changes in the scenarios/hypotheses. Monique's style was collaborative. It wasn't obvious, except in retrospect, how she posed tasks in such a way as to ensure the independence of each researcher. But in the end, the tasks were like puzzle pieces that eventually cohered to make a full picture.

Led by Vince and with all researchers present, every Monday there would be a plenary research session to discuss the progress of the previous week and the necessary follow-ups and tactics. Occasionally, different experts, such as investigative psychologist and offender-profiling expert Bram van der Meer, would visit, and thoughtful discussions would ensue.

The Amsterdam City Archives became one of the most important sources for research and was like a second home to the full-time researchers. The main archivist, Peter Kroesen, had worked there for twenty-five years and was often approached by people asking for his help in finding the betrayer of their relatives. Every time Vince or Pieter visited, there might be a new story; they were immensely valuable to the team because they gave a sense of the texture of life during the war.

Sometimes Kroesen was able to solve cases in short order, such as the case of the man who walked in one day wanting to know who had betrayed his parents. The man knew the address of their hiding place, so Kroesen simply checked who the official resident was at the time. It was a woman who had lived there with her nephew since the 1930s. Two months after the betrayal of the man's parents, she moved to a bigger house—the house that had belonged to the people she betrayed. Meanwhile, the nephew changed his official address every two months, which was typical of collaborators who feared being tracked down by the resistance. Kroesen soon found the work records of the nephew. He'd been a student at the secret German spy school in Antwerp and had then worked for the SD as well as for the Einsatzstab Reichsleiter Rosenberg (ER), the Nazi organization dedicated to appropriating cultural property. It was not difficult for Kroesen to conclude that it must have been the nephew who betrayed the man's parents, who had no idea that they were being hidden by the aunt of a dedicated Dutch Nazi.

Once the Cold Case Team's office in the north of Amsterdam was set up, visitors started to come. Perhaps most important for Thijs was the visit of the Dutch military's chief rabbi, Military Police Colonel Menachem Sebbag. Thijs had met him through the commander of the Royal Navy barracks when he had been searching for a new office. On that occasion they had established an immediate rapport.

Thijs wanted to know what it would mean if the team actually found the betrayer of Anne Frank. Did the rabbi worry that they would stir up emotions they'd be better off avoiding? What if the betrayer were Jewish? Should the matter be left alone?

Rabbi Sebbag was very clear. "Hardly anything is of greater importance than the truth," he said. "If the betrayer turned out to be Jewish, so be it." The rabbi reminded Thijs that the Nazis had tried to dehumanize the Jewish people. "The truth," he said, "is that Jewish people are human *at all levels.* As humans can or will betray each other, then there will also be Jewish people among them."

In the office, the Cold Case Team kept a thick binder containing copies of the *Kopgeld* receipts that Vince had found at the National Archives in College Park, Maryland. Each of the 956 notes is forensic proof of payment of head money for the betrayal of one or more people. With bureaucratic precision, each is furnished with stamps, signatures, an amount in guilders, and the name of the recipient. Sometimes the names of the betrayed are mentioned, but other times only the number of betrayed men, women, and children is noted.

Rabbi Sebbag knew of the existence of *Kopgeld* but had never seen the receipts. When Thijs showed him the binder, he did not touch it. He stiffened. So many men, women, and children sentenced to death. Their absence was palpable in the profound sadness that filled the room.

20
The First Betrayal

Over the course of the investigation, various researchers worked on different scenarios and new information came in all the time. Vince saw the investigation as less chronological and more of an arc, which began with a betrayal far earlier than the 1944 call to the SD.

By the end of 1934, business at Opekta was picking up, and Otto rented larger offices at Singel 400. As is often the case with fledgling businesses, he found himself performing many roles, including salesman visiting housewives and wholesalers across the country. Business again improved in 1935 after Otto convinced a number of small wholesalers to stock pectin. He was finally able to employ more staff and hired a secretary,

Isadora "Isa" Monas, and at least two product demonstrators.

One was a woman named Jetje Jansen-Bremer, whose job it was to attend various trade shows and explain the use of pectin. At the same time, Otto gave part-time jobs to Jetje's husband, Josephus Marinue "Job" Jansen, and their eldest son, Martinus. Job built the wooden display cases, and Martinus helped with packaging and dispatch duties at the warehouse.

After the war Job Jansen was accused of collaboration. The Cold Case Team was able to obtain his profile from the police investigative report on him included in his CABR files at NIOD. There was also material on him in the Dutch National Archives. It seems that the man had a fraught past. Brought up in a strictly Catholic household, he'd joined the seminary of the Brothers of the Immaculate Conception of Mary (Broeders van de Onbevlekte Ontvangenis van Maria), intending to become a priest. Having failed at that, he married at age twenty and worked in theater: in administration, in advertising, and occasionally onstage. After eight and a half years his marriage disintegrated, and his wife and two children left him. Unable to cope, he attempted suicide, shooting himself in the lung. During his recuperation he met Jetje Bremer, who worked at the Dutch

Theater (Hollandsche Schouwburg); they married and had six children. By 1935, Jansen was no longer able to support his family through the theater, and Jetje opened a florist shop in Amsterdam and also went to work part-time for Otto.

It seems that Jetje's financial independence galled her husband, and the marriage deteriorated. In his paranoia and sense of impotence, Jansen soon came to believe his wife was having an affair with her boss. (He would later apologize for "implicating" Mr. Frank in adultery and "tarnishing" his name.)[1] The tension caused Otto to cut all ties with the Jansens.

When the Germans invaded, Jansen immediately re-joined the by then ruthlessly anti-Semitic Dutch Nazi Party, to which he had belonged in the mid-thirties. That made life unendurable for his wife, who was Jewish. Eventually Job left Jetje to live with a widow who was a like-minded NSB sympathizer.

Job Jansen was almost a blueprint of a rank-and-file member of the NSB. When Vince asked Dr. Roger Depue, the forensic behavioral scientist who often advised the Cold Case Team, to look at the biographical material they'd collected on Jansen, he said it was clear that belonging to the National Socialist Movement gave Jansen a sense of authority and access to power. In truth he was only a common bully, taking out his frustrations on his fellow citizens, especially the group that was deemed the scapegoat.

An anecdote in Jansen's file makes this clear. At the funeral procession for the NSB member Hendrik Koot, who'd died in the violent confrontation between Dutch Nazis and young Jews in February 1941, Jansen and a fellow NSB member, Martinus J. Martinus, accosted a Jewish man for passing through the parade barriers and crossing the street. They marched Isidore Rudelsheim into a nearby police station, saying that the Jew had been disrespecting the procession, even though the procession had not yet begun, and demanding that he be locked up.

In March 1941, Jansen and Otto bumped into each other on the Rokin, a busy street in downtown Amsterdam. Though he did not like the man, as a courtesy Otto stopped for a short conversation. With leering condescension, Jansen asked if, being a Jew, Otto was still able to get goods from Germany. Otto replied that he had no difficulty doing so. Jansen then said, "The war will be over soon." Otto replied that he wasn't convinced and said that the Germans were still having a tough time of it. Such a comment, implying that the Germans could lose the war, at that time and place was treasonous.

A few weeks later, on April 18, 1941, a young man

paid an unexpected visit to Opekta and asked to see Otto Frank. When he was ushered into Otto's office, he introduced himself as a courier between the NSB and the German SD and asked Otto if he knew a man named Jansen. Slowly the courier removed a letter from his pocket and handed it to Otto. The letter was addressed to the NSB.

Otto looked at the signature: Job Jansen, Member 29992. The letter was a denunciation of Otto for "publicly insulting the Wehrmacht" and "attempting to influence him." Jansen requested that the SS be informed and that the Jew Frank be arrested. Otto immediately understood that Jansen was reporting him for his remarks about the German Army during their brief encounter on the Rokin. The very appreciative Otto gave the young man the cash he had in his pocket, a mere 20 guilders, to thank him for intercepting the letter. At the time, he was convinced that the young man had saved his life.[2]

Otto later told the police that he'd let Miep read the letter and then had given the original to his lawyer for review. After taking a few notes, his lawyer destroyed it, with Otto's permission, since it was deemed too dangerous to keep.[3]

After the war and when searching for the person responsible for the raid on the Annex, Otto didn't forget about his former disloyal employee. It was unusual for Otto to react as he did, but on August 21, 1945, he wrote a scathing letter to the authorities in Amsterdam to inquire if they had Jansen in custody. He claimed that the man had committed treacherous acts against him. He was careful to insist that Jansen's wife, who was Jewish, had in no way been involved but said she might be able to help them find him if he was not yet in jail.[4] Perhaps it was Jansen's disloyalty that cut Otto so deeply. He'd helped the man and his family by employing them in a time of great economic distress, and the man had betrayed him. Had Jansen's letter reached the SD on Euterpestraat, Otto would certainly have been arrested and, at the least, been sent to a concentration camp.

Because Otto initially suspected Job Jansen of being responsible for the raid on the Annex, Vince believed it was logical for the Cold Case Team to begin their investigation with him. They were able to locate Eric Bremer, a relative of Jansen's wife, Jetje, and Vince interviewed him on April 23, 2017, at the Tolhuistuin restaurant in Amsterdam-Noord. Bremer had nothing to say about the betrayal of Otto and the other people in the Annex, but he did claim that there was a rumor in the family that Jansen had been responsible for betraying his own sons to the Nazis.[5] Of course, this was critical information for the team. Someone capable of such a betrayal would not hesitate to betray his former Jewish employer, against whom he held a grudge.

In the Jansen CABR file the team found Jetje's testimony about the arrest of her sons:

> *In September 1941, at four in the morning, two of his sons were arrested, taken out of their beds, and taken to Overtoom police station by two Dutch police officers. My husband was not present during the arrest, as he was staying at a different address. After the arrest of my two sons, I said to my husband, "What do you think about that? Two of your children have been arrested, and you're an NSB member." And to that he replied, "Oh, well, in a war there simply must be casualties."*[6]

It's a chilling statement. What kind of father would respond to the arrest of his sons in such a way? Was he hiding his guilt?

The statement is all the more devastating given the fate of Jansen's sons. One was shot in Neuengamme concentration camp on August 18, 1942, as he walked toward the electrified fence, saying he'd suffered enough. The other endured the horrors of Auschwitz and Dachau, though he did survive the war.

Soon, however, the team found a September 10, 1947,

postwar declaration by Jansen's surviving son, Josephus, in which he stated that he and his brother had been betrayed by a postman who kept a list of all members of their resistance group. (Apparently, the man was on holiday, got drunk, and bragged about the list of names he held.) Josephus claimed that his father had tried to intercede with the Germans to get them released.

That testimony was an interesting early warning for the Cold Case Team's researchers that nothing could be taken at face value. The bitter words of a wife must be checked against the facts. Even then, the acceptance of one statement over the other involves an interpretation: Did the first statement simply reflect the acrimony between husband and wife? Was the son covering for his father? In the end, what sways is the facts. The postman was found to have betrayed others along with the Jansen sons.

But that still left the team with the question: Was Otto right in suspecting that Jansen reported the people in the Annex to the SS? Vince was beginning to use the law enforcement axiom "motive, knowledge, and opportunity" to examine each case.*

---

* The original law enforcement axiom is "means, motive, and opportunity." The Cold Case Team developed a hybrid: "knowledge, motive, and opportunity."

In Jansen's file, the team found a postwar psychological assessment by Dr. W. Ploegsma, written in 1948 and obviously commissioned by the Amsterdam police, in which Jansen is described as a narcissist who played the victim and wallowed in self-pity. "Grudges, excessive guilt, impulsive behavior, restraint, servitude, excessive sense of dignity, lust for power; one can find all this within him."[7] Jansen was jealous of Otto Frank because Frank was "a man who could earn his own money." Jansen first joined the NSB in 1934 but had had to withdraw after two years because he could not afford the membership fees. He later rejoined because, as he told the psychologist, "he wanted to show that he was a man."

This would seem to suggest that Jansen had sufficient motivation to betray those in the Annex. Or it might be simpler: If he betrayed Otto once, why not twice? The real test would rest on whether he had knowledge and opportunity to commit the crime of betraying Jews.

To confirm that Jansen possessed knowledge of Otto's hiding in the Annex was more difficult and perhaps possible only through making assumptions. Even though Jansen was separated from Jetje during all or part of the time that the Annex was occupied, could it be assumed that he remained in contact with her? Since she was technically still married to a non-Jew, she was exempt from having to emigrate and continued working in her flower shop. Was it possible that she heard about Otto and the others hiding in the Annex and mentioned them to Job? Or was it possible that he or his new NSB-sympathizer girlfriend had a connection to someone who lived in the neighborhood or was supplying food to the helpers? The Cold Case Team came up empty in their efforts to find any information that could conclusively answer these questions.

That left the team to consider whether Jansen had the opportunity to betray the people in the Annex. A deep dive into Jansen's CABR file revealed that by 1944 he was working for a Dutch theater troupe that performed in German and was living in Winterswijk, near the German border. On August 15, eleven days after the raid on the Annex, he was jailed in the city of Munster, Germany, for theft.[8] Had he managed, in the eleven days between the raid and his arrest, to return to Amsterdam, to somehow learn of the Jews hiding in the Annex, betray them, and get back to the other side of the country at a time when travel was very difficult? It seems unlikely but can't be dismissed entirely, given Jansen's vendetta against Otto.

However, the most convincing argument against Jansen's guilt is that, had he made the so-called anonymous call, he wouldn't have had the contacts to be put through directly to the man at the top, Lieutenant Julius Dettmann. He would have been handed over to the IV B4 unit under Sergeant Abraham Kaper at the Bureau of Jewish Affairs.

In 1946, Jansen was convicted of assisting the enemy in wartime. One of the charges against him was the denunciation of Otto Frank. Tried for collaboration, his self-defense was creative. He claimed to have joined the NSB in 1940 in order to be able to help his Jewish wife. He said that he'd become a beneficiary member of the SS in the Netherlands in order to be able to do something for his sons, who'd been captured by the Germans.[9] His lies were easily contradicted, and he was sentenced to a term of four years and six months. Since he'd spent time in preinternment beginning March 31, 1945, his incarceration terminated on September 30, 1949.

Was there anything more to the story of Job Jansen? The team tracked down a grandson living in Australia. After obtaining a telephone number, Vince attempted to speak with him about his family's memories of Job. After the grandson listened intently to Vince's explanation of what the team was attempting to do, he refused to speak about Job, claiming that he was doing his own investigation. It was clear from the grandson's tone that the family was still embarrassed by the patriarch's affiliation with the Nazis.

This scenario, like many others the team investigated, was ultimately eliminated. But it was particularly interesting because it intersected with another theory under consideration. That theory involved a man to whom Otto Frank was initially grateful, a man whose story was ignored for more than sixty years, until he was named by the British author Carol Ann Lee in her book *The Hidden Life of Otto Frank.* That man had boldly walked into Otto's office with Jansen's letter of denunciation. That man was Anton "Tonny" Ahlers.

21
The Blackmailer

"The stranger said: 'You can keep the letter. Or perhaps you'll do better to tear it up. I took it out of the file of incoming reports.'"[1]

So said Ahlers as he handed an envelope to Otto Frank in his Opekta office on April 18, 1941. The first published account of this incident is found in Ernst Schnabel's book *The Footsteps of Anne Frank.* Otto described to Schnabel a moment when "danger came very close." He referred to Job Jansen simply as an "acquaintance" who stopped him in the street and to Tonny Ahlers as a "stranger" who had come to his office. He did not name either man. It's a poignant moment because Otto told Schnabel that he had escaped danger that time and had then survived the camps, the only one in his family to do so. "But I do not like to speak of a guardian angel. How could any angel have had the heart to save a man alone, without his family?"[2]

Vince contacted Carol Ann Lee, who had first identified Tonny Ahlers as the courier for the NSB, and on November 8, 2018, flew to England to interview her at her home in Yorkshire. One of his first questions was how she'd come to write a biography of Otto Frank. She explained that she was intrigued by his life and wanted to know who he was independent of his daughter's diary. Eventually Vince asked her how she'd happened upon Tonny Ahlers. "It's a long story," she replied. It had begun when she had contacted Otto's nephew Buddy Elias, the chairman of the Anne Frank Fonds and the person who had taken over Otto's house in Basel after Otto's and Fritzi's deaths. Lee had told Elias that she was writing a biography of Otto Frank, and he had invited her to visit.

It turned out that Otto had left behind a massive collection of documents. The attic and basement of the house contained stacks of photos and papers, including letters Otto had written and received over the years. It seemed to Lee that Elias had no real idea of their significance.

At one point, Elias directed her to a wooden bureau full of stacks of papers. As she was looking through them, she came across a letter Otto had written that referred to an A. C. Ahlers. It was addressed to the Dutch authorities, notifying them that A. C. Ahlers had come to Otto's office and given him the denunciation letter penned by J. Jansen that Ahlers had intercepted. Otto wrote that the man had saved his life. Lee recognized the story Otto had told Schnabel even though names had not been used. Since Tonny Ahlers had not been mentioned in past investigations, Lee decided to probe further.

Based on her investigation into the encounter between Otto Frank and Tonny Ahlers in 1941, she developed one of the more complex theories about who betrayed Anne Frank. She argued that after that first encounter, Ahlers saw the opportunity to continue to blackmail Otto.

Vince enumerated for me the assumptions that Lee had made. First, Ahlers had to have been aware that Otto Frank and his family were hiding in the Annex. Lee claimed he had known this because the annex of Prinsengracht 263 was similar to the one attached to his mother's nearby residence at Prinsengracht 253, where he'd lived for some time in 1937.[3] Second, Ahlers had kept the information about the hiders to himself until, in the summer of 1944, his business was floundering and he needed money. The bounty he could receive for reporting Jews proved too tempting.[4] Tipped off by Ahlers on August 4, 1944, a team of SD agents stormed into the Opekta office, demanding to know where the Jews were hiding. Neither the blackmail nor the betrayal came out after the war because Ahlers continued to have the power to blackmail Otto Frank. Ahlers's leverage, according to Lee, was the knowledge that Otto Frank's company had delivered goods to the Wehrmacht during the war.[5]

The Cold Case Team found Lee's deductions intriguing, but they would have to be proved. Monique set up the evidence board in the office and assigned each of her researchers a stage in Lee's deductions. The first question was: What would Ahlers's motive in taking the Jansen letter to Otto have been? Was it blackmail? Ahlers did pay a second visit to Prinsengracht 263, at which point Otto gave him another few guilders. But if it was blackmail, even Otto suggested that far more could have been extorted. It's clear from Otto's postwar account in his letter to the Bureau of National Security (Bureau Nationale Veiliheid; BNV) that his and Ahlers's paths did not cross again before Otto and his family went into hiding.[6] Otto said that he felt grateful and indebted to Ahlers for saving his life. That was of course absurd: Ahlers was an unscrupulous Dutch Nazi and a petty thief. But Otto did not know that.

In his CABR file, there are statements from witnesses that Ahlers worked for the SD. Couriering letters from the Dutch Nazis to the SD, he would have had little compunction about opening them. He was known to have kept a list of the names and addresses of Jews in hiding. It was also his job to report all persons found to be listening to the BBC on illegal radios, which he'd sometimes confiscate and resell. There is evidence that he informed on numerous people, including his mother's new husband, who was sent to Camp Vught, as well as a butcher and greengrocer who were friends of the family. He was said to have been a fierce anti-Semite even before the war.[7]

Ahlers was not the kind of man to be motivated by sympathy or generosity toward Otto Frank. Rather, he would have seen a good opportunity for a shakedown. It's likely that he intended to return a third time for more money, but by then Otto had disappeared.

At the time of his encounter with Otto, Ahlers was twenty-four years old. In his identity photo, he looks rather handsome, with fine cheekbones, square chin, and high forehead, his dark hair greased and combed back severely in the fashion of the day. Yet one might also say that he has the aggressive features of his fellow Dutch fascists, with an arrogant, even smug, look about the mouth and eyes. He was a cocky opportunist, trading on his affiliation with the SD to maneuver himself into a position with more power and money.

Vince and his team examined Ahlers's childhood as recorded in his CABR file. Born in Amsterdam in 1917 to working-class parents, in his early years Ahlers contracted polio and spent nine months in a sanatorium. He would always be slightly lame in one leg. His parents divorced when he was eleven, and both lost custody of their children. He and his five siblings were placed in a Salvation Army children's home and then in Vereeniging Nora, a home for neglected children.[8] When he was twenty-one, he tried to drown himself, apparently after a failed love affair.

Ahlers's working life was unstable. He started out as a hairdresser's assistant and then worked in a factory in France. His ID file at the Amsterdam City Archives indicated that he had lived with his mother for three months at Prinsengracht 253, a few doors down from Prinsengracht 263, but that his mother had relocated long before Otto moved his business there. Other than knowing that the buildings had similar annexes, what would that have told him?

Ahlers joined the NSB as early as 1938 and, according to his CABR file, was soon involved in an assault on personnel and customers at the Jewish-owned Bijenkorf department store. In March 1939, with a group called the Iron Guard (De IJzeren Garde), he vandalized the Amsterdam office of the Committee for Jewish Refugees (Comité voor Joodsche Vluchtelingen; CJV) and ended up in jail for nine months in the northern province of Friesland.[9]

The Cold Case Team researchers brought in an abundance of information confirming that Ahlers was not the man Otto Frank took him to be. After the German invasion, he immediately aligned with the enemy. He acted as the official photographer during raids made by the WA (Weerbaarheids Afdeling), the uniformed paramilitary wing of the Dutch fascists. He was often seen at Café Trip on Rembrandtplein and other places where Nazi sympathizers could be found, bragging about his connections with German officials.[10] In the February 18, 1941, issue of *De Telegraaf* reporting on the funeral of Hendrik Koot, killed when Dutch Nazis invaded the Jewish Quarter of Amsterdam, there is a photograph of Ahlers standing proudly next to high-ranking German officials.[11] He is wearing a white belted raincoat and looks as if he's posing as a detective. That was the same funeral before which Job Jansen, the author of the betrayal note, and Martinus J. Martinus illegally arrested a Jew for disrespectfully crossing in front of the procession. Although the Cold

Case Team could not confirm a relationship between Jansen and Ahlers, they did confirm that both Martinus and Ahlers were involved in the arrest of a man falsely claiming to be a member of the Gestapo and SS in November 1940. Clearly Ahlers and Jansen moved in the same political circles.

By November 1943, Ahlers's work for the SD enabled him to move into an elegant house that had previously been occupied by a Jewish family. His neighbors included SD Sturmführer (assault leader) Kurt Döring, who was in charge of tracking down resistance organizations and Communists. Ahlers's CABR file indicates that after the war, when he was under interrogation in Amsterdam prison, Döring admitted that he had known Ahlers well. He had "found him too stupid" for serious work and so had sent him to the Fokker airplane factory to report on Communist propaganda. He added, "Later I made him a V-Man [a paid informant]. He never did anything big." But he did admit that Ahlers was a dangerous man.[12]

After the Netherlands was finally liberated in April 1945, Ahlers was one of the first to be arrested by the Political Investigation Service (Politieke Opsporingsdienst; POD) of the National Police Corps. He was accused, among other things, of acting as an informant for the SD and was sent to prison in The Hague. In the chaos of those first months, he escaped several times but was soon recaptured.[13] One wonders if the incarceration of prisoners was half-hearted. In December 1945, the Dutch daily *De Waarheid* reported that between 100 and 150 prisoners were escaping each month.[14] After serving four years, Ahlers was released on October 3, 1949. His possessions were confiscated, and he was stripped of his Dutch nationality.

When Otto Frank returned from Auschwitz, he was not seeking revenge for the crimes committed against him and his family; he was seeking accountability. It was almost as if he believed that justice could be restored. Therefore, he wrote to the POD, denouncing Job Jansen for his slanderous letter. By November, he'd tracked down two of the Dutch policemen who'd been part of the raid team sent to the Annex, hoping to find out who had betrayed him and his family. And he looked for Tonny Ahlers.

On August 21, 1945, Otto wrote to the Bureau of National Security (BNV) to say he'd heard that it had Tonny Ahlers in custody.[15] He wanted to testify to the fact that the man had saved his life. However, when he finally went to the bureau that December, the personnel there were able to set him straight. As he explained cryptically, "I went to the Committee and said: 'That man once saved my life.' But they showed me the documents on him, and I saw that I was the only person he saved. He had betrayed a great many others."[16] The BNV showed Otto an illegal underground publication from 1944 called *Signalementenblad* (Description Booklet), produced by the resistance to warn citizens of the presence of provocateurs and betrayers. Tonny Ahlers's name was listed among the dozens of the most dangerous individuals.[17]

As Vince explained, the question confronting the Cold Case Team was whether Lee's accusations stood up. She claimed that Ahlers continued to extort money from Otto even after he and his family went into in hiding.

However, that would have meant that the office staff would have witnessed Ahlers's visits and might even have been responsible for paying him. That seemed an unreasonable hypothesis. If the office staff had any inkling that Ahlers had been blackmailing Otto, they wouldn't have hesitated to report him to the postwar authorities.

Lee suggested that Ahlers's failing business had left him with no other option than to betray Otto Frank for the *Kopgeld.* Like Lee, the team first thought that a person could earn a tidy bonus by passing a quiet tip about Jewish hiders to a Dutch SD policeman. However, Vince's discovery of the *Kopgeld* receipts in the

National Archives in Maryland made it clear that a reward was paid not to the informant but to the Dutch detectives who made the arrest. At their own discretion, the detectives might share a small portion of the reward with the informant. Tips from regular citizens were likely to come from someone who ran afoul of the law for theft or minor infractions such as forgetting to put up air-raid blackout curtains at night.

In any case, would Ahlers have known that Otto and the others were hiding in the Annex? The Cold Case Team could find no proof of it. About a month after Ahlers delivered the Jansen letter, the Nazi law forbidding Jews to own businesses came into effect and the name on the building at Prinsengracht 263 was changed from Opekta to the Aryanized Gies & Co. The change of name would have signaled to anyone who did not know otherwise that Otto was gone. Keeping in mind that Ahlers first visited in 1941 and the arrest was almost forty months later, if he knew that there were Jews in hiding, he did not seem like someone who would keep the information to himself for such a long time.

In her book, Lee noted that according to Ahlers's family members, he liked to boast that he himself was the betrayer of the by then famous hiders in the Annex.[18] It is a peculiar, though perhaps sadly not uncommon, psychosis to want to claim fame as a villain. Even Ahlers's family didn't really believe him.

To complete their due diligence, Vince had the Cold Case Team review Lee's claim that Ahlers continued to extort Otto after the war over his alleged business dealings with Germany. With the Anne Frank House providing extraordinary access to its archives, the team was able to dig into the Opekta and Gies & Co. order books and found out that Opekta did receive pectin from the parent company in Frankfurt and ultimately did supply the Germans, but so did many other Dutch companies.

The order book for 1940 indicated that pepper and nutmeg were supplied to the Wehrmacht in The Hague. But the Gies & Co. profit-and-loss books for 1942, 1943, and 1944 do not indicate any direct deliveries to the Wehrmacht. After the war the Netherlands Administrative Institute (Nederlandse Beheersinstituut; NBI), which monitored wartime trade with the enemy, indicated that it was not concerned about small businesses, as long as they did not actively seek German orders. If Otto's firm had ever worked with the Germans, it was on a very small scale and surely not worthy of blackmail. Otto Frank was not a war profiteer.[19]

Vince, it turns out, is something of a bulldog. Once

he finds the scent, he proceeds in a straight line and is relentless. "During my investigations in the FBI," he said, "I never allowed anything to get in my way. In fact, when I was teaching new agents how to approach major case investigations, I told them if they ran into administrative roadblocks my advice was 'If you can't go around them, go through them.'" You have to admire his intensity.

In this case the team revealed another aspect of Dutch society under the occupation. Tonny Ahlers and Job Jansen were grudging opportunists who viewed the Nazis' rampage as a neutral system to benefit themselves. They had no moral qualms about the murder of Jews, of Sinti and Roma ("Gypsies" in the parlance of the day),* of hostages, of resistance fighters. If they thought of them at all, those people were enemies who deserved their fate. Though prone to violence, they themselves didn't commit murder. But they condoned it.

---

* It is estimated that the Nazis killed 500,000 Roma and Sinti.

22
The Neighborhood

Prinsengracht 263 is on the edge of the Jordaan district of old Amsterdam where the houses lean against each other and face the canal. During wartime, the neighborhood was relatively poor. People were crowded together into small apartments and often spilled out onto the streets, adults walking to the shops and gathering along the canal, children playing. Neighbors knew one another.

In his book *The Phenomenon of Anne Frank*, former NIOD researcher David Barnouw suggested that the betrayer might have lived in the neighborhood because neighbors living cheek by jowl would probably have known if there were Jews hiding nearby. He further suggested that not only is there a sea of windows in homes on the adjacent streets Keizersgracht and Westermarkt that are visible from the Annex but also that the Annex can be seen from the windows in the rear of the houses that share the courtyard.

If the raid was indeed caused by a tip from a neighbor, the Cold Case Team had to find out who lived in those houses. That was when Vince came up with the idea of the Residents Project. He tasked three of the researchers with locating and compiling all available information on persons working and residing in the Annex neighborhood in the time period 1940–1945. That involved locating and retrieving thousands of records from five different archives in three different countries.

In Amsterdam, anytime a person moved and established a new residence, he or she was required to file the new address with the city. The Amsterdam City Archives gave the Cold Case Team unprecedented access to those records, which tracked the flow of people—when they arrived in the city and when they moved to a new address. Population registry cards recorded where and when a person was born; the names of their parents, spouse, and children; and all addresses where they lived. One section of the card indicated religious affiliation. On a few cards, the researchers noted that *NI*, which stood for "Netherlands Israelite," was crossed out, meaning that the person had somehow managed to get him- or herself "Aryanized" and off the deportation lists.

Once the list of residents and those who worked in businesses in the neighborhood was complete, the next step was to determine who among them were NSB members, collaborators, informants, and/or betrayers.

The team turned first to Yad Vashem in Israel since the institute's archive indicated that it possessed the records of all Dutch NSB members recovered after the war. NIOD and the Amsterdam City Archives held copies of the *Signalementenblad*, compiled by the Dutch resistance, regularly updated, and containing incredibly detailed information on known collaborators, their modi operandi, and occasionally a photograph. (As noted above, Tonny Ahlers made the list.) Vince was also able to locate a list of SD informants in the NARA files in Maryland in the same collection where he'd found the *Kopgeld* receipts.

There should have been *proces-verbalen* (police reports) that could have provided critical details on collaborators, but according to Jan Out, a policeman working as an archivist for the police, due to lack of space and money, the records from that period were all (one might say conveniently) destroyed. What did survive were the daily police reports kept by every precinct in the city. Anyone who was arrested or otherwise involved in an incident that required police or even came into the precinct to report something was noted in the record book, often together with the officer involved. Twelve-year-old Anne Frank is in one of the books, reporting the theft of her bicycle on April 13, 1942, a little less than three months before the Franks went into hiding.

In the mid-1990s, the archivist Peter Kroesen discovered daily police reports from the period 1940–1945 among a huge batch of files about to be destroyed. He saved them by smuggling them to a safe storage location. (These files, which can be viewed but not scanned, are among the most visited at the Amsterdam City Archives.) The Cold Case Team painstakingly reviewed the police reports for all incidents and calls for service originating from the Annex neighborhood, looking for any clues that might shed light on who or what could have initiated the raid.

The team of researchers assigned to the various portions of the Residents Project entered the information into a database and then uploaded it to the AI platform so they could cross-reference the names on residence cards, NSB membership lists, SD informant lists, known V-Men and V-Women, and daily police reports, as well as purge files and social services files, focusing on Prinsengracht and the surrounding streets: Leliegracht, Keizersgracht, and Westermarkt.

Computer scientists from Xomnia provided the foundation for the Microsoft AI program, which created a virtual picture of where the persons resided in the neighborhood. Complicating the process was the fact that many of the Amsterdam street names had changed since the war. However, the scientists were able to write a program that converted the street names from a current map to a wartime map and then geolocate all of the addresses of the residents and potential threats.[1]

Xomnia's offices are in a historic building just off the Prinsengracht, five blocks south of Anne Frank House. The Cold Case Team was invited for a demonstration. The researchers said they were speechless when the visual of the neighborhood appeared on a large wall-mounted monitor. Colored dots representing the various categories of threats, such as NSB members (blue), collaborators/V-people (red), and SD informants (yellow), were so close together that they appeared as one large mass over the greater Jordaan neighborhood. As the visual zoomed in on the streets directly surrounding the Annex, the dots were less dense, but the number of threats was still astonishing. An SD informant named Schuster owned a bike shop a block and a half away from Otto's business; a collaborator named Dekker, a waiter by profession, whose name the team found on the resistance's wanted list, lived a few doors down from the Annex; and multiple NSB members resided in the buildings bordering the back courtyard.

After the Cold Case Team's project was announced publicly at the end of September 2017, Kelly Cobiella, a reporter for NBC's *Today* show, traveled to Amsterdam to interview the team. Vince demonstrated the virtual program showing the concentration of threats surrounding the Annex and said that instead of asking what caused the raid, maybe they should be asking how the hiders lasted for more than two years before being captured.

For David Barnouw's neighborhood theory to be valid, it wasn't enough that neighbors be fervent NSB members; they would also have to have knowledge that Jews were hiding in the Annex. The team found that some neighbors seemed to know that the Annex was occupied, including those in the businesses in the two buildings on either side of Prinsengracht 263: Elhoek, an upholstery shop at 261, and Keg, a tea and coffee business at 265.

Bep claimed that an employee of Keg asked the staff of Opekta/Gies & Co. about the building's drainpipes. He wanted to know "if people were staying in the building." He often worked late at night and heard water flowing through the drainpipes after everyone had gone home. An Elhoek employee said that they sometimes ate their lunch in the wide gutter between 261 and 263 and occasionally heard voices coming from the Annex.[2] As Anne mentioned in her diary, the residents were occasionally careless, peeking out of windows and sometimes forgetting to close the curtains.

Yet, assuming that some neighbors were suspicious, it wouldn't have been an automatic conclusion that the hiders were Jewish. By August 1944, a vast number of Dutch citizens (estimated at more than three hundred thousand) were hiding to avoid being sent to Germany for mandatory work duty or were wanted for escaping from the work duty camps. The occasional sound of voices, the noise of water running, or smoke from the Annex chimney could just as easily have been caused by Dutch citizens in hiding as by Jews. Given the Nazi anti-Semitic propaganda of the time, it seems that some people were willing to betray Jews (one-third of Jews in hiding were betrayed). But they were less willing to betray Dutch citizens who were refusing to work in the enemy's country, which would only prolong the war, which, by the summer of 1944, the Germans were clearly losing.

It was important for the Cold Case Team to determine what could actually be seen and heard from the buildings whose rear windows faced the shared courtyard, which was roughly two hundred feet long (two-thirds the length of a football field). Vince wanted to conduct a 3D laser and audio scan of the courtyard, but there were too many buildings involved and it would have been outrageously expensive. Instead, he and Brendan Rook, the former investigator with the International Criminal Court in the Hague, used the gumshoe method.

They approached the Anne Frank House and asked for access to the roof of the administrative offices and museum, which occupy the corner of the block next to the Prinsengracht 263 address. The Anne Frank House was entirely cooperative and pointed out the stairs to the roof. Luckily, most of the buildings surrounding the courtyard are essentially the same as they were during the war, except for the one they were standing on. From there they had a bird's-eye view of the entire courtyard but only a side view of the Annex. It immediately became clear that the buildings on the Prinsengracht to the left and right of the Annex did not have a view of its rear-facing windows. Only a select number of windows in buildings on Westermarkt, Keizersgracht, and Leliegracht possessed a line-of-sight view of the Annex.

Certain views would have been further obscured by the large chestnut tree that once stood behind the Annex; Anne often referred to it in her diary. (In 2010, the almost one-hundred-year-old tree was felled by high winds, although it still lives today. Chestnuts from the tree were rooted, and the saplings were planted all over the world in Anne's memory.) Looking at time-period aerial photos of the courtyard during the summer, it's clear that the tree's foliage would have almost completely eliminated a view of the Annex from most of the buildings on the Keizersgracht side of the courtyard.

Because their rooftop perspective didn't allow them to see the windows of the Annex, Vince and Brendan searched for another location. A building directly across the courtyard from the Annex on the Keizersgracht, now a very popular comic book store, seemed to offer the best vantage point. When they explained to the owner what they needed, he was immediately accommodating. He said he'd inherited the building from his father and lived on the floors above. They were very welcome to see what could be observed from the upper windows. As they were about to climb the stairs to the top floor, he told them, with some embarrassment, that a few family members had been pro-Nazi during the war.

Vince and Brendan sat at the owner's bedroom window, staring across the courtyard at the Annex and wondering what could have been seen and heard while it was occupied by the hiders. Today, all the Annex windows are covered by shutters except for the lone window of the attic where Anne, Margot, and Peter used to retreat to escape their parents. From their vantage point the two men could see the steeple of the Westerkerk church, its bells still loudly ringing on the quarter hour as they had during the war. Also visible was the stump where the chestnut tree had once stood. The courtyard was mostly empty of people, with the exception of a few residents watering plants and several workers doing a patio renovation at the far end of the courtyard.

From their brief survey, Brendan and Vince were able to draw several conclusions: Even though people who had a direct view of the rear of the Annex might have been able to detect movement inside, it would have been very difficult to identify whether it was caused by workers or residents, Jews or non-Jews, especially at night with the air-raid blackout curtains in place. In addition, because the courtyard is surrounded by mostly brick and block buildings, sounds would have bounced around and deceived listeners as to their point of origin.

Occasionally the Cold Case Team was contacted by people who had new theories about the betrayer of Anne Frank that related to the neighborhood. One of the more interesting came from Arnold Penners, a retired physiotherapist in Amsterdam-Noord. In 1985, he said, he'd had an elderly woman patient—he didn't remember her name, only that it began with a *B*—who claimed she'd been living on the Prinsengracht only a few houses down from 263 and had witnessed the arrest. The team became very excited at this news since it would be the first and only known witness statement regarding the arrest by someone other than the helpers, Jan Gies, and Willy Kleiman.

According to the woman, it was a beautiful day. She was hanging out the window of her house looking down into the street when she saw a truck coming from the Rozengracht. It stopped in front of number 263, and from the front of the truck a German officer and a man she recognized as one of Gies & Co.'s warehousemen, Lammert Hartog, stepped out. Some German soldiers and Dutch police leapt from the back of the truck, and the soldiers blocked the road in both directions. Hartog pointed upward at number 263, and the other men entered the building. Sometime later she saw them coming out with the prisoners from the Annex. Lammert Hartog walked over to the other side of the canal and shouted something anti-Semitic at the prisoners. When the truck started moving, she noticed a small group of women standing by the road and spotted Hartog's wife, Lena. Lena also shouted something anti-Semitic and banged the side of the truck as it drove past.

The woman claimed she had reported what she'd seen to the detective in charge of the 1947 investigation, but since nothing had been done, she had let the matter drop.

In fact, her account was an ingenious fiction contradicted by all witness, suspect, and victim accounts of the raid. The raid party did not arrive in a truck; the street was not cordoned off by soldiers; none of the helpers ever mentioned either of the Hartogs' anti-Semitic remarks; Jan Gies and Willy Kleiman were watching from the other side of the canal and heard nothing. One can only say that it's curious how many people want to be part of the Anne Frank story.

23
The Nanny

Though Vince was hoping that people with information about the case might contact them, he was stunned at the number of letters that poured in. The *Today* show was one of the first to respond to the Cold Case Team's press release at the end of September 2017. But the team received interview requests from news outlets in the United Kingdom, Canada, Australia, Colombia, Russia, France, the United States, the Netherlands, Germany, Israel, Italy, and many other countries. And then the Dutch newspaper *Het Parool* ran a long article on the cold case investigation, which led to further tips from a number of people.[1]

One of the early tips came from an eighty-two-year-old woman who'd grown up in Jordaan, just a few blocks from Prinsengracht 263. Jansje Teunissen currently lives in a small farming community about two hours south of Amsterdam.* Christine Hoste organized the trip, and she, Monique, and Vince drove together to conduct the interview. It turned out that Christine knew the area well since she'd spent her childhood among its rural farms and her family still lives there. Jansje's home was a modest single-story dwelling off the rural highway. It was decorated with family photographs and lovely curio cabinets. The interview was filmed and conducted in Dutch, with Monique translating for Vince.

It was obvious that Jansje was nervous, but she soon relaxed as she recounted her numerous stories of Jordaan. A wonderful raconteur, she spoke in long monologues and with excellent recall about the early part of the war, describing the terrifying sound of the air-raid sirens and her father holding her hand as they rushed to the shelter. At least at the outset of the war, there was still plenty of food. Making phone calls was still possible, and the family were fortunate to have a telephone in their home, something usually reserved

---

* This is a pseudonym to protect privacy. Jansje was unaware that her father had worked for the National Socialist Motor Corps (Nationalsozialistisches Kraftfahrkorps; NSKK) and was surprised to discover that her mother had also been an NSB member and both of them had lost their Dutch citizenship.

for businesses or people friendly to the German occupiers. In the summer of 1944, Jansje was sent to live at a boarding school in the small town of Noordwijkerhout, where she would be safer than in the capital.

Jansje told Vince and Monique that her childhood had not been easy. Her father belonged to the NSB, though what that meant she understood only in retrospect. He had a drinking problem; he sometimes made money playing the piano in bars in the area but then would drink away his earnings. She was often left alone during the day because her mother had to support the family by working at a local fish shop. At some point, her parents decided that Jansje should spend her days with a nanny at her residence.

To get there, she would take a short walk down her street to the Prinsengracht, opposite Otto Frank's business. She would then cross over the canal to where the Westerkerk church stands and onto Westermarkt. It was easy to identify her nanny's house, Westermarkt 18, since there was a Dutch Nazi poster prominently displayed in the front window.

Her nanny, Berdina van Kampen (nicknamed "Tante Kanjer," or "Auntie Whopper") was a childless woman who lived alone with her husband. Jansje always regarded Tante Kanjer as a warm, generous woman who gave her sweets, cookies, and hugs, something she did not often receive at home. The nanny was married to a man Jansje called "Uncle Niek," a composer who had garnered some notoriety by writing a few popular Dutch songs. She said she was scared of Uncle Niek, but she felt sorry for Tante Kanjer.

Jansje was never allowed into the kitchen at Tante Kanjer's home.

A self-described "naughty" and "inquisitive" child, she did enter the kitchen once, climbing onto the countertop and seeing a basket with a rope and pulley hidden behind a curtain. Only years later did she realize that her nanny's home was directly adjacent to the Annex. She wondered if Nanny had been using the rope and basket to lower food down to the people hiding in the Annex. From the window in the kitchen, she could see the courtyard with the tree that Anne described in her diary, and there was a clear view of the Annex behind it.

Vince and the Cold Case Team found Jansje's story compelling: a fervent NSB member, whose wife was supposedly supplying food to the hiders, living so close to the Annex—that definitely needed to be investigated. The team began to examine the details of the story by querying their massive database to confirm the various names and addresses that Jansje had provided. The results showed that the nanny, Berdina van Kampen–Lafeber, and her husband, Jacobus van Kampen, did indeed live at Westermarkt 18 from May 1940 to February 1945. Uncle Niek was identified as a composer by profession.

That span of time was, in itself, interesting: the couple lived at Westermarkt 18 from the beginning of the German invasion; they moved out exactly at the point when it was clear that the Germans had lost the war and collaborators were fleeing Amsterdam. A search of Uncle Niek's CABR file confirmed that he was indeed an NSB collaborator, but the Cold Case Team had not expected to find that Jansje's sweet auntie was a card-carrying member of the NSB, too—and that she rented rooms to young NSB men. Perhaps instead of being a helper of the people in the Annex, she had something to do with their betrayal.

Though it was unlikely that a card-carrying member of the NSB would have fed Jews in hiding, Vince and Monique allowed for the possibility that the nanny was secretly against the Germans and belonged to the NSB only to accommodate her husband. But did she live close enough to deliver food without being seen?

Unfortunately, the building at Westermarkt 18 had been torn down and replaced by updated apartments. Switching to period photos from the war revealed that the rear of Westermarkt 18 actually faced the side of the Annex and did not provide a view of the Annex's rear-facing windows, as Jansje remembered. Also, the building was far enough away that her theory of her nanny lowering food to the hiders would have required the helpers to emerge from the Annex through the back of the warehouse and walk several dozen meters to retrieve it. Surely such activity would have been too risky for all concerned. Furthermore, if it did happen the way Jansje imagined it, there would have been some documentation of such assistance, either in Anne's diary or in the helpers' statements. As far as the nanny possessing a rope on a pulley and a basket, many multistory canal homes had narrow hallways and steep, twisting stairs, so it was a very common delivery method in Amsterdam at the time.

Uncle Niek's CABR file contained evidence of just how impassioned an NSB member he really was. Witnesses described him as sometimes walking around in a Landwacht* uniform with two pistols and flying the NSB flag from his home on holidays. Evidently, he held on to his radical beliefs right to the very end of the war, since there were several statements from people who

---

* Beginning in the summer of 1943, many male members of the NSB were organized in the Landwacht, which helped the government control the populace.

had witnessed him giving a pro-German speech on the street the day before liberation. The same witnesses against Uncle Niek claimed that his wife, the good nanny, had assisted him with the speech. Memories may have edited the date somewhat, since the couple had reportedly moved from the street in February, but the anecdote indicates just how much the locals loathed Uncle Niek.

But no matter how vehement a Nazi sympathizer Uncle Niek might have been, the team could find no evidence that anyone ever accused him of turning someone in. After the war he was convicted of having been an NSB block leader and writing pro-Nazi propaganda songs that were sold to a popular broadcaster. For his collaborationist actions he received a sentence of twenty-two months in prison.[2]

In the end, a snippet of information found deep within his social file proved crucial to the team's conclusion that Uncle Nick was not the betrayer: during 1944, he was not in Amsterdam but in the distant eastern city of Arnhem. He may have had motivation, due to his radical NSB affiliation, but he did not have opportunity. Nor could the team find any evidence that, despite having lived in close proximity to the Annex, he possessed knowledge that the Annex was occupied.

Normally that scenario would have been put to rest,

but the team found the identity cards of Jansje's parents at the Amsterdam City Archive and discovered that they lost their Dutch nationality after the war. Merely being an NSB member did not usually result in losing one's nationality; it took more than just misguided ideology to make that happen. The team located a CABR file for Jansje's father indicating that he was a member of the National Socialist Motor Corps (Nationalsozialistische Kraftfahrkorps; NSKK) and worked in Germany from 1942 to 1944. A paramilitary group, the NSKK provided mechanics and drivers for the various branches of the German military. It was probably his membership in the NSKK that lost him his Dutch citizenship. His collaboration activities may also explain how the family was able to possess a residential phone late into the war. What was more surprising was the discovery that Jansje's *mother* was also a member of the NSB. Her name was on the list that Yad Vashem had provided Vince early on in the investigation. She, too, lost her citizenship, which shocked Jansje; she'd had no idea how involved the family had been with the Nazis.

The team then discovered that Jansje's mother had been arrested on August 3, 1944, at 10:10 p.m., a mere twelve hours before the raid on Prinsengracht 263. That she was only fined and quickly released aroused the team's suspicion, since quick release often meant that people had traded information for their freedom.[3] Could Jansje's mother have seen or heard something about Jews hiding in the Annex close to where the nanny lived and given the information to the police after her arrest?

It was an interesting hypothesis, but it didn't hold up. The records show that the woman was arrested for violating curfew, which was at 8:00 p.m. However, it was still light out until 9:30, so there was likely nothing sinister about her walking around at that hour; she didn't seem to pose any danger. Besides, that late in the war, when everyone knew that the Germans were in trouble, the average beat cop would probably not have bothered to get mixed up with the Dutch SD detectives of the dreaded Jew-hunting unit. When the war was over, everyone wanted to have been on the right side.

24
Another Theory

In 2018, a message came into the office from an older Dutch gentleman who declared that Vince and his team were wasting their time trying to solve the Annex arrest because he already knew what had happened. After a few emails, Pieter established telephone contact with Gerard Kremer, who, as a small child, grew up at Westermarkt 2, the same stately building that housed two floors of Wehrmacht offices, around the corner from the comic book store from whose attic Vince and Brendan observed the interior courtyard and the back of the Annex.

As was typical of that Dutch neighborhood, Westermarkt 2 was a building that housed several different businesses and residences. Kremer's father, Gerardus Sr., worked there as a caretaker and lived with his wife and son on the sixth floor. The third and fourth floors were occupied by a Wehrmacht unit that collected confiscated goods from the Netherlands for shipment to Germany. Part of the cellar was also requisitioned for the storage of food and medical equipment.

In May 2018, Kremer's book *De achtertuin van het achterhuis* (The Backyard of the Annex) was released, and although it met with some skepticism, it also created a sensation. He had written it as an homage to his parents and their resistance work. He claimed that his mother and father secretly pilfered food from the cellar of Westermarkt 2 and with the help of a Dr. Lam, a physician who had an office in an adjacent building, distributed food packages to the resistance. Once acquired, items such as cheese and dry goods would be lowered with a hoist and rope from the Westermarkt 2 building to the small courtyard of Dr. Lam's residence on the Keizersgracht. The stolen items were then distributed by the resistance, including to the people in the Annex. When Pieter asked Kremer how his father had known that people were hiding in the Annex, he repeated a story his father had told about seeing and hearing the girls from the Annex loudly playing around the chestnut tree in the courtyard.[1] In addition to helping the Annex residents with food, Dr. Lam was supposedly providing medical services.

Although finding a new supplier of food to the Annex piqued the team's interest, the part of Kremer's story that Pieter most wanted to hear was his version of the raid. Kremer claimed that his father had recognized a frequent visitor to their building as the infamous Jewish V-Frau Anna "Ans" van Dijk. Using the false name of Ans de Jong, she often came to drink coffee with the secretaries at the Wehrmacht office. Gerardus Sr. once greeted her and mentioned that he recognized her from the hat shop Maison Evany, where she'd worked before the war. But the woman insisted that he was mistaken and walked away.

In describing the raid on the Annex, Kremer maintained that in early August 1944, his father overheard snippets of a phone call Ans van Dijk made to the SD reporting that she'd heard children's voices coming from a house on Prinsengracht. Supposedly that phone call resulted in the raid.

Gerard Jr.'s wife obtained that remarkable account from Gerardus Sr. just before his passing in 1978 as a kind of deathbed confession. Oddly enough, she did not inform her husband of that statement until years later. Gerard Jr. held on to the revelation for several years before deciding to publish the account in his 2018 book.[2]

Kremer's father was arrested over a month after the

Annex raid. According to Gerard Jr., his father believed he was betrayed by Ans van Dijk, though that was never proven. The family assumed that his arrest was related to his assisting Jews in hiding. He was taken to the SD headquarters on Euterpestraat and tortured. Dr. Lam was also arrested but was released a short time later. Gerardus Sr. ended up in the notorious Nazi prison the Weteringschans, but luckily a German officer who lived in the same building as the Kremer family at Westermarkt 2 put in a good word for him. Gerardus Sr. was released on October 23, 1944, the same day that an SD officer, Herbert Oelschlägel, was murdered by the resistance. The very next morning, twenty-nine men were selected from the prison Gerardus Sr. had been held in, transported to the south of the city, and executed as a reprisal for the killing.

After Pieter ended what would be the first of many and sometimes irate phone calls with Kremer, the team began to dissect this new information. It certainly met the elements of NIOD researcher David Barnouw's theory that someone from the neighborhood saw or heard something and notified the SD. It also involved an infamous V-Frau who was already on the team's radar because she was known to work that area of Amsterdam.

The first investigative step was to attempt to confirm

some of the information that Kremer provided about his father, Dr. Lam, and the location of the Wehrmacht office. Through the Residents Project, a few keystrokes on the computer showed that Kremer and his parents indeed lived at that address during the war and his father was employed as a caretaker of the building. It also confirmed that Dr. Lam had his office and residence in the adjacent building just around the corner at Keizersgracht 196. He had moved there with his wife in March 1942, just four months prior to the Franks entering the Annex. However, establishing that the Wehrmacht occupied two floors of the building proved to be more difficult. The only government-type office listed in the archive records showed offices of the Department of Social Affairs, Public Health Department. But it was wartime; the Wehrmacht most likely seized the two floors of the building and nothing was ever recorded in the city registry.

The team then turned their attention to Kremer's claim that his father was providing food to the Annex. In her book, *Anne Frank Remembered*, Miep Gies described in great detail obtaining vegetables from a friendly greengrocer, Hendrik van Hoeve, whose store was on the Leliegracht, a few hundred yards from the Annex.[3] A friend of Kleiman, W. J. Siemons, who owned a chain of bakeries, delivered bread to the office two or three times a week. There was also Piet Scholte's butcher shop, where Hermann van Pels had arranged with the owner to supply the Annex's meat. (Anne mentioned the shop in the menu she drafted for Miep and Jan's anniversary dinner at the Annex.) Bep Voskuijl shared the food collection duties with Miep, often bicycling at great risk to farms outside the city or traveling to Halfweg, a town west of Amsterdam, for milk.[4]

The helpers gave generous credit to all their food suppliers, and there is no reason to assume that they would not have acknowledged Gerardus Sr., who would have been putting his life at risk to supply them. But the team found nothing to corroborate Kremer's claim that his father supplied the Annex with food. This doesn't mean that Kremer's father was not assisting the resistance by supplying food to other people in hiding. Similarly, if Dr. Lam was providing medical services to those in the Annex, as Kremer insisted in one of his frequent phone calls, Anne would likely have mentioned it in her diary or Otto Frank and the helpers would have said so. Dr. Lam may well have been treating people in hiding, just not those in the Annex.

To follow up on the other parts of Kremer's claim, Pieter and Christine Hoste set out to determine whether it was possible to hear voices coming from the Annex.

Westermarkt 2 has changed little since the war. It is a six-story brown brick building with its front side entirely dominated by large windows. The ornate lobby is still period correct, making it easy for Pieter and Christine to imagine what it was like during the war. Speaking with various tenants, they learned that the building had a very large cellar area, just as Kremer described it, where confiscated goods could have been stored.

Inspection of the building's rear outer wall made it clear that there was no window, nor, as period photos showed, had there ever been one; people working in offices there could not have had a direct view of the Annex. Even with the side windows open, it would have been very hard to hear, let alone pinpoint the location of, voices emanating from the Annex. As for Gerardus Sr.'s account of seeing the girls playing in the courtyard—he may well have seen children, but certainly not the Frank daughters. Anne made it clear in her diary that none of the residents left the Annex for more than two years.

Vince and the team rejected Kremer's theory about the raid on the grounds that it was hearsay, based on the deathbed testimony of Gerardus Sr. to his daughter-in-law, who later told her husband with intervals of years between. There are simply no corroborating statements or documents.

25
The "Jew Hunters"

Who were the men (and occasionally women) who hunted down Jews for a living? Who, for the magnificent bounty of 7.5 guilders ($47 today), would turn in a Jew simply for the "crime" of being Jewish? (If the Jew had actually committed what the Nazis considered a real crime—owning a radio, for example—an extra 15 guilders was added to the bounty.) As the Cold Case Team began investigating the CABR files, they found that some of the Jew hunters were members of the Referat IV B4, headed by Adolf Eichmann in Berlin. Standardized in every occupied territory, that subdepartment of the Reich Security head office oversaw the categorization of Jews, anti-Jewish legislation, and eventually the mass deportations to extermination camps. The IV B4 unit in Amsterdam, including the

Dutch policemen who joined it, was under the German Security Service (Sicherheitsdienst; SD).

By the end of 1941, the Nazi noose tightened around the necks of the Netherlands' Jewish population. Day by day, the regulations became stricter. On December 5, all *non-Dutch* Jews were ordered to report to the Zentralstelle für Jüdische Auswanderung (Central Agency for Jewish Emigration), usually referred to simply as the Zentralstelle, to register for "voluntary emigration." The Nazis already had the registration files of all *Dutch* Jews. The next call was for forty thousand Dutch and non-Dutch Jews to report for *Arbeitseinsatz*, mandatory work duty in Germany; that began on July 5, 1942, the day Margot Frank received her summons. By 1943, the well-oiled machine was well on its way to reaching its "emigration" goals. The Nazis simply totaled up the number of Jews in the Netherlands and subtracted those who had already been processed or were exempted by working for the Jewish Council. It didn't take a statistician to calculate that there were a significant number of Jews unaccounted for, roughly twenty-five thousand, most of whom were assumed to be in hiding.

To reach their goal of making the Netherlands a *judenfrei* (Jew-free) nation, the Nazis ordered that those twenty-five thousand people be found. In a postwar interrogation, Willy Lages, the head of the SD in Amsterdam, admitted to having been present at a meeting in the SD headquarters in The Hague at which a decision was made to incentivize the search for the missing Jews by offering a bounty. The bounties were to be paid to Dutch policemen, mainly men from the Amsterdam police, Bureau of Jewish Affairs. The actual investigative squad within the Zentralstelle, known as the Henneicke Column (Colonne Henneicke), was made up of civilian contract employees.[1]

Staffed almost entirely by Dutchmen with NSB affiliation, the members of the Henneicke Column were an eclectic bunch coming from a number of different professions: 20 percent were traveling salesmen, 20 percent office clerks, 15 percent from the auto industry, and 8 percent small-business owners. Some of the notables, such as Henneicke and Joop den Ouden, were mechanics. Den Ouden had worked for Lippmann, Rosenthal & Co. and was notorious for his ruthlessness in stealing Jewish property. Eduard Moesbergen, a wireless radio operator by profession, was a skilled bookkeeper and was responsible for the efficient management of the Henneicke group.

After the group was disbanded on October 1, 1943, the hunt for Jews fell to men with police powers, namely the SD Jewish Affairs squad known as unit IV B4.

The chain of command started with the German-born SS Lieutenant Julius Dettmann at the top with fellow German Otto Kempin directly under him in charge of the Dutch SD detectives. Those two were in place from 1942, but the Cold Case Team discovered that Kempin was transferred just days before the Annex raid. His absence is probably the reason that the phone call regarding the Annex went upstairs to Dettmann. As a German SD officer, Karl Silberbauer, who conducted the raid, would have reported to Kempin, but since Kempin was no longer there, Silberbauer was taking his orders directly from the top.

After the war was over, all of the Dutch members of IV B4 were accused of collaboration, and thus a CABR file under each of their names exists in the Netherlands' National Archives. Some of the non-Dutch members were prosecuted for war crimes; Kempin was sentenced to ten years, and Dettmann was arrested but committed suicide in jail before he could be prosecuted. Yet others, such as Silberbauer, had already slipped out of the Netherlands.

It was clear from the files that the IV B4 Dutch detectives depended heavily on civilians to inform them about Jews in hiding. These V-Men and V-Women could be Jew or Gentile. Most had done something to cause them to fear for their lives if they didn't turn on others. In return for their cooperation, they remained free but under the watchful eye of their handlers, who profited nicely from their work. They might be paid expenses and given a place to live. They might even, on occasion, receive some additional token of nice clothing or food products, but the *Kopgeld* reward and any plunder would go into the pocket of the detective handling them.

The best-known V-Frau, Ans van Dijk, later identified Gerrit Mozer and Pieter Schaap, two of the most prolific handlers of the V-people, as the detectives to whom she passed information. Eduard Moesbergen, who joined IV B4 after the Henneicke Column was disbanded, successfully ran a productive V-Frau by the name of Elisa Greta de Leeuw, who went under the code name "Beppie." These informants tricked unsuspecting Jews into trusting them. It all came down to the detectives and V-people understanding what Jews in hiding needed (e.g., a new hiding spot, false papers, food) and then making it known in the right circles that they could help. They set up apartments known as "Jew traps," offering safe shelter to desperate and unsuspecting Jews. This was the ruse used on May 10, 1944, to capture the husband and son of Otto's second wife, Fritzi Geiringer, which led to the capture of Fritzi and her daughter, Eva, the following day, coincidentally Eva's birthday.[2]

Another trick the SD detectives used was to place V-people in jails or camps to elicit information from prisoners about addresses where other Jews were hiding or valuables were stowed. In his postwar interrogation, Schaap admitted to sending a V-Man named Leopold de Jong to Westerbork to collect addresses from recent prisoner arrivals. He would become a potential suspect in the Annex betrayal.

Non-Jewish informants were also used, but they expected some form of payment for their information or, at a minimum, forgiveness for some prior infraction of the law, such as petty theft. People who were caught hiding Jews were given the chance to escape their fate by becoming V-people and supplying other addresses where Jews were hiding or their resistance contacts. One postwar trial involved a man who ran a boardinghouse on Weteringschans in Amsterdam and offered Jews safe accommodations. After collecting the rent in advance, he would contact the authorities to pick up the Jews. During his interrogation, he identified SD detective Frederick Cool as the officer who ordered him to call when new tenants arrived. He claimed that he followed Detective Cool's orders because he feared that if he didn't, he, too, would be arrested. So he made the calls—but only after he collected and deposited the rent money.

The men of IV B4 eventually found themselves making less money as the number of Jews easily found in hiding started to dwindle. Fewer arrests meant fewer bounty payments at the end of the month. To compensate for that, the Jew hunters would often steal whatever valuables the Jews or hiders possessed. For example, Dutch police officer Pieter Schaap from the Bureau of Jewish Affairs was not immune to helping himself to some of the loot. When the postwar arrest team went to pick up Schaap, they found furs, paintings, jewelry, and other valuables that had somehow made their way into the Schaap household. Witnesses claimed to have often seen Schaap's wife wearing furs and jewelry while out on the town.

Vince was intrigued to see the name of the Dutch detective Willem Grootendorst in one of the NIOD documents. His name appeared on a number of the *Kopgeld* receipts, and, of course, he was one of the Dutch policemen who accompanied Silberbauer in the raid on the Annex. The other policeman on the raid, Gezinus Gringhuis, was reported for extorting a Dutch woman who was harboring a Jew. He demanded 500 guilders to "make things go away." Instead, she went to the local police to report him. When Gringhuis went back to her house to collect his 500 guilders, police officer Hendrik Blonk was waiting behind the curtains to apprehend him. Unfortunately, a gust of wind blew the curtains open, exposing Blonk and ruining the sting. When Blonk went to Sergeant Kaper to report Gringhuis, Kaper told Blonk in the presence of his men that if he ever interfered in their business again, he would give his men the right to shoot him.[3] Such was the extent of the corruption within the force.

In order to know which SD detectives worked together, Vince established the Arrest Tracking Project, an investigative initiative by which the Cold Case Team researched all arrests of Jews in 1943 and 1944 in order to determine the MOs of the Jew hunters: who worked with whom, what methods they used, how they obtained information, and so forth.

When they catalogued the information in the CABR files with Amsterdam police daily journals, *Kopgeld* receipts, and other sources, the group was able to see that the Annex raid was unusual in at least one regard. That day was the first time SD man Silberbauer and Dutch SD Detectives Gringhuis and Grootendorst worked together. (There was evidence of Silberbauer and Grootendorst participating in prior arrests as late as June 1944, but not with Gringhuis.) Though no one has ever categorically determined the identity of the third SD detective who joined Silberbauer and the others that day, Vince and his team came to believe that it might have been none other than Pieter Schaap. Thanks to Nienke Filius, a brilliant young Dutch data scientist who wrote a program to analyze the data from the Arrest Tracking Project, the team learned that Schaap and Silberbauer worked together in August 1944.

Often the CABR files contained mitigating statements regarding the IV B4 men's wartime conduct. Usually the reports about "good behavior" began in late 1943, when even the SD likely suspected that the Germans would lose the war. Driven by self-preservation—everyone knew that there would be postwar reckonings—the Dutch SD detectives occasionally started helping people and letting suspects go. After the end of the war, notes flew out of the prisons asking Jews and others who'd been spared to put in a good word. In his file, Eduard Moesbergen claimed that he'd helped a prominent Jewish Council member by going to his home to warn him of an impending arrest. The council member, who was a notary by profession, was not there. Checking back a few days later and seeing that the notary was still absent, Moesbergen assumed that he'd gone into hiding.[4] Of course, most of the people the IV B4 members did not help couldn't be contacted and couldn't testify one way or the other about their experiences at the hands of the Jew hunters; they hadn't survived the war.

In the postwar period, the special courts took keen notice of the behavior of the IV B4 members as well as the informants and V-people who worked for them and reflected it in their sentencing. Nearly one-fourth of the IV B4 members tried received the ultimate sentence of death, though most of the sentences were commuted. Abraham Kaper, Pieter Schaap, Maarten Kuiper (a police agent assigned to the SD who specialized in tracking down and arresting members of the resistance), and Ans van Dijk were executed. Only those guilty of the most egregious crimes were executed, which led the Cold Case Team to exhaustively examine their CABR files to assess what role, if any, they might have played in the betrayal of the hiders in the Annex.

26
The V-Frau

Anna "Ans" van Dijk was born in Amsterdam in 1905. Her parents were lower-middle-class secular Jews. She had one brother. When she was fourteen years old, her mother died, and her father soon remarried. At the age of twenty-two, she married but separated from her husband eight years later. In 1938, after her father was confined to a mental hospital, where he eventually died, she officially divorced her husband.

Her story might have remained unremarkable except that when she turned thirty-three, as she later testified in court, she fell in love with the female nurse who nurtured her through an illness.

Van Dijk worked in a hat shop, Maison Evany, owned by Eva de Vries–Harschel, who was also Jewish. (That was where Gerardus Kremer remembered meeting her.) After it was forbidden for Jews to own businesses, the shop was seized, and van Dijk lost her job. Soon after, she began a romantic relationship with a woman named Miep Stodel. Stodel, also Jewish, left Van Dijk in 1942 to seek safety in Switzerland. How different Van Dijk's life might have been had she managed to flee with her.

During her postwar collaboration trial in 1946–1948, Ans van Dijk claimed that from the beginning of the invasion she had defied the German occupiers, refusing to wear the yellow star or obey any of the discriminatory laws against Jews. She said she had worked for a resistance group of mostly young Jewish people who met clandestinely on Tweede Jan Steenstraat, the majority of whom would be arrested and not survive the war. With fake identity papers in the name of Alphonsia Maria "Annie" de Jong, she distributed forged documents and successfully placed many Jewish people in hiding. Van Dijk stated that she had also worked for the resistance newspaper *Vrij Nederland*.[1]

The Cold Case Team could find no record to corroborate those details, but that does not necessarily mean they are untrue since resistance members worked in small cells and seldom exchanged names, let alone kept records. In case of capture, the less they could reveal under torture, the better. If a group was largely Jewish, the chances of its members surviving to testify in someone's favor were small.[2] At her trial, which was obsessively followed in the newspapers, someone could easily have come forward to debunk her assertion of having helped the resistance. No one did. But neither did anyone come forward to support her.

Van Dijk claimed that she engaged in resistance work for almost two years but, as the situation worsened, decided to go into hiding in Marco Polostraat. Sadly, she miscalculated: her hiders, a woman named Arnoldina Alsemgeest and her daughter, betrayed her.[3]

On Easter Sunday, April 25, 1943, Van Dijk was arrested by Pieter Schaap, the notoriously cruel Dutch officer working for the IV B4 unit. He'd begun his police career before the war working with the dog brigade; by the end of the war, he was responsible for the betrayal and execution of hundreds of Jews and resistance fighters. Schaap gave Van Dijk the usual ultimatum: either cooperate or face certain death in one of the eastern camps. She claimed that on her third day in captivity, she agreed to cooperate. She became one of the most prolific V-Frauen in the Netherlands.

Pieter Schaap had many V-persons working for him, and he saw the advantage of pairing up collaborators to work together. Van Dijk was assisted in her "work" by Branca Simons, a Jewish seamstress who was no longer protected from deportation as her Christian husband, Wim Houthuijs, had been arrested for theft. After she was turned by Schaap, her apartment at 25 Kerkstraat became a Jew trap.[4] People who needed to hide were lured to the apartment with the promise of safe shelter and food stamps. After a few hours or days, the SD would come by to make the arrest.

It's difficult to contemplate the transition from working for the resistance and saving people to becoming a V-Frau who betrayed them. However, when you are thirty-eight years old and faced with death, many might choose life. Van Dijk claimed that she was terrified of Schaap, who threatened her at gunpoint with deportation to Mauthausen.

In the late 1930s, when Ans van Dijk declared herself a lesbian to her lover, homosexuality was not a criminal offense. There were gay and lesbian bars in Amsterdam. Worldly people knew about homosexuals, while people who were less sophisticated just pretended that homosexuality did not exist. Men who lived together were called confirmed bachelors; women were called spinsters. However, one could certainly not risk being openly gay in public.* Police officers often went out of their way to target homosexuals, outing them with dire social consequences. In Van Dijk's CABR file, the Cold Case Team found extensive statements in which people expressed their disgust at her lifestyle, including a statement from the daughter of her lover. Van Dijk was an outcast and a pariah.

In 1936, Heinrich Himmler created a division within the Gestapo called the Reich Central Office for the Combating of Homosexuality and Abortion (Reichszentrale zur Bekämpfung der Homosexualität und der Abtreibung). Both threatened the growth of the master race. Male homosexuals were imprisoned, often in concentration camps, where they were sometimes used as subjects in scientific experiments, particularly to cure homosexuality. But oddly enough, lesbians were not widely persecuted.[5] It seems that female homosexuality was deemed passive and nonthreatening and was, if not tolerated, at least overlooked. That held true in the Netherlands. To her SD handlers, Van Dijk's sexual-

* Article 248 bis of the Wetboek van Strafrecht (of Criminal Code). Homosexuality had not been a criminal offense in the Netherlands since 1811. Homosexual contact between adults (over twenty-one) and minors (under twenty-one) was prohibited in 1911.

ity did not seem to be a matter of concern. They were pragmatic and tolerated her lesbianism because she was useful to them.

Two months after being turned by Pieter Schaap, Van Dijk met her new girlfriend, Johanna Maria "Mies" de Regt, in a café and moved into her apartment at Nieuwe Prinsengracht 54-2, among elegant houses along the canal. Both women worked as V-Frauen, and the apartment soon became a Jew trap to which people trying to hide were lured with the promise of safety. De Regt would later testify that she and Van Dijk attended parties at nightclubs with the German elite where the food and the vintage wine flowed freely, even as most people lived on food stamps.[6] For the first time Van Dijk was part of the in crowd, and the money she earned so ruthlessly brought her luxury. It clearly wasn't hard to be seduced by the status she'd gained and to grow indifferent to the price others paid as a result of her actions. Though it does produce heroes, war is never the best context in which to hone one's conscience.

The cold criminality of the V-Frauen was stark. In her court testimony, Van Dijk described how they found the family of a man named Salomon Stodel by coincidence when they were looking for another family altogether:

Because we had no address from Klepman (about whom they had heard that he had hidden money in his chimney), we inquired about the family in a nearby milk shop. We pretended to be members of the resistance. We were told that the Klepman family had already been arrested by the Germans and that their home was inhabited again. Because we presented ourselves as good Dutchmen, the woman in the milk shop said that Jews lived next to them, who were in difficulty and in need of help.[7]

The women contacted Schaap to come arrest the Stodel family. Ronnie Goldstein–van Cleef recalled her interaction with Van Dijk. Goldstein–van Cleef was from a very liberal Jewish family in The Hague, and going undercover and joining the resistance was natural: "Certain circumstances and requests from friends forced you to act." Her family kept a printing press belonging to the resistance under the floor of their house. Her aunt Dora often hid people in her home and also found a perfect hiding place for *onderduikers* in a condemned apartment nearby. Goldstein–van Cleef remembered meeting Van Dijk there:

I was to take a boy to Twente. Aunt Dora knew Ans van Dijk from the time she was little and consid-

ered her to be completely trustworthy. Ans van Dijk asked if I could take another girl along. She gave me a picture of the girl, and I obtained an identity card for her. Later she proposed, "If you are at Central Station at such and such a time with that boy I will be there with the girl, and you can take both of them." That's what we agreed to do. At Central Station I gave the boy my purse to hold because I wanted to get tickets at the ticket office. I turned around, I saw that the boy was being arrested, and holding only my change in my hand, I ran out of the station as fast as I could, jumped onto the streetcar, and went back to Aunt Dora's, where I burst into tears. I was so terribly shocked. Then I said, "That Ans van Dijk is not good; she is no good." And later that turned out to be the case.[8]

Goldstein–van Cleef was haunted by that moment. The victim was a child, and she had to abandon him. She herself was finally betrayed in June 1944, ending up in Westerbork, where she met the Frank family. She survived the war.

One strategy Ans van Dijk used to gain information was dubbed "cell espionage." She would be put into a holding cell together with other prisoners who were suspected of knowing the locations of Jewish people in hiding. After falsely claiming to have been severely tortured during interrogation, she would convince her cellmates that the SD was releasing her and offer to warn any of their friends or relatives to relocate. She said that there was always the risk that the prisoners might be forced to give up information if the torture became too unbearable.[9]

Like all V-people, Ans van Dijk used a combination of chance, contingency, and betrayal to do her job. Vince recounted an extraordinary story about van Dijk that he had learned from Holocaust survivor Louis de Groot, whom he'd been able to interview at his Washington, DC, apartment in May 2018.[10]

De Groot said his parents had owned and operated an appliance store in Arnhem. His father, Meijer de Groot, was friendly with the policemen in the area, who promised to warn him of any Nazi raids about to happen. His family went into hiding on November 17, 1942, after they were warned of an upcoming raid. They were split up and placed in different locations in Amsterdam. De Groot and his parents hid in a house at Prinsengracht 825, but in December 1943 he was relocated to the countryside by a Dutch detective whom his father knew. His older sister, Rachel de Groot, was in hiding at a different location in the city.

In the early evening of April 8, 1944, the day before

Easter, Ans van Dijk, Branca Simons, and her husband, Wim Houthuijs, were strolling through the Prinsengracht neighborhood, where De Groot's parents were hiding. Van Dijk recognized Israel de Groot, Louis's uncle, walking alone on the street. She approached him, mentioning that she could arrange safe passage to Spain. Israel told her that he didn't need her help and kept walking.

Van Dijk, Simons, and Houthuijs followed Israel and watched him enter the building at Prinsengracht 825. From a nearby bar, Van Dijk made a phone call to the Zentralstelle and relayed the tip to SS Lieutenant Otto Kempin, who ordered Grootendorst and several other Dutch SD detectives to the address. The V-people waited nearby and pointed out the location to the raid team.

Israel de Groot had left the Prinsengracht address just prior to the arrival of the Dutch SD men. Sadly, Louis's sister Rachel was at that moment visiting her parents, and all three were taken away. While still in hiding, Louis was told that his parents and sister had been captured, but only after the war was over did he learn that they had all perished in the camps. His uncle Israel, who was working with the resistance, was never captured and survived the war.

Louis discovered that his mother, Sophia, and his

sister were sent to a jail in The Hague. Though it cannot be proven, he suspects that after the arrest of his family, Van Dijk was put into the cell with his sister to gain information on other Jews in hiding. His father was taken to a jail in Amsterdam where, by chance, his jailer was known to him, and he was able to convince the man to allow him to write a note to his brother Israel recounting the details of the arrest. The jailer passed on the note, which was how Louis eventually learned who was involved in the arrest and betrayal of his family. From the note he also learned that his father, Meijer, knew the arresting officer, Grootendorst; they had played marbles together when they were children.

As it was becoming evident by the fall of 1944 that the Allies had won the war, Van Dijk turned to Otto Kempin and asked for help to get a visa to travel to Germany. Kempin refused. However loyally she may have worked as a V-Frau, she was not to be rewarded.[11] She then moved with her lover, Mies de Regt, to The Hague, where she made her living from black-market trade.

After the liberation, Van Dijk was arrested and tried by the Special Court of Justice. She was convicted of twenty-three cases of betrayal involving sixty-eight people and sentenced to death. Her CABR file is massive and suggests a much higher number, probably closer to two hundred betrayals, but many cases simply couldn't be proven because so few witnesses had survived.

Launching an appeal, Van Dijk's lawyer asked for a psychological investigation, claiming that both her parents had died while suffering from mental illnesses; his attempt to suggest that her behavior was a result of some inherited condition did not impress the judges. On January 14, 1948, Ans van Dijk was executed at Fort Bijlmer after having been baptized a Catholic the previous day.

Van Dijk had the distinction of being the only woman sentenced to death and actually executed in the Netherlands. The other women she had worked closely with, Miep Braams and Branca Simons, were also sentenced to death, but their sentences were commuted to life in prison. It has been argued that part of the reason Van Dijk was executed was that she was an outspoken and openly homosexual woman.

If it had not been for the Nazis, it is unlikely that Van Dijk's life would have been exceptional. In 1940, she was a thirty-five-year-old clerk in a hat shop with a female lover. As a lesbian she would have been an outsider, which clearly angered her, though there is no suggestion that she acted on her anger. Perhaps, initially, that fact even gave her courage. In the early days of the occupation, she refused to cower before the Nazis' rules and supposedly helped some fellow Jews find safe hiding places. However, in the last two years of the war, from April 1943 to April 1945, she turned into a grotesque monster capable of betraying several hundred people. Fear for her life may have led her to become a V-Frau, but what happened after that, according to her handler Pieter Schaap, was that she took to the work; she became one of his most effective informants.

Her lover Mies de Regt testified that she believed that Van Dijk had been seduced by the "irresistible excitement of the hunt."[12] Excitement of the hunt! It's an astonishing phrase. Coerced by fear for her life, then seduced by power. Is it possible that one thing we can learn from Ans van Dijk is that totalitarian regimes achieve their power not just through repression but through the seduction of insiderism, which turns people into craven sycophants? They believe that they are among the elite until, like Van Dijk, the power turns on them and spits them out.

For a time Van Dijk seemed to be a likely suspect in the raid on Prinsengracht 263. In the Arrest Tracking Project, her name came up again and again. Clearly, working as a V-Frau, she had a motive. Did she have knowledge? The Prinsengracht area was part of her regular turf, and, at least according to Gerard Kremer, she was often seen there. Could she have overheard something about the hiders in the Annex? Could she have become suspicious and staked out the building, watching the stream of suppliers who provided what seemed an excess of food? And did she have opportunity? Where was she in the days preceding August 4, and who was she in contact with? Those were the questions the Cold Case Team had yet to answer.

27
No Substantial Proof, Part I

From the beginning of their work, the Cold Case Team collected a wealth of material related to the original 1947–48 police investigation into the raid on the Annex. It included multiple CABR files, personal and official correspondence, court documents, and the nine-page Amsterdam police report. Vince said that one thing was clear: by today's standards, the quality and thoroughness of the investigation were subpar. One reason for this was that just after the war, the Dutch police force was purged of collaborators. That led to 2,500 people losing their jobs and many others being demoted. Sixteen percent of the force was suspended and investigated. As a result, inexperienced and understaffed investigators had to deal with an overwhelming backlog of cases of collaboration, war crimes, and betrayal.

It was also clear that the investigation might not have occurred at all except for pressure from Otto and his employees at Opekta/Gies & Co. Johannes Kleiman and Victor Kugler took the initiative to push the postwar authorities to take up the case. They, along with Miep and Bep, concluded that Opekta's warehouse manager, Willem van Maaren, was the most likely betrayer. Kleiman wrote the Amsterdam Political Investigation Service (Politieke Opsporingsdienst; POD) in the summer of 1945, demanding an investigation of Van Maaren. Nothing happened.[1]

On November 11, 1945, Otto wrote a letter to his mother saying that he, together with Kleiman and Kugler, had gone to the Bureau of National Security (Bureau Nationale Veiligheid; BNV) to check police files for photographs of the Dutch policemen who'd arrested them. He said they'd been able to identify two men—murderers who had been responsible for the death of his family. He was hoping that the men might be able to identify the traitor who had betrayed them to the SD in the first place, though he wasn't optimistic since such men always said that they had just been following orders.[2] (In a letter dated May 2, 1958, Kugler recalled that he and Kleiman had accompanied Otto to the BNV in 1945.) Among the mug shots the police showed them, they recognized Willem Grootendorst and Gezinus Gringhuis, the Dutch policemen attached to the IV B4 unit who were currently serving sentences for collaboration in Amstelveenseweg prison.

Later that November, Otto, Kleiman, and Kugler made a visit to the prison to interview Grootendorst and Gringhuis. Both men admitted to having taken part in the raid at Prinsengracht 263, though later, under official interrogation, they would conveniently forget having done so.[3] Both said that Sergeant Abraham Kaper of the Bureau of Jewish Affairs had summoned them. They claimed, probably truthfully, to have no information about an anonymous morning phone call to Julius Dettmann reporting Jews in hiding. Dettmann could not be questioned; he'd hanged himself in his jail cell on July 25, though it was rumored that he'd been helped.

Otto then made a second visit to the prison to interview Gezinus Gringhuis. He made a notation to that effect in his agenda on December 6, 1945, along with the name Ab. That likely refers to Otto's close friend Abraham "Ab" Cauvern, whose wife, Isa, worked as Otto's secretary.

Otto was clearly hoping to have his case taken up quickly by the POD, but in 1945 he was just one of

5,500 survivors returning from the camps. Nothing happened. It wasn't until June 11, 1947, almost two years later, that he next visited the Bureau of National Security in person. Again nothing. Then, after a conversation with Otto, on July 16 Kleiman sent another letter to the Political Investigation Department (Politieke Recherche Afdeling; PRA) (the POD had been renamed in March 1946 after the Allied military forces had handed power over to the civil administration). He asked, on behalf of Otto and himself, that the case be "addressed again."[4]

On January 12, 1948, three and a half years after the raid on the Annex, Police Brigadier Jacob Meeboer opened an investigation into the warehouse manager, Willem van Maaren, the only person ever officially investigated as the betrayer. Brigadier Meeboer interviewed fourteen people, among them the helpers Johannes Kleiman, Miep Gies, and Viktor Kugler but not Bep Voskuijl;* the Dutch detectives Gezinus Gringhuis and Willem Grootendorst; Johannes Petrus van Erp and Dr. Petrus Hendrikus Bangert, both of whom knew Van Maaren; the other warehouse worker, Lammert Hartog, and his wife, Lena; and finally, Van Maaren

* Why he did not interview Bep Voskuijl is unclear. Perhaps he concluded that he had enough witness statements.

himself. Despite Kleiman's expression of shock in his July letter that Karl Silberbauer had never been brought over to the Netherlands for questioning, seeing that he had "played an important role in the apprehension of 'Jewish and other absconders,'"[5] Silberbauer was not called to testify. Nor was Otto Frank, probably because he'd already told the police that he and his family had been in hiding in the Annex well before Van Maaren was hired and he did not know the man.

Brigadier Meeboer's official report begins with Kleiman's testimony, in which he gives a detailed account of the raid and also outlines Van Maaren's questions and suspicious behavior. Shortly after he was hired, Van Maaren asked the staff about someone being in the stockroom after hours. He'd found a wallet on a table in the stockroom, where Van Pels must have forgotten it during one of his nightly ventures into the warehouse. Van Maaren presented the wallet to Kugler and asked if it was his. Kugler reacted quickly, saying that, yes, it was his and he'd forgotten it the night before. The contents of the wallet were intact, except for a missing ten-guilder note.

Kleiman explained that Van Maaren certainly knew of the existence of the Annex. He'd seen it when Kugler had sent him to fix a leak in the roof, and in any case, a back annex was a feature of many of the narrow buildings in the area. There was also a door at the back of the warehouse opening onto the courtyard. A man as curious as Van Maaren would likely have gone outside; from there, he could see the entire Annex attached to the building. It would have been only normal for him to wonder why the large "appendage" was never mentioned by anyone or used for business purposes. And he would have asked himself where the access to the Annex was located, since there was no clear indication of an entryway. Absent an obvious entrance, he would likely have suspected a concealed door.

Kleiman explained to Detective Meeboer that they would come across pencils balanced on the edges of desks and flour strewn onto the floor, clearly placed there by Van Maaren to confirm his suspicion that people were in the building after hours. Van Maaren once asked Kleiman whether a Mr. Frank had worked in the building, implying that he was conducting his own investigation. Everything suggested that Van Maaren surmised there were people living in the Annex.

Kleiman reported that after the raid on August 4, Opekta's accountant, Johannes van Erp, visited Dr. Petrus Bangert, a homeopathic doctor, and mentioned that the Jews hiding at Prinsengracht had been arrested. The doctor asked if the address was 263. He said he'd known for about a year that there were

Jews in hiding at that address. When Van Erp told that to Kleiman, apparently Kleiman responded that Van Maaren must have been the source of the information since he was a patient of the doctor.

When Dr. Bangert was interrogated, however, he insisted that Opekta's accountant was mistaken. He'd never said any such thing, he said, and after he checked his patient records, he claimed that Van Maaren had become his patient only on August 25, 1944, three weeks after the arrest. Was that accurate or simply an evasion? It was 1948, three years after the war ended. Everyone wanted to wash their hands of the catastrophe and get on with the peace.

The most revealing part of Brigadier Meeboer's investigation was his interrogation of Van Maaren himself as to what he had known about Jews hiding in the Annex. Van Maaren testified that he had not known for certain that there was anyone in hiding, though he'd had his suspicions. He explained the pencils on the edges of desks and the flour on the floor as his strategy to trap thieves he believed were stealing from Opekta. As for his asking about a Mr. Frank, he said he'd heard office talk about "Papa Frank" and had been told by Miep Gies and Kleiman that the former owners, Frank and Van Pels, had fled, supposedly to the United States.[6]

More damning was the fact that his assistant, Lammert Hartog, swore that Van Maaren had told him fourteen days before the raid that there were Jews in hiding at Prinsengracht. Van Maaren emphatically denied that he'd said any such thing.

Though Van Maaren did eventually admit to stealing from Opekta/Gies & Co., he also accused Miep and Bep of theft. He accused both women of heading up to the Annex after the arrest and, before an inventory could be made by the Germans, grabbing "clothes and papers and a lot of other things to keep for themselves."[7] Van Maaren was a bitter man and turned the accusations against him back onto his accusers.

The investigation was dropped on May 22, 1948. The report concluded that there was no proof of the warehouse manager's culpability.[8] Van Maaren was given a conditional discharge, put under surveillance by the Political Delinquents Surveillance Department for three years, and stripped of his right to vote for ten years.

Van Maaren was outraged at receiving a conditional discharge and appealed. During the hearing, his lawyer argued that the appeal itself was proof of Van Maaren's innocence. "If the accused had felt even the smallest amount of guilt, he would not have appealed against his conditional discharge, since the restrictions imposed are so slight."[9] On August 13, 1949, a district court dismissed all charges.

Van Maaren likely thought that that was the end of his ordeal, but fifteen years later the matter of who betrayed the people in hiding at Prinsengracht 263 would resurface and he would again find himself the prime suspect. Everyone on the Cold Case Team thought that the first investigation of Van Maaren had been perfunctory; the official report was only nine pages long. At that point, they began to collect all information relevant to the second investigation in 1963–1964, hoping that it might have had a broader focus and delved more deeply into what had precipitated the raid.

28
"Just Go to Your Jews!"

The Cold Case Team found no conclusive evidence that the betrayer of Anne Frank was someone in the neighborhood, but their investigation turned up disconcerting evidence with regard to a closer circle, the helpers. The team had become emotionally attached to the helpers, but, as Vince put it, it was necessary to remain objective to protect the integrity of the investigation. Through the Mapping Project, they learned that the next-door neighbor of Johannes Kleiman was not only a fervent NSB member but also an employee at the SD office on Euterpestraat. Both Kleiman's wife and his brother knew about the hiders, and it seems that their daughter, Corrie, also deduced from a casual remark by her father that the Franks were still in Amsterdam, though she probably didn't know they were hiding in the Annex.[1] The team also discovered that the adoptive brother of Miep, as well as Kugler's brother-in-law, had been accused of collaboration. Could an unintentional remark by any of them have given the hiders away?

The team began by researching the collaboration file of Kugler's brother-in-law and discovered that his "collaboration" amounted to operating a movie theater that had played pro-German films during the occupation. As for Miep, any doubts about her were easy to dismiss. She was hugely self-disciplined and able to compartmentalize; as she herself said, during the war she had lost the habit of speech. Regardless, the Cold Case Team found documents indicating that her adoptive brother, Laurens Nieuwenburg, Jr., went to Germany in November 1943 and reregistered at his parents' address in August 1945; it appears that he was in Germany at the time of the Annex arrests. Finally, Kleiman's neighbor, too, was a very unlikely suspect; if he was the one to give up the Prinsengracht 263 address, he would not have phoned SS Lieutenant Julius Dettmann with the information. As an employee of the SD, he would have known that the person to call with tips about hiders was Sergeant Abraham Kaper at the Bureau of Jewish Affairs. Kaper was in charge of the Jew-hunting unit and could be nasty when others went around him, poached on his territory, or tried to claim the *Kopgeld* rewards.

War brings conflict between countries, between strangers, between neighbors, and between family members. The team discovered that the conflict of war within a family had come right to the door of Prinsengracht 263. There were grounds to believe that Bep's sister Nelly Voskuijl could have been the one who betrayed the people in the Annex. In his book *Anne Frank: The Untold Story* (coauthored with Jeroen de Bruyn), Bep's son Joop van Wijk made what seems a strong case against his aunt.

Vince was able to contact Joop through his social media site and discovered that he was eager to talk with the Cold Case Team. On a freezing day in December 2018, Joop and his wife traveled from their home in the eastern Netherlands to the Amsterdam office, where Vince and Brendan were waiting to interview him.[2] Joop was remarkably candid. He said that *Anne Frank: The Untold Story* was a labor of love for his mother and a tribute to his grandfather, whose efforts in support of the hiders had never been adequately acknowledged. He added that in writing the book he could not avoid expressing his concerns about his aunt Nelly's role in the betrayal.

Joop began by explaining his relationship with his

mother. He is the youngest son in a family of four children and was seven years old when he realized that his mother had helped Anne Frank's family. He became fascinated by the Annex story. He fondly recalled visits by Otto Frank, whom he addressed as "Uncle Otto." During the interview Joop became emotional when he recounted an incident that occurred in 1959, when he was ten. He heard his mother crying in the bathroom, and when he opened the door, he could see that she was consuming pills. She looked at him in dismay and stopped. His intrusion undoubtedly saved her life. Only later did he realize how much she'd been traumatized by the war; she told him she felt she'd failed the people hiding in the Annex.

Joop gave the Cold Case Team a detailed profile of Nelly. She was the fourth of eight children, four years younger than her sister Bep, who was the oldest. They lived in a working-class district in west Amsterdam in a house too small to accommodate a family of ten, so as a result the older girls often had to live elsewhere. At the beginning of the war, Nelly and her sister Annie worked as live-in maids for a wealthy family who proved to be Nazi sympathizers. German soldiers often visited the villa. One of the regulars was a young Austrian named Siegfried with whom the eighteen-year-old Nelly soon fell in love.

On November 1, 1941, Nelly was arrested while walking along Nieuwendijk with Siegfried. The Cold Case Team found her police file in the Amsterdam City Archives indicating that she was charged only with breaking curfew.[3] Because Nelly was still considered a minor, her father was called to pick her up at the police station the next morning and was almost apoplectic when he learned that his daughter had been out with an enemy soldier. Johannes Voskuijl was profoundly anti-Nazi and insisted that Nelly break off the relationship.[4]

It seemed impossible, however, to deter Nelly. Her younger sister Diny reported in a 2011 interview with the Anne Frank Foundation that Nelly had brought her Austrian boyfriend home to ask her father's permission to date him. Peeking through a crack in the door, Diny had watched the young man click his boots and say to their father, "Herr Voskuijl, Heil Hitler!"[5]

According to the family story, Johannes tried to dissuade his daughter from having any further contact with Siegfried. It didn't work. Tensions in the family grew unbearable until, in December 1942, Nelly applied for a Dutch passport.[6] The Cold Case Team was able to track down her application. It bore the stamp "A.B.," which meant that the Amsterdam employment office had approved her for work in Germany. It also carried the words "With consent." As a minor, Nelly required parental permission to travel, but it seems unlikely that her father would have consented. Joop concluded that his aunt had simply lied on her application about having parental consent.

Joop told the Cold Case Team he believes that the Voskuijl family underestimated or deliberately concealed his aunt's involvement with members of the German Army. They claimed that she moved to France after a falling-out with Siegfried and that she remained there until the war was over. While researching his book, though, Joop found a different story.

According to her sister Diny, Nelly went to Austria to live with Siegfried's sister while he fought at the front. Then she discovered a letter to him from his fiancée,[7] which sent her home to Amsterdam brokenhearted. But her relationships with Nazis did not end there. Bep's boyfriend at the time, Bertus Hulsman, was often to be found at the Voskuijl residence. He claimed that after her return to Amsterdam, Nelly continued to consort with the occupiers. He recalled that she "could often be found in the building of the Veronica skating club, opposite the Concert Building. The Germans made this into a so-called *Wein, Weib und Gesang* (wine, wife [woman] and song) establishment where they'd hold parties."[8]

Joop discovered that in May 1943, Nelly traveled to

northern France to work for the Wehrmacht at a military air base in Laon. She was the base commander's secretary. This was serious collaboration, since it meant she would have known the schedules of German bombing raids. It seems she lasted a year. By May 1944, she decided to return home.

As she continued to date Germans, the tension in the home accelerated. Diny said that her father occasionally beat Nelly. She remembered one occasion when the beating was so severe that Nelly fell down on the hall floor and her father continued to kick her. It was so shocking that Diny asked her mother why her father had lost his temper, but her mother refused to answer. Although Diny remembered that the incident occurred in the summer of 1944, she could not recall whether it was before or after the arrest of the people in the Annex.[9] If after, her father's anger might have been a consequence of his belief that Nelly was involved in their betrayal.

At this point in the investigation of Nelly as a suspect, the Cold Case Team came across an anomaly. In *The Diary of a Young Girl: The Definitive Edition*, edited under the supervision of Otto Frank and published in 1947 all over the world, no mention is made of Nelly Voskuijl. Of course, this could have been simply a matter of producing a readable book of 335 pages;

much had to be cut. When NIOD published *The Diary of Anne Frank: Critical Edition* in 1986, many deleted passages were restored.

In one mysterious entry, dated May 6, 1944, Anne records that M.K. was in northern France, which had recently come under allied bombardment. M.K. was terrified and desperate to return to Amsterdam. She was also asking forgiveness for the trials she had put her father through.

The Cold Case Team knew that Nelly had worked as a secretary to the commander of a German airbase in Laon in northern France. Obviously, her name had been replaced by initials. There was also a curious footnote in the Critical Edition.

The editors explained that, at the request of an unidentified person, they had disguised the name of the person Anne was referring to, selecting the initials M.K. at random to replace it. They also indicate that, at the request of this same person, twenty-four words had been deleted from the May 6 entry. Three other passages in the May 11 and May 19 diary entries were also excised, for a total of ninety-two words.

Clearly, it was imperative for the Cold Case Team to find out who had made this request and what text had been removed. When they contacted David Barnouw, one of the editors of the Critical Edition, he told the team that it was Nelly herself who'd made the request. She had obviously gotten word of the pending publication of the Critical Edition and contacted NIOD, requesting that the passages regarding her be deleted. NIOD said it would keep the passages but remove her name.

What was in the deleted passages that was so damning that Nelly needed to remove them? Did they give any hint that she might have been the betrayer of the secret Annex?

The Cold Case Team contacted Jeroen de Bruyn, Joop Voskuijl's coauthor of *The Untold Story*. He was generous enough to send the team an extensive collection of documents and notes that he'd accumulated in his own research. One was a document with four entries from Anne's diary, which identified the missing words that Nelly had asked the editors to delete.

Bep must have talked freely with Anne Frank about the battles between Nelly and their father over her dalliances with Germans, since this is the subject in most of Anne's entries regarding Nelly.[10]

It turns out that the first excision, of twenty-eight words, refers to Anne's comment that Nelly could plead her father's illness as a reason to return to the Netherlands, but Anne adds that this would work only if her father died.* The next deletion, of four words, refers to the fact that Nelly is desperately anxious to see her father.[11]

The third deletion, of twenty-eight words, is equally harmless. Nelly must have asked for permission to leave. The commander of the base made it clear that he was annoyed to be disturbed before supper. Anne reports Nelly responding that if her father died before she could see him, she would never forgive the Germans. Finally, in the last redaction, Anne refers to Nelly's father's sadness. He was dying of cancer, and his daughter, who was back home, was making him even more wretched by consorting again with Germans.[12]

The entries on May 6 and May 19 make it clear that Nelly had returned from France and was carrying on an affair with a German pilot. It's possible that she wanted the words deleted because she felt guilt at her father's suffering, to which she'd contributed, though of course at the time of the book's publication, he was long dead. It's more likely that in 1986, even forty

---

*Unfortunately, we did not receive permission to quote the entries from *The Diary of Anne Frank: The Revised Critical Edition*, edited by David Barnouw and Gerrold van der Stroom (New York: Doubleday, 2003).

years after the end of the war, to be identified as a collaborator working with the Nazi occupiers still evoked contempt and outrage. And Anne's diary would clearly have identified Nelly as such. In any case, the deleted words were innocuous. They provided the Cold Case Team no further insight into the possibility that Nelly was the betrayer.

The most direct accusation that Nelly might have known about Jews hiding in the Annex came from Bep's boyfriend, Bertus Hulsman.[13] In an interview with Dineke Stam of the Anne Frank Stichting in 2007, he remembered an argument at the family table when Nelly's sisters "bullied [her] because she had dealing with krauts. And one time—I'll never forget it—she shouted at the table, 'Just go to your Jews!' I don't remember when exactly this was."[14]

The interview took more than two hours, and the exchange between Nelly and her family was referred to in different ways. In one instance, Hulsman clarified Nelly's exclamation: "That family relationship, there was always a field of tension. You know, all those girls. . . . And then she said, 'You go to your Jews.'"[15]

At another point, Hulsman added that the remark should be taken as a more general utterance: "A sneer was made at her, and then she sneered back, 'Go and see your Jews.'"[16]

He then reflected on his own uncertainty about the source of the information: "But how do I come up with that, 'Go to your Jews,' that happened sixty years ago? I will doubt that myself, you know [. . .] I hope I am wrong, that my suggestions are wrong."[17]

Was Nelly's statement, which at first appears to refer to the people in the Annex, a retort rather than a specific accusation? "Just go to your Jews!" could have been her response to her sisters or father yelling that she should go to her "krauts." Was Nelly making it clear that she knew something? Or was she simply responding to the sympathy her father and sister Bep no doubt expressed for Jews in the occupied Netherlands?

Shortly after the liberation in May 1945, Nelly moved to the city of Groningen, not far from Amsterdam. According to Melissa Müller, she was arrested on October 26. She spent several years in custody and was not able to pick up her life again until 1953.

The Cold Case Team searched for Nelly's CABR file. A file on every postwar conviction for political offenses is kept in the National Archives. But there was no file on Nelly Voskuijl. Vince contacted Müller to ask her for the source of her information about Nelly's arrest and conviction. She recommended that he talk to her researcher.[18]

The researcher did not recall the source, either.[19]

During two interviews with the team, he did, however, explain his theory. According to him, Nelly Voskuijl was first held in a theater in Groningen with other young women who were suspected of collaboration. Later, according to the researcher, she was transported to a prison for about a year. The team searched the Groningen Archives but did not find any documentation or proof to back that up. According to the researcher, Nelly's records would have been destroyed because, as a minor at the time, she would have been judged in juvenile court. Corroborating the story of Nelly being arrested is the statement by her sister Willy that she remembered being interrogated just after the war, possibly about Nelly, though she did not recall the details.[20]

At that time in 1945, Nelly was actually over twenty-one and would have been judged in adult court; therefore, there should have been records. To find proof of this theory or any other information on the whereabouts of Nelly during the period 1945–1953, the Cold Case Team conducted a search into postwar camps, specifically looking for young female prisoners in Groningen, and read the files on political prisoners held by the Groningen authorities.[21] No direct leads pointed toward Nelly Voskuijl. The absence of a CABR file led the team to suspect that Nelly was never arrested.

One day the Cold Case Team's researcher Circe de

Bruin returned to the office in a state of high excitement. She had discovered a document indicating that Nelly Voskuijl had registered in the municipality of Groningen on October 26, 1945, the same day Müller claimed she had been arrested.[22] Müller's researcher seems to have mistakenly assumed that the registration document was the record of Nelly's arrest.* Vince said that the roller-coaster ride from excitement to letdown is a normal part of any investigation, but he was somewhat disappointed. Had Nelly been arrested, her CABR file would have provided a narrative of her activities and her German contacts during the war. Whether or not she took part in the Annex betrayal might have become clearer.

By fleeing Amsterdam, Nelly passed under the radar and evaded conviction for whatever crimes of collaboration she might have committed. At the very least, she escaped the fate of women who had had sexual relationships with Germans. Dragged from their houses, their heads shaved, they were drawn in carts through the city streets as bystanders shouted abuse.

---

* Possibly what happened was that Müller's researcher may not have visited the archive in Groningen but relied on someone else who lived there to make an inquiry on his behalf. Other than that, we cannot explain the mistake.

After decades of silence, Joop van Wijk renewed contact with his aunt Nelly in 1996. She was living in the small village of Koudum in the province of Friesland in the northern Netherlands and was still in close contact with her sisters, particularly Diny and Willy. Joop recalled, "I was always welcome, but this changed when I brought up the subject of the war and her behavior in the Voskuijl family."[23] Nelly understood that he was writing a book about his mother, but she said that it was difficult to speak about those times; she greatly regretted that period of her life.

Then rather startingly, Joop recounted that "One of the last times I visited her and mentioned Anne Frank and the raid on the Annex, she had a serious fainting spell."[24] He offered to take her to the hospital, but she refused and told him that her fainting was probably a result of the blows her father had given her. Joop was suspicious, believing his aunt was not above using a dramatic performance to obscure her culpability. However, he told the Cold Case Team that, fearing for her health, he stopped asking about the war.

Of course, the most surprising aspect of Joop's account is that it seems that all he had to do was mention the Annex and Nelly fainted. Could that have been a ruse, Nelly's way of getting out of having to respond? But he also recounted that he'd actually seen her faint on three earlier occasions, which suggests that she might have had some kind of chronic condition. In his book *Anne Frank: The Untold Story: The Hidden Truth About Eli Vossen, the Youngest Helper of the Secret Annex* he also mentioned the fainting incident but said that it was occasioned by his mentioning the war and not the raid on the Annex. The Cold Case Team was left wondering: Was Nelly hiding things with her fainting spells and her refusal to speak?[25] Or did Joop, already convinced that his aunt was guilty, have tunnel vision? After Joop's last visit, Nelly moved to an assisted living residence, where she died in 2001. Joop received a final postcard from her with the short text "An embrace, Nel."

Calling on his twenty-seven years of experience as an FBI undercover agent, Vince said he'd learned to read people—for his own safety. He liked Joop very much, but he felt he was somehow obsessed with proving his aunt Nelly's guilt. Vince told him not to worry about the betrayal; he should focus on celebrating his mother and grandfather, which had been his motive for writing *Anne Frank: The Untold Story.*

As expected, Vince went about his investigation coolly, applying the law enforcement axiom "knowledge, motive, and opportunity" to the Nelly Voskuijl scenario. Did Nelly have a motive? Joop visited his aunt fifty years after the war ended, at which point Nelly seemed ashamed of her younger self, but back then, she was rebellious, thoughtless, combative, flirting with the enemy. Could she, in a moment of rage—after a fight with her father, for example—have told the wrong person about the secret her father and sister were keeping? And did that person, possibly one of her German friends, then pass the information on to the SD?

Did she have knowledge? Though her father and sister were very discreet, it's possible that she overheard them talking about the bookcase. Perhaps she grew suspicious of the goods Bep always seemed to be collecting, sometimes with the help of her siblings. But even Bep's mother didn't know about the hiders in the Annex. When she found out after they were arrested, she was furious that her husband and daughter had put their family into such jeopardy

Nelly had opportunity, having returned to Amsterdam in May 1944. Her father complained that she was still meeting her German friends.

But the team was skeptical that Nelly might have been lashing out at her father, Johannes, when they discovered that the details she'd requested be redacted from Anne's diary were affectionate toward him. More likely, by 1986 she did not want her past as a German sympathizer known, which could have been damaging not only to herself but also to her father's memory and to that of her sister Bep, both of whom were now celebrated as helpers in the Anne Frank story.

It seemed that there was no substantial proof that Nelly, however inadvertently, betrayed the residents in the secret Annex. But the Cold Case Team was not yet ready to set that scenario aside.

29
Probing Memory

Vince reminded me that anyone relying on eyewitness statements as an accurate record of a historical moment will quickly learn that memory is fluid. People claim things with great certainty that either are contradictory or simply cannot be true. They are not lying; rather, their memory has been polluted by experiences they have gone through later. The same moment filtered through different emotions can also change the so-called objective record. Vince said that every time the Cold Case Team recorded a scenario, they had to take that fact into account. One of the most compelling cases was that of Victor Kugler.

In one of his accounts of the raid, Kugler recalled that as he was working in the office that morning, he suddenly heard footsteps and saw shadows running past the window in his office door. He opened the door and saw a Gestapo officer climbing the stairs with gun drawn, followed by others.[1] The raid team spread to the office, where Kleiman, Bep, and Miep were working. Leaving behind one policeman to guard the helpers, Silberbauer ordered Kugler to precede him up the stairs to the next level of the building. Kugler was alone with the Nazi. As he climbed the stairs, Silberbauer shouted, "Where are the Jews?"[2] Kugler led him to the bookcase.

In an article in *Life* magazine in 1958, Kugler's version of events was somewhat different. He described the raid team taking him to the front storeroom and looking around until eventually they pulled their guns and led him to the bookcase.[3] His account in Ernst Schnabel's 1958 book *The Footsteps of Anne Frank* repeated that version. During the 1963–64 investigation, he explained to Detective Arend Jacobus van Helden that, hoping the Nazis were just looking for weapons or illegal IDs, he first showed Silberbauer his office, opening the cabinets and bookcases. He then led him to the back of the building and showed him Kleiman's office, the washroom, and the little kitchen. Silberbauer had then ordered him up to the next floor. They went first to the stockroom in the front part of the building and then to the Annex corridor in the back. As they came to the bookcase, Kugler noticed that another nearby bookcase and boxes had already been searched, presumably by the Dutch policemen. He saw them trying to move the swinging bookcase. At first, they could not budge it, but then they figured out that the hook had to be unfastened and swung it open.[4]

Who would expect Kugler's account nineteen years after the raid to be the same? But it seems that a kind of emotional revisionism was at work.

1. *In the first version, Kugler revealed the location of the secret bookcase almost immediately under mortal threat from Silberbauer, who demanded, "Where are the Jews?"*

2. *In later versions, the raid team searched the building; they determined that the bookcase concealed something, confirmed by the marks of the moving wheels on the wooden floor beneath it. The bookcase yielded, and the secret door was exposed. Kugler added that he then understood that the Green Policeman "knew everything."*[5]

The most likely scenario is number one. Vince remarked that Silberbauer's aggressive question was a familiar tactic he recognized from FBI raids: you let a suspect think you're already in the know. From everything else about the raid, it's clear that Silberbauer did know that there were Jews in the building but probably not where. With a gun to his back, terrified, Kugler led the raid team to the bookcase entrance to the secret Annex. That must have been painful for a man of Kugler's integrity. He had hidden eight people faithfully despite enormous stresses over two years, and now he carried in his mind the responsibility for exposing them. He must have felt terribly vulnerable and filled with an irrational guilt, irrational because there was nothing he could have done to save them. It's not surprising, then, that his account of the tragic event morphed somewhat over the years; he becomes more wily, more devious in misleading Silberbauer, more composed.

It might have assuaged Kugler's guilt to have realized that Detective Van Helden had reported Otto as saying in December 1963 that "if Silberbauer claimed that one of those present pointed the door [hidden behind the bookcase] out to him, then he [Otto] understood that you couldn't remain silent for long in the case of an armed SD raid." There was no blame. Otto knew that as soon as Silberbauer and the Dutch policemen entered the building, those in hiding were bound to be found.[6]

Given the variations in Kugler's account, it's been suggested that Silberbauer and his team were not looking for Jews at all. Gertjan Broek, a researcher at the Anne Frank House, suggested that the SD were after illegal food coupons and forged documents and came across the Jewish hiders by chance. Maybe there was no betrayer. Monique Koemans thought Broek's idea interesting enough that she proposed it to her team of cold case researchers during their weekly review of possible scenarios and they decided to pursue it.

As she went over possible sources to use in her research, Monique decided to begin with Ernst Schnabel. For his book *The Footsteps of Anne Frank* he had spoken to Otto and all the helpers, including Jan Gies. He'd started the book in 1957, just twelve years after the war had ended, and had been able to include the first-person testimony of forty-two people somehow connected to Anne Frank.

Monique discovered that the original manuscript of Schnabel's book was stored at the German Literature Archive Marbach near Stuttgart, Germany. When she contacted the archive, she was told that part of Schnabel's personal notes and some of Otto Frank's letters were available as well. Schnabel had not made recordings of his interviews, and some critics argued that he'd been imprecise in his notes. Regardless, it could be valuable to examine the notes personally. Maybe she'd find corroborating evidence to support Kugler's assertion that Silberbauer had demanded, "Where are the Jews?," clearly indicating that he'd been tipped off about their presence in advance.

Monique set out for Germany with the researcher Christine Hoste. After an eight-hour drive in wind, rain, and light December snow, they arrived at a deserted hotel near the archive. There were no other guests, which enhanced the feeling of diving into unknown territory. Given the strict German bureaucracy, it had not been easy to get permission to look at the notes in the archive, but when they arrived the next morning, after some misunderstanding, the papers were more or less ready for their perusal. The two women were escorted to a small room with a glass wall (so the librarian could keep an eye on them), a Formica-topped table, and retro lamps.

Schnabel's notes were in German in old-fashioned cursive writing. Some were not difficult to read; others felt like a puzzle with words scribbled in corners. At the time of writing, either paper was still scarce or Schnabel had retained the wartime habit of not squandering it.

Monique and her colleague worked feverishly. Monique said it was strange to feel so close to Otto, knowing that he'd held some of the papers and letters in his own hands. This was no longer just history. Reading the notes felt personal.

Suddenly Monique said to Christine, "Here's the evidence!" She'd found two instances in Schnabel's notes from different interviews in which he'd copied the sentence *"Wo sind die Juden?"* (Where are the Jews?). To judge from the notes, the helpers apparently agreed with Kugler's first memory—that the raiders specifically demanded to know where the Jews were hiding. That was exciting. It meant that Silberbauer and the Dutch detectives were not looking for food coupons or weapons; they did not happen on the hiders by chance.

There was another mysterious scrap of paper among Schnabel's notes. It was simply the end of a sentence: ". . . and she knew the betrayer." There was nothing more. The "she" would likely have been Miep, certainly not Bep. Otto did not confide in Bep, and Miep was the only one who had ever claimed to know the name of the betrayer. Had Miep told Schnabel what she knew? Schnabel had died in Berlin in 1986. If he had known the name of the betrayer, he had never disclosed it.

There was still another piece of the puzzle to investigate, however. If there was a betrayer, as the Cold Case

Team was now convinced there was, did the tip actually come, as had always been assumed, through a phone call? How prevalent were phones in homes during the war? Were there public phones on the streets that could easily be used by a potential informer? To find out, Vince and Brendan turned to Jan Rijnders, a historian and expert on Netherlands telecommunications during World War II, who provided the team with a report on the public phone system (PTT) during the war.

Four days after the Dutch surrendered on May 15, 1940, the German authorities appointed Dr. Werner Linnemeyer director of the municipal telephone services. Huge amounts of cables and equipment were stolen for the German military, but, according to Rijnders, that only meant that the high quality of the Dutch network dropped to a lower level. By 1944, only a few private homes still had a telephone, since a permit was needed to own a phone. Though public phone booths on the streets had been dismantled, most functioning businesses still had a phone. The cold case researchers tracked down a telephone directory for 1943. There was no edition for 1944, but that is not proof that there were no more phones; it's just as likely that there was no paper on which to print a phone book.

After September 1944, the Germans were aware that calls could be set up by the resistance to the liberated southern part of the country. They therefore switched off all long-distance exchanges, but generally local calls still functioned, in part because the Germans wanted to continue to wiretap local businesses as well as their own personnel.[7]

Anything the Cold Case Team knew about a phone call initiating the Annex raid came from Silberbauer. In his testimony to Austrian authorities, he stated that at 10:00 a.m. on the fourth, a call was received by SS Lieutenant Julius Dettmann of Referat IV B4, who then ordered Silberbauer to carry out the raid along with a number of detectives chosen by Sergeant Kaper.

The team was doubtful that things could have been that simple. As they had discovered from the Arrest Tracking Project, raids led by German SD officers such as Silberbauer were rare, so if this case was a deviation from the norm, it suggests that the call, too, might have been handled differently from the norm. If the call had been an anonymous tip, it would certainly not have gone directly to Dettmann, who was much too high up in the German organization to take a call from an unidentified informant.

The Cold Case Team tended to believe that the call was for Dettmann but was either an internal call from within the German organization, maybe from someone in his immediate vicinity such as Willy Lages or Ferdinand aus der Fünten, the head of the Zentralstelle, or, if an external call, was from another Zentralstelle, possibly in Groningen, Zwolle, or The Hague, or perhaps even from Westerbork internment camp. In any case, it was probably a call from someone Dettmann knew and trusted.

A 1964 statement made by Willy Lages, then imprisoned in Breda, seems to confirm this view:

> *So finally, you are asking me if it is logical, after receiving a telephone call about Jews in hiding at a certain, specifically named location, one would immediately go to that building to arrest the Jews found there. I would have to respond that this is illogical. In my opinion one would first check the validity of such information, unless the tip came from someone who was trusted by our department. If Silberbauer's story about receiving a tip by telephone is correct and immediate action followed that same day, my conclusion would be that the person calling in this tip was known to us and that their earlier information had also been reliable.*[8]

Obviously, if the caller was a highly placed source, many of the scenarios the team had considered so far could be dismissed. Someone such as Willem van

Maaren, for instance, would not have had the clout to get an important man such as Dettmann on the telephone.

There are only two people who could know for sure who the mysterious caller was: the caller him/herself, and Dettmann, who received the call. But then the team thought it possible that when Dettmann called Abraham Kaper and told him to pick his raid team, he might also have told Kaper where he had gotten the information. Would there be some reference to the caller in Kaper's files? And where would those files be after all this time?

Vince assured me that in his many years in law enforcement, he's learned a lot about cops. Kaper might well have kept copies of the files he considered important in his own home. Though the team knew that finding any of Kaper's descendants was a long shot (Kaper was executed as a collaborator in 1949) and it was even less likely that any of them would know about specific files, Pieter began the search.

According to records in the Amsterdam City Archives, the Kaper family originated from a region north of Amsterdam. Pieter found several people listed in that region's phone book with the name Kaper and soon narrowed his search to a man who seemed to be the grandson of Abraham Kaper. However, every time he phoned, a woman answered and denied that her husband was in any way related to the infamous collaborator. It must not have been easy to be the grandson of one of the most notorious Dutch war criminals. At Kaper's postwar trial, numerous witnesses attested to his ruthless brutality against Jews and resistance prisoners, few of whom had survived his interrogations.

After the war, the shame directed at collaborators and their families was intense. Most lost their jobs and had to go to the social services office of their municipality to apply for aid. The civil servants who vetted them would canvass their neighbors to ask if they knew whether the applicant was working on the side or otherwise in violation of regulations. The reports are all on file in the Social Services Archive of the City of Amsterdam.

In Kaper's file, Pieter discovered that his wife was named Grietje Potman, and they had a daughter and two sons. From the reports of inspectors canvassing the neighborhood in the immediate postwar period, it was clear that most people detested Abraham Kaper but liked his wife.

Since Pieter was 90 percent sure that he'd found Kaper's grandson, he decided simply to go to the Kaper residence and see what would happen. On a sunny day in June 2019, armed with a cream cake he'd bought along the way, he drove to Kaper's apartment, let himself into the building as someone was leaving, and rang the doorbell.

Kaper himself opened the door. Pieter handed him the cake and said he had interesting information about his family. Along with his wife, Kaper turned out to be very friendly and, now in his eighties, talked freely about his past experiences with his grandfather, though he barely remembered him since he'd been a child during the war.

Abraham Jr. accepted that his grandfather was a war criminal, but he took consolation in what his neighbors, the Van Parreren family, had told him about his grandmother. Apparently, Grietje secretly worked against her husband by collecting all the betrayers' notes that were anonymously pushed through the mailbox of their front door or that she found in her husband's pockets. She would copy out the names and give them to Van Parreren so that he could warn people in advance. (Abraham Jr. was also proud to report that his uncle Jan was a sailor for the Allies and that his aunt Johanna worked for the resistance.)

In addition, Abraham Jr. confirmed something else for the team: his grandfather had indeed kept files and documents in a cardboard box at his house and he even knew where he had kept them. Pieter was thrilled when he heard that. He felt as if he was about to reach the mother lode. Then Kaper told him that all the documents were destroyed in 1960, when the rural area where his grandparents lived was flooded and everything was lost.

That was an enormous letdown, to say the least.

30

"The Man Who Arrested Frank Family Discovered in Vienna"

In 1957, at the Austrian premiere of *The Diary of Anne Frank* in the city of Linz, a group of young demonstrators rushed into the theater interrupting the play and shouting that it was a fraud. This incident came to the attention of Simon Wiesenthal, already well known for tracking down fugitive Nazi war criminals. In his book *The Murderers Among Us*, Wiesenthal described what happened:

> *At half-past nine one night in October 195[7],* a friend called me in great excitement in my apart-*

* Wiesenthal misremembered the date as 1958. The play premiered in 1957.

ment in Linz. Could I come at once to the Landestheater?

A performance of The Diary of Anne Frank had just been interrupted by anti-Semitic demonstrations. Groups of young people, most of them between fifteen and seventeen, had shouted, "Traitors! Toadies! Swindle." Others booed and hissed. The lights went on. From the gallery the youthful demonstrators showered leaflets upon the people in the orchestra. Those who picked them up read:

"This play is a fraud. Anne Frank never existed. The Jews have invented the whole story because they want to extort more restitution money. Don't believe a word of it! It's a fake!"

. . . Here in Linz, where Hitler had gone to school and Eichmann had grown up, [young people] were told to believe in lies and hatred, prejudice and nihilism.[1]

Two nights later, Wiesenthal was having coffee with a friend in a Linz coffeehouse. Everyone was talking about the demonstration. His friend called over a young man he knew and asked him what he thought about it all. The young man said it was exciting: "The diary may be a clever forgery. Certainly, it doesn't prove that Anne Frank existed." "She's buried in a mass grave in

Bergen-Belsen," Wiesenthal replied. The boy gave a shrug. "There's no proof," he said. If he could prove that Anne Frank existed, if he could come up with the Gestapo officer who arrested her, would that be proof? Wiesenthal asked. "Yes," the young man said. "If the man admitted it himself."[2]

That exchange was the impetus for Wiesenthal's quest to track down the SD man who led the Annex raid. The main clue that Wiesenthal had to go on was the last name of the SD officer, which he thought was Silbernagel. He also remembered that Miep said she'd recognized the SD officer's Viennese accent, but that really wasn't very helpful since more than 950,000 Austrians had fought on the German side in World War II. Through various sources, Wiesenthal was able to locate eight men with the name Silbernagel who'd been Nazi Party members. However, none of them had been stationed in Amsterdam in the service of the SD. Surely something was off.

In his memoir, Wiesenthal admitted to not having contacted Otto Frank to confirm the name of the SD man. A Holocaust survivor himself, Wiesenthal said he had not wished to upset Otto by forcing him to search his memory of that fateful day. He also worried that, like many other survivors he'd approached, Otto might not wish the SD man to be found. Wiesenthal had come across others who'd asked, "What's the use? You cannot bring back the dead. You can only make the survivors suffer."[3] But Wiesenthal felt he was looking at the bigger picture: if he could locate the SD man and get him to admit to the arrest, he would have proven that Anne Frank did exist and her diary was real. More important, in the late 1950s, when Germans and Austrians were once again talking nostalgically about the "great past," they would be confronted with proof of the Holocaust.

What appeared to the Cold Case Team to be crucial was that although Otto learned of Wiesenthal's mission to identify and locate the SD man, he did not offer his help despite knowing Silberbauer's real name. In a 1985 interview, Miep explained that Otto had asked her to change the name because he did not want the man's family harassed and she'd come up with Silberthaler.[4] According to Wiesenthal, Victor Kugler was the source of the name Silvernagl.[5] Prior to Ernst Schnabel's book *The Footsteps of Anne Frank*, there had been no public mention of the SD man who led the raid on the Annex. The ruse of using a false name for Silberbauer must have begun with the interviews Schnabel conducted with Miep, Otto, and the other helpers in 1957. Vince suddenly remembered how during his visit with Pieter and Thijs to the Anne Frank Fonds in Basel, the president, John Goldsmith, had taken him aside and said, "You know that Otto lied to Wiesenthal about knowing the identity of Silberbauer. Why do you think he did this?" Vince now believed that answering Goldsmith's question would be key to the investigation.

During a trip to Amsterdam in the spring of 1963, Dutch friends told Wiesenthal that he should not be searching for Silbernagel but rather for Silberthaler, the name Miep had invented. Then he had a fortuitous meeting with Ynze Taconis, the head of the National Criminal Investigation Department (Rijksrecherche) regarding his investigation. As Wiesenthal was about to leave, Taconis handed him what he called a little "travel literature." It was a photostat copy of a 1943 directory of the SD in the Netherlands with about three hundred names in it. On the plane back to Vienna, Wiesenthal started flipping through the directory, looking for Silberthaler. He never found it, but running his finger down the list of forty or so IV B4 members' names, he came to the common Austrian name "Silberbauer." Elated, Wiesenthal finally had his man—or at least his last name, since the roster did not contain first names.[6]

It was now an astonishing six years since he had come up with the idea of tracking down the SD man. Known for his searches for Josef Mengele and his tracking down of Adolf Eichmann, he would have been the first to admit that Silberbauer was not a high-ranking Nazi. His goal was not so much to punish him as to get him to admit to the arrest of Anne Frank and her family. In early June 1963, he provided the information he'd gathered on Silberbauer to Dr. Josef Wiesinger, his contact at the Austrian Federal Ministry of the Interior responsible for war crimes investigations.

At that point it was not clear if Silberbauer had even survived the war. For the next five months, Wiesenthal regularly contacted Wiesinger to learn if there was any progress in identifying and locating the Silberbauer on the list. He was always met with the same response: "We are working on it." The last such comment was in October 1963. What Wiesenthal didn't know, and the Cold Case Team discovered in an Austrian Federal Ministry of the Interior report dated August 21, 1963, was that the Austrian authorities had already identified, located, and interviewed Silberbauer. They just weren't telling Wiesenthal.

The team learned from the report that Inspector Karl Josef Silberbauer, an employee of the Vienna police, was quietly summoned before a Ministry of the Interior inquiry panel. During the interview he admitted to having been assigned to the Amsterdam SD, stationed there from November 1943 until October 1944, when he was injured in a motorcycle accident. He confirmed having worked under Willy Lages and Julius Dettmann as well as receiving reward payments for the capture of Jews in hiding. He also admitted to never having mastered the Dutch language and needing a translator to conduct interviews. Most important, he confessed to having been present at the arrest of Anne Frank and her family.

In doing a background investigation on Silberbauer, the team learned that after the war, in April 1945, he returned to his native Austria, where he ended up serving a fourteen-month jail sentence for using excessive force against Communist prisoners prior to his assignment in Amsterdam. After his release he was recruited by the West German Federal Intelligence Service (the Bundesnachrichtendienst; BND) and, according to a *Der Spiegel* report, worked as an undercover operative. His past membership in the SS served to blind targeted neo-Nazis to his changed loyalties.[7] After his time with the BND he was hired by the Vienna police, where he rose to the rank of inspector.

On November 11, 1963, nearly three months after Silberbauer provided his initial statement, Wiesenthal read the news in a headline of the Austrian newspaper *Volksstimme*: "The Man Who Betrayed Anne Frank."[8] It seemed that someone within the Vienna police department had leaked the story to the local newspaper.

The world press descended on Vienna. They also immediately requested comments from Otto, Miep, Bep, Kugler, and even the formerly accused, Willem van Maaren. Many followers of Anne's story and even its participants thought that finally, now that the SD man who led the Annex raid was located, he would reveal the name of the betrayer.

Probably feeling both outraged and hurt, Wiesenthal immediately penned a letter to Dr. Wiesinger, reminding him that *he* was the one who had provided the name "Silberbauer" and requested a photo that he could send to Otto Frank for identification purposes.[9] To preserve their relationship, Wiesinger eventually told Wiesenthal that he'd been ordered by his superiors not to inform him that they'd found and interrogated Silberbauer.

Based on the text of his letter, Wiesenthal still had no idea that Otto and the other witnesses had known Silberbauer's name all along. But one week after he sent the letter, he likely learned the truth. In one of his interviews after the news broke, Otto admitted to the Amsterdam newspaper *Het Vrije Volk* that he had known all along that Silberbauer was the man who led the raid. He further commented, "I have never had contact with Mr. Wiesenthal in Vienna. The reason why he wanted to have Silberbauer in particular is, therefore, a riddle to me."[10] In one of her interviews, Miep also confirmed that she had known Silberbauer's name but had not revealed it because Otto had asked her to use a fake name.[11]

So Otto had asked those who knew Silberbauer's real name to call the man something else? Why would he do that?

Cor Suijk, a past director of the Anne Frank House and Otto's friend, speculated years later that Otto felt somewhat sympathetic toward Silberbauer because he showed him respect as a fellow German officer when arresting him. He said that Otto wanted to protect the family of Silberbauer from undue attention, though in fact Silberbauer had no children.[12]

This seems a sentimental—and pat—explanation. Otto was not a sentimentalist. Silberbauer was the man whose actions led to the horrific deaths of his wife and children. At the time of the raid, the Nazi had yelled at Miep—she remembered him "almost bent over with rage"—berating her for helping "Jewish garbage."[13] During their interrogation at SD headquarters, he'd greeted Kugler and Kleiman: "Mitgefangen, mitgehangen" (Caught together, hanged together).[14] Silberbauer didn't deserve any empathy, especially from Otto. There must have been some other reason for his deliberate obfuscation.

Miep, too, had concealed Silberbauer's identity, and the unexpected announcement about locating the SD officer in Vienna presented somewhat of a problem. Out of the blue five months earlier, on May 3, 1963, she'd been contacted by a detective from the National Criminal Investigation Department regarding her knowledge of the Annex raid. In that interview she'd claimed not to know the name of the man who had led the raid team, even though she'd previously supplied it during the 1947–48 PRA investigation.[15] She'd also suggested that they speak with Otto Frank, a hint that he might know more.

Meanwhile, perhaps as a rebuke to the Austrian authorities for failing to tell him that they'd identified Silberbauer, Wiesenthal quietly provided Silberbauer's home address to a Dutch student journalist, Jules Huf. On November 20, 1963, the ambitious Huf went to Silberbauer's home without an appointment and knocked on his door, requesting an interview. At first Silberbauer's wife dismissed the request, but from deep within the house Silberbauer shouted to let the reporter in. Huf spent several hours interviewing Silberbauer about his recollection of the Annex arrest. In a play for sympathy, Silberbauer complained that after he had recently been called in for questioning, he'd had to turn over his gun, badge, and tram pass. "I was suddenly forced to buy my own tram ticket. Imagine the way the conductor looked at me." His wife occasionally chimed in, complaining that her husband's overtime pay had been cut: "We had to buy our furniture on loans." In the end, the bombshell headline that should have led every international newspaper was that Silberbauer claimed the raid was caused by a warehouse employee of Otto Frank making a call to the SD.[16] But the heavily edited interview ran in the Austrian newspaper *Kurier* on November 22, and whether because of the paper's limited circulation or the fact that the world was consumed by the news of the assassination of President John F. Kennedy, there was no marked public reaction.

However, the Austrian authorities clearly saw the story and were likely furious, since Silberbauer had been ordered to keep his mouth shut.[17] Just three days after the Huf story broke, Silberbauer was summoned and reinterviewed. His new statement was quite different from the version in the Huf article:

> *I want to make clear that I was never made aware of whoever reported the family Frank. I was not made aware whether it had been a Dutch or German individual. So, I as the only German and the only police officer went together with the arrest team to the said house. In the storage area on the ground floor*

> *was a man standing around, but he did not seem to have been waiting for us. He was questioned by the Dutch arrest team, during which he pointed in an upstairs direction with his hand.*[18]

The Cold Case Team could find no explanation for why Silberbauer changed the story he told Huf about the caller. What is consistent is that in the three official statements Silberbauer supplied to the Austrian authorities (in August 1963, November 1963, and March 1964), he never said that the call was placed by a warehouse employee. In fact, he asserted that he'd never been made aware of who had reported the Frank family, nor whether the caller had been Dutch or German, male or female. That stark contradiction of Huf's article left the team in a bit of a quandary as to who was more believable, Huf or Silberbauer.

Could Huf's version of what Silberbauer said be true? The authors Jeroen de Bruyn and Joop van Wijk made an excellent point: Silberbauer's claim that the traitorous phone call occurred half an hour before the arrest eliminates the warehouse manager, Willem van Maaren. The team's analysis of all available data has the raid occurring at approximately 10:30 a.m. Van Maaren always arrived at work at 9:00 a.m. All public telephone kiosks in the streets had been eliminated on German orders years earlier. The only phone Van Maaren could have used was located in the front office, but Bep, Miep, and Kleiman had been there all morning.[19] The only other possibility is that he used a phone in one of the neighboring businesses. The Cold Case Team were confident that if that had happened, given the notoriety of the case, someone from that business would have eventually come forward.

The complete Silberbauer interview did not become available to the public until twenty-three years later, when it ran in the Dutch weekly newspaper *De Groene Amsterdammer* in 1986.[20] It was interesting, but it didn't answer the most important questions: Had Silberbauer actually been told by his superior SS Lieutenant Julius Dettmann who the caller was? Or had he just been grandstanding for the young reporter Huf in one last bid for notoriety?

31
What Miep Knew

Among the helpers, it is hard not to find Miep Gies the most compelling. She saved Anne's diary, intending to give it back to her when she returned at the end of the war; Otto lived with her and her husband for seven years after his return from Auschwitz; she was the one who kept Otto's secrets after the war. Following Otto's death in 1980, she became the de facto spokesperson for the story of Anne Frank. The world press interviewed her on dozens of occasions, and she was invited to speak internationally.

Vince organized what he called the Statements Project: the Cold Case Team was to collect all statements made by the witnesses over the years in print, audio, or video with regard to the betrayal. They were placed on a timeline to identify contradictions or corroborations.

As part of the Statements Project, the Cold Case Team collected all available print, audio, and video material involving Miep.

One day in 2019, while he was reviewing a recording of one of her international speaking engagements, Vince stumbled upon something totally unexpected. In 1994, she gave a lecture at the University of Michigan and was accompanied onstage by Professor Rolf Wolfswinkel, who served as moderator and also assisted her when she occasionally struggled with an English word or phrase.[1] Lying on his couch listening to the speech through headphones, Vince almost fell asleep. It was essentially the same speech he'd heard Miep give in most of the other recordings he'd reviewed. Then, at the conclusion of the speech, Wolfswinkel invited questions from the audience, and a young man posed the question "What gave the Franks away?" In the course of answering, Miep made the startling statement, "After fifteen years . . . we began again to search for the betrayer. But that was 1960, and by this time the betrayer had died." She concluded by saying, "So we have to resign ourselves to the fact that we will never know who did it." Vince sat up in shock. Both things couldn't be true. If Miep had known the betrayer was dead by 1960, she must have known who the betrayer was.

Vince turned to the writings of University of Texas at Austin psychologist Art Markman to explain the discrepancy. In an article by Drake Baer for *The Cut*, "The Real Reason Keeping Secrets Is So Hard, According to a Psychologist," Markman explained that the mind has a limited capacity to process information, and to keep track of what is privileged and what can be divulged is a multifaceted cognitive maneuver. Sometimes the temptation is to unburden oneself by letting slip a part of the secret.[2] Vince believed that that was what happened to Miep: she admitted that she had known who the betrayer was and left a clue: that he or she was dead by 1960. What else did she know?

Though she clearly knew the name of the betrayer, she never disclosed it. When her friend Cor Suijk asked her directly if she knew the name of the betrayer, she asked, "Cor, can you keep a secret?" Very eagerly he answered, "Yes, Miep, I can!" And she smiled and said, "Me, too."[3]

Vince decided to contact Father John Neiman, who was a close friend of both Otto and Miep. He had been with Miep at the Academy Awards party in 1996 hosted by Leslie Gold, a coauthor of Miep's book *Anne Frank Remembered.* The book had been made into a documentary film and won an Oscar for Best Documentary

Feature. Neiman recalled that he was talking privately with Miep when, out of the blue, she told him that Otto Frank knew the betrayer of the Annex and the betrayer was dead. It wasn't clear to him if she meant that Otto knew the betrayer personally or just the betrayer's name. "You could hear a pin drop." He asked if she also knew who it was. She said she did, and there the conversation ended.[4]

According to Bep's son Joop, his mother told him that in the late 1950s, a "spontaneous agreement" was reached between Otto and the helpers. From then on, Otto would be the spokesman who addressed the media. "The helpers would remain non-committal as much as possible regarding their role in the hiding."[5]

The aggression of neo-Nazis and Holocaust deniers and the manipulation by journalists writing about the story of the Annex were reasons enough for Otto to want to control the narrative. Bep, Miep, and Jan Gies had no problem with the arrangement, so annoyed were they by the frequent press errors.[6] Yet it seemed that for Otto, something deeper was at stake; the team was determined to probe this mystery.

It occurred to Vince that he should follow up with Rolf Wolfswinkel. Maybe he'd had personal conversations with Miep about the Annex raid. After a few

Otto Frank (*center*) with the people who helped hide him and his family. *Left to right:* Miep Gies, Johannes Kleiman, Victor Kugler, and Bep Voskuijl. *Courtesy of the Anne Frank House, Amsterdam*

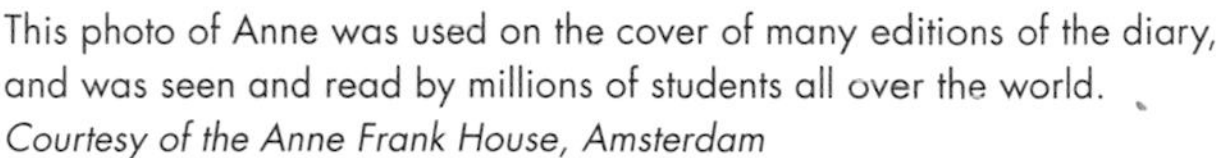

This photo of Anne was used on the cover of many editions of the diary, and was seen and read by millions of students all over the world. *Courtesy of the Anne Frank House, Amsterdam*

Left: Otto Frank, before the war. Friends "smiled at his Prussian self-restraint." *May 1936, courtesy of the Anne Frank House, Amsterdam.* *Right:* Born in Germany, Edith Frank married Otto in 1925. They were forced to flee with their two daughters, Anne and Margot, to Amsterdam in 1933. She died in Auschwitz of starvation. *May 1935, courtesy of the Anne Frank House, Amsterdam*

Margot Frank, older than Anne by three years, was called up for forced labor in July 1942. *May 1942, courtesy of the Anne Frank House, Amsterdam*

The Franks and friends on their way to the wedding of Jan and Miep Gies. *Amsterdam, July 1941, copyright © Granger*

The elusive Karl Josef Silberbauer. He arrested the Franks and the others in the Annex and started them on their way to the concentration camps. He eventually became a police officer in Vienna. *Private collection. Heritage Images/TopFoto*

Ans van Dijk was a V-Frau (a collaborator who betrayed Jews in hiding). She was the only Dutch woman to be executed for her wartime activities. *1947, AFH/IISG, International Institute of Social History, Amsterdam*

Left: Like Otto Frank, Auguste van Pels and her husband were born in Germany but moved to Amsterdam to escape the rise of Nazism. *Right:* Hermann van Pels had been an herbalist with Otto Frank's company before he, his wife, and his son joined the Franks in hiding. *Fotobureau Actueel, courtesy of the Anne Frank House, Amsterdam*

Peter van Pels, who went into hiding with his parents, the Franks, and the dentist Fritz Pfeffer. *1942, courtesy of the Anne Frank House, Amsterdam*

The Jewish Council for Amsterdam, 1942. A very powerful, controversial group. Some prominent members included (*seated, left to right*) Abraham Asscher (*first*), David Cohen (*second from left*), and Arnold van den Bergh (*fifth from left*). *The College of the Jewish Council for Amsterdam, 1942, copyright © Image Bank WW2—NIOD—Joh. De Haas*

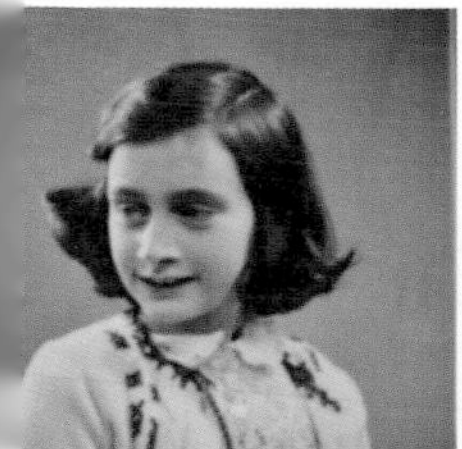

Some snapshots of a young, happy Anne. *May 1939, courtesy of the Anne Frank House, Amsterdam*

ons, in de schoolbanken zou kunnen zitten!
O lala, heb ik niet net nog verteld dat ik
niet voorbarig wil zijn? Vergeef me, ik heet
heb niet voor niets de naam dat ik een
bundeltje tegenspraak ben!

je Anne M. Frank.

Dinsdag 1 Aug. 1944.

Lieve Kitty,
„Een bundeltje tegenspraak" is de laatste zin van
m'n vorige brief en de eerste van m'n huidige.
„Een bundeltje tegenspraak", kun jij me precies
uitleggen wat dat is? Wat betekent tegenspraak?
Zoals zovele woorden (kan het op twee manieren
uitgelegd worden) heeft het twee betekenissen, tegenspraak van buiten en tegenspraak van binnen.
Het eerste is het gewone niet neerleggen bij
andermans meningen, het zelf beter weten,
het laatste woord hebben, enfin alles onaange-
name eigenschappen waarvoor ik bekend
sta; het tweede, daar sta ik niet voor bekend,
dat is m'n eigen geheim.
Ik heb je al eens meer verteld (gezegd), dat m'n
ziel als het ware in tweeën gesplitst is. De ene

The last page of Anne's diary, written three days before the family was arrested. It was one of the pieces of writing Miep kept in her drawer as she awaited Anne's return. *1944, copyright © Tallandier/ Bridgeman Images*

Amsterdam. Note how close together the residences are. The building highlighted in blue houses Otto Frank's business, Opekta, and the section in green illustrates the Annex. Note the courtyard with the chestnut tree that Anne wrote about in her diary. *Copyright © Luchtvaart Museum Aviodrome*

The "Wall of Shame" in the Proditione office in Amsterdam. The SD photos are of police officers involved with the Nazis' intelligence agency. The V is for V-men and -women, paid informants who worked to help find and capture Jews. *Courtesy of Vince Pankoke*

The anonymous note that would turn the case. *Courtesy of Monique Koemans*

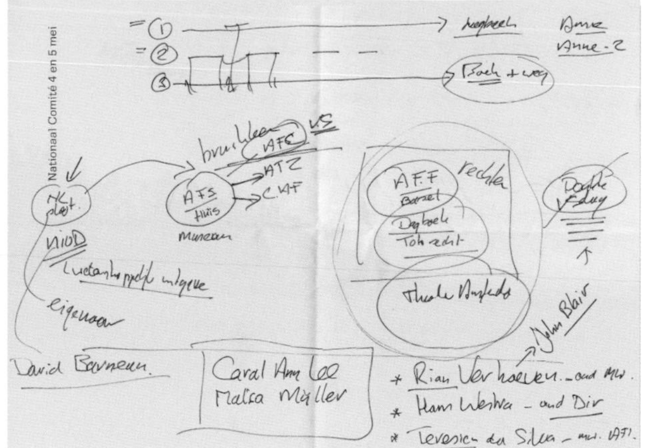

The diagram showing just how complicated the relationships between the Anne Frank organizations are. *Courtesy of Proditione*

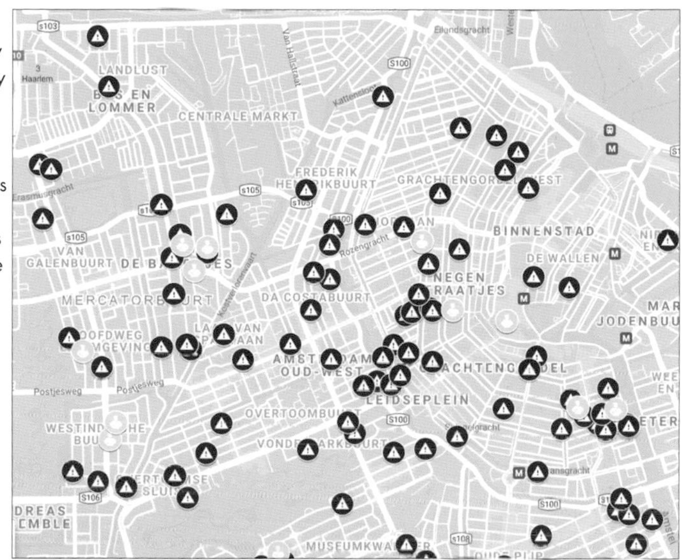

The interactive map produced by Xomnia, the Dutch data company to which the Cold Case Team provided raw data. The red circles with triangles show the addresses of known collaborators obtained from lists compiled by the Resistance. The yellow circles indicate SD informants who were identified from a list found in the US National Archives and Records Administration (NARA).

Prinsengracht 263–267, the hiding place, now a museum and landmark. *2018, courtesy of the Anne Frank House, Amsterdam*

FOUR REASONS FOR ARREST

1. Chance 2. Betryal 3. Carelessness
4. Mass Arrests (not viable DNA)

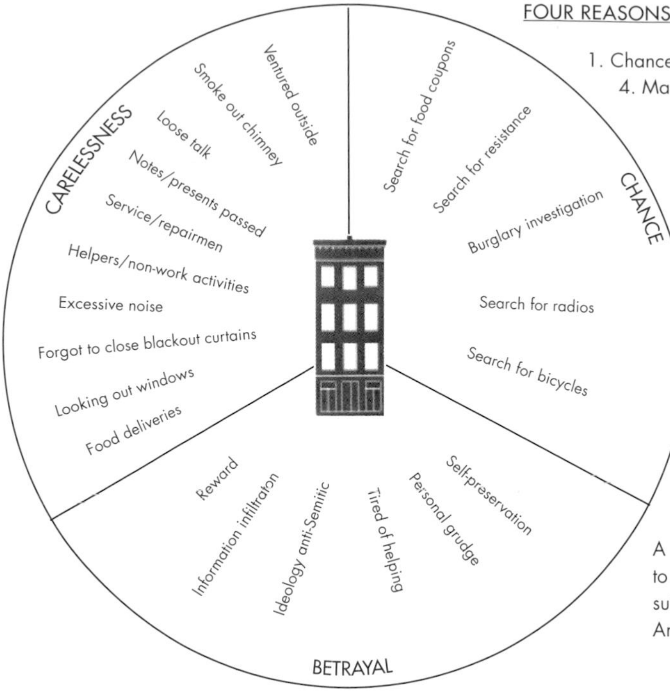

CARELESSNESS
Ventured outside
Smoke out chimney
Loose talk
Notes/presents passed
Service/repairmen
Helpers/non-work activities
Excessive noise
Forgot to close blackout curtains
Looking out windows
Food deliveries

CHANCE
Search for food coupons
Search for resistance
Burglary investigation
Search for radios
Search for bicycles

BETRAYAL
Reward
Information infiltraton
Ideology anti-Semitic
Tired of helping
Personal grudge
Self-preservation

A diagram Vince Pankoke made to narrow down the motives and submotives behind the raid on the Annex. *Courtesy of Vince Pankoke*

A model of the warehouse and the Annex. *Illustration of the Anne Frank House by Chantal van Wessel and Frédérik Ruys, www.vizualism.com © 2010, 2012 Anne Frank Stichting, Amsterdam*

Director of research Pieter van Twisk, reviewing some of the latest discoveries with researcher Circe de Bruin. *Courtesy of Proditione*

Two more views of the Wall of Shame, with detailed notes, "Escaped to Argentina" for the SD officer (*left*) and "Executed" for Ans van Dijk (*right*). *Courtesy of Proditione*

Left to right: Cold Case Team researchers Circe de Bruin, Nienke Filius, and Nina Kaiser meticulously examining thousands of archival documents. *Courtesy of Proditione*

Left to right: Pieter van Twisk, Thijs Bayens, and Vince Pankoke in the early days of the investigation. *Courtesy of Vince Pankoke*

Bernhard Haas, legendary document examiner. The team consulted him at his home in Winnenden, Germany. *Courtesy of Bernhard Haas*

Left to right: Monique Koemans, Vince Pankoke, and Brendan Rook. *Courtesy of Proditione*

computer searches he located Wolfswinkel at New York University, where he was a professor of modern history. Vince reached out to him and had a long conversation with him regarding the Cold Case Team's project and his relationship with Miep. It turned out that he was a close friend of Miep's, often accompanying her to lectures and helping with translation.

Wolfswinkel told Vince that his father, Gerrit, had been an Amsterdam policeman during the war. His father claimed that he'd accompanied the SD on a few arrests but would only stand outside the location to guard the door. For those actions he was found guilty of collaboration and served a jail sentence. Rolf's mother divorced his father while he was incarcerated, and he had only limited contact with him after that.

Later in his life he reconnected with his father and inquired about his wartime activities. Strangely, his father, who had previously been a mainstream Christian, said that he'd become a Jehovah's Witness and could confess anything done during the war only to God. At the time, Rolf's statement about his father's unexplained change of religion meant nothing to Vince, and since he didn't seem to know much more about Miep, Vince didn't think much more about Rolf.

But Wolfswinkel is a hard name to forget, and Vince

had the feeling he'd seen it somewhere before. The name Gerrit Wolfswinkel kept swirling in his head. Prior to the Microsoft AI program, the Cold Case Team had been relying on printed records and crude spreadsheets to keep track of information. Vince pulled up the spreadsheet for the nearly one thousand *Kopgeld* receipts he'd found and did a quick name search for Wolfswinkel. There in black and white was Professor Wolfswinkel's father. He was much more than a policeman who guarded the door during a raid; he was a member of the IV B4 Jew-hunting unit. Vince wondered if Rolf knew that about his father. How incredible was it that the man who was a friend of Miep Gies was also the son of an IV B4 member, the same SD unit that conducted the Annex raid? At the time Vince thought: You just can't make this stuff up!

It got even stranger. While examining the *Kopgeld* receipts chronicling the elder Wolfswinkel's work, Vince found one that was not for arresting Jews. A receipt dated March 15, 1942, showed that he was paid a bounty of 3.75 guilders for the arrest of a Jehovah's Witness. Had Gerrit Wolfswinkel felt so guilty about the arrest that he converted to his victim's religion? Or was the conversion expedient, since Jehovah's Witnesses can confess only to God?

The last of the strange coincidences was that Rolf had

also told Vince that he was remotely related to Tonny Ahlers, who had blackmailed Otto Frank in 1941 with the Jansen note. Rolf's grandmother had married several times, and one of her husbands was Tonny Ahlers's father. Wolfswinkel has the wedding ring given to his grandmother with "ACA 1925" engraved inside.

32
No Substantial Proof, Part II

Vince concluded that it was now time to turn the Cold Case Team's attention to the second investigation into the Annex raid, conducted by Arend Jacobus van Helden, a veteran detective of the Dutch police force. The first question the team faced was: Why, suddenly, in 1963–1964, did the Dutch government authorize the investigation? It didn't seem to be the result of any new information. Most likely it was a response to Simon Wiesenthal's search for Silberbauer that had generated so much international press attention. The Dutch wanted to take back control of the case.

Vince noted that the second investigation was conducted in a more professional manner than the one in 1947–1948, although it, too, had its weak points. Not only had memories faded in the twenty-year interval, but evidence had been lost and witnesses had died, including Johannes Kleiman (on January 30, 1959), Lammert Hartog (on March 6, 1959), and Hartog's wife, Lena (on June 10, 1963).

The problem with the second investigation was that it, too, was narrow. The focus was once again only on Willem van Maaren. That was in part due to Silberbauer's remark in Vienna that a warehouse employee of Otto Frank made the call to the SD. Though he would later retract that, Silberbauer claimed that when he arrived on the scene, he witnessed a Dutch detective ask the warehouse manager, "Where are the Jews?" The man pointed toward the upper floor, which led Silberbauer to conclude that Van Maaren had phoned in the tip about the Jews and had been waiting for the raid team.

Detective Van Helden was methodical. He tracked down and questioned the two Dutch policemen, Willem Grootendorst and Gezinus Gringhuis, who assisted Silberbauer in the raid. Grootendorst was released from prison in 1955 on the tenth anniversary of the liberation of the Netherlands. Gringhuis, whose death sentence was commuted to life in prison, was released in 1958. Both claimed that they could not recall having taken part in the Annex arrest. But Gringhuis went further, claiming that he was not there because he would have remembered the arrest of eight Jews, a crafty obfuscation.[1]

Van Helden also interviewed another of Van Maaren's coworkers, Johannes de Kok, who was a warehouse assistant for a few months during the second half of 1943. De Kok admitted to having helped Van Maaren sell the goods he stole from Opekta/Gies & Co. on the black market, but he added that Van Maaren never exhibited any sympathies toward the Nazis.

As Van Helden probed Van Maaren's past, he uncovered a checkered career of failed businesses, bankruptcies, years of unemployment, and charges of petty theft. But throughout it all, Van Maaren seemed anti-Nazi. Shortly before the war, he'd been supported by a Dutch charity. After the Nazis closed down all private charities and replaced them with Winterhulp Nederland (Winter Aid Netherlands), according to a former charity committee member, Van Maaren refused on principle to accept aid from the fascists. The detective made inquiries among Van Maaren's former neighbors, and although people reported that he was "financially untrustworthy," no one suspected him of having had contacts with "people who had served the enemy or the enemy's henchmen." He was known to often visit a neighbor in the resistance, and "there had never been any hint of treachery."[2]

When Van Maaren himself was questioned, he refuted Silberbauer's version of events. He said that Silberbauer did not speak Dutch and misunderstood the exchange. When the raid team arrived and the Dutch policeman approached him, the man simply asked, "Where is the office?" and Van Maaren pointed upward.[3]

Van Maaren was also accused of having spoken to employees from the neighboring businesses about the Jews in the Annex. He clarified that, saying that only after the arrest did he speak with them. He pointed out that people in the adjacent businesses already knew that something strange was going on within the Opekta/Gies & Co. building. Jacobus Mater, who ran an herb business at Prinsengracht 269 and was a member of the NSB, had once asked Van Maaren, "What have you got hidden there?"

The Van Maaren file was closed on November 6, 1964. The final report to the prosecutor stated that "the inquiry did not lead to any concrete results."[4]

The Cold Case Team decided to dissect Van Maaren's interviews from both the 1947–48 and the 1963–64 investigations for any false statements or inconsistencies. Van Maaren claimed that he would not have called attention to himself by telling the Nazis about the

Annex because his oldest son, Martinus, was avoiding work duty, a fact the SD would have easily discovered. However, the team found no record of Martinus van Maaren's being wanted for failing to report for *Arbeitseinsatz.* Unfortunately, this is not a definitive statement on his status since he might have been placed on one of the SD's wanted lists after March 1944, by which time the lists were notoriously incomplete.

Several people who were interviewed commented that Van Maaren did not seem pro-Nazi, thus eliminating ideology as a motive. However, a person would not necessarily need to be pro-Nazi or anti-Semitic to provide information on Jews in hiding in order to save a son from arrest. If, for example, Martinus van Maaren had been found to be disobeying the law, to keep his son safe, the father could have been coerced into revealing that there were people in the Annex.

But at that stage the Cold Case Team remained unconvinced of Van Maaren's guilt. It seemed more likely that he was happy with the status quo. He could steal money from lost wallets or desk drawers without being questioned. He could take produce from the warehouse and sell it with impunity on the black market. The staff might have had their suspicions about his questionable actions, but they would never have risked confronting or firing him for fear that he would retaliate by betraying them.

With Van Maaren looking less likely to be the betrayer, other suspects were also considered. The first was Lammert Hartog, who had only recently joined Opekta and was working illegally, since he'd ignored his call-up to do forced labor in Germany. And then there was his wife, Lena, who was employed intermittently as a cleaning lady at Opekta/Gies & Co.

In her biography of Anne Frank, Melissa Müller pursued the theory, already mentioned earlier, that Lena Hartog gossiped about Jews hiding in the Annex not only to one of the clients she cleaned for but also to Bep Voskuijl, who immediately reported it to the other helpers. She and the others in the warehouse discussed the impossibility of relocating the eight people in the Annex and so didn't tell Otto. That was only about five weeks before the raid. But logic suggests that it would not have been in Lena's best interests to call in such information. Her husband was working illegally at Opekta/Gies & Co., after all, and such a call could well have cost him his job, his income, and his freedom. The Nazis did not take evasion of work duty lightly.

Father John Neiman, a close friend and confidant of Otto, was staying with Miep at her home in Amsterdam in November 2000. He recounted telling Miep that he'd read Melissa Müller's *Anne Frank: The Biography*, in which she suggested that Lena Hartog was possibly the betrayer. He asked, "Miep, was it Lena? Did she betray them?" Miep looked straight at him and said, "No. She did not."[5]

One reason Müller thought Lena might have been the culprit was the theory that the person who placed the anonymous phone call to SD headquarters was female. That idea was perpetuated by the ABC miniseries *Anne Frank: The Whole Story*, based on Müller's biography. But the contention that the caller was female has never been substantiated. The source of the rumor was supposedly Cor Suijk, a former director of the Anne Frank House, who claimed he had learned that through a conversation he'd had with Silberbauer. However, there is no evidence of his ever having interviewed Silberbauer.[6]

Suijk died in 2014, but the Cold Case Team interviewed a close contact and fellow Anne Frank House employee, Jan Erik Dubbelman. Dubbelman claimed that Suijk told him that when Silberbauer was first identified, Otto Frank asked Suijk to go to Vienna and speak with Silberbauer. At the time (1963–1964), Suijk was not employed by the Anne Frank House but claimed to be good friends with Otto. It seems improbable that Otto would make such a request, since he'd sworn he wanted nothing further to do with Silberbauer.[7] Furthermore, after his 1963 interview with the Dutch journalist Jules Huf, Silberbauer refused to grant any further interviews, likely on orders from the Austrian authorities. It seemed that Suijk was known to exaggerate. His daughter told Dubbelman that you couldn't believe a word her father said.

As for Lena's husband, Lammert Hartog, being the betrayer, the team was doubtful. Yes, he'd made it clear in his 1948 statement that he'd learned from Van Maaren, approximately fourteen days before the raid, that Jews were hidden in the building.[8] According to Johannes Kleiman, as soon as Silberbauer and his team arrived, Hartog "immediately took off and we never saw him again."[9] But it is hardly incriminating that someone working illegally would run at the sight of a German SD officer.

Notwithstanding their dismissal of the Hartogs as suspects, the team was still intrigued by Melissa Müller's research. On February 13, 2019, Vince and Brendan flew to Munich to interview her. She was open and generous in describing her research and still passionately attached to Anne Frank. It turned out that Müller was no longer all that convinced of Lena's involvement and felt the case was still very much open.

She told Vince she'd managed to interview Miep Gies, whom she described as a "tough interview. . . . It was hard to get information out of her." She strongly suspected that both Miep and Otto knew much more about the circumstances of the raid but for some reason were unwilling to share that information.

Vince said that it was as if alarm bells went off. The question that had been dogging the team all along was: What had changed between the 1948 investigation and the one in 1963–1964? The answer was, not much—except for the way Otto Frank behaved. In 1948, he'd been intent on finding out who'd betrayed the Annex residents. By the second investigation, he was barely present. At most, he was watching quietly from the sidelines. He and the helpers no longer seemed convinced of Van Maaren's guilt. In several interviews Miep Gies even said that she did not believe Van Maaren was the betrayer. A key puzzle now became: Why did Otto Frank change his mind? What does he know now that he didn't know before?

Or, as Melissa Müller put it, something happened that made the identity of the betrayer "less a mystery unsolved than a secret well kept."[10]

33
The Greengrocer

Hendrik van Hoeve owned a greengrocer's shop on Leliegracht, around the corner and not more than 100 yards from Prinsengracht 263. He supplied fresh vegetables and potatoes to the Annex, secretly delivering the food at midday when the warehouse employees were out for lunch. He worked with the resistance. During the war, he allegedly used a handcart with a hidden compartment to distribute illegal foodstuffs to a list of addresses that he picked up each morning. "He never saw any of the recipients. Either he placed the bags outside the door or someone appeared from inside the house to take them from him."[1] Sometimes he pasted posters on walls. He would always treasure a photo of a large poster bearing the word *VICTORIA!*

with Hitler's head trapped between the two arms of the *V*.[2]

In the winter of 1942, a Jewish resistance worker named Max Meiler contacted Van Hoeve and asked if he would be willing to hide a Jewish couple. When he agreed, Meiler arranged for a trusted carpenter to construct an ingenious hiding place in Van Hoeve's attic. The Weiszes moved into an extra bedroom at the back of the house equipped with an alarm bell that could be rung in case of danger, at which point they would climb to the secret attic compartment.[3] They stayed with the Van Hoeve family for at least seventeen months.

On May 25, 1944, an arrest team headed by Pieter Schaap, the handler of Ans van Dijk, raided the house and shop of Van Hoeve and discovered the Weiszes in hiding.[4] The couple and Van Hoeve were arrested, although Van Hoeve's wife was not. That was not unusual. When there were children involved, the arrest teams often let the wife stay behind.

Immediately the Cold Case Team wondered if the raid was one of the "daisy chain" arrests—Jews who had been arrested being forced to give up the addresses of other Jews in hiding. The obvious question was whether there was a connection between the arrests of Van Hoeve and the Weisz couple and the subsequent raid on Prinsengracht 263, since Van Hoeve's house and shop were so close to Otto's business. In that neighborhood news traveled fast. That same day, Anne Frank wrote in her diary that their vegetable man had been picked up by the police, along with two Jews he'd been hiding; they would now be entering the concentration camp universe. As for herself and her family, they would have to eat less. Maybe they'd be hungry, but at least they still had their freedom.[5]

After six weeks in prison in Amsterdam, Van Hoeve was sent to Camp Vught. Set up in 1942 in the south of the Netherlands by Reich Commissioner Arthur Seyss-Inquart, Vught was the only concentration camp run directly by the SS in Western Europe outside Germany.[6] It was a terrifying place. Surrounded by barbed wire and watchtowers, the camp had its own gallows, an execution grounds in the nearby woods, and a mobile crematory oven to dispose of the dead.

By that time in the Netherlands, it was generally understood that those who had the courage to save Jews, if discovered, usually ended up in such places.

During the war Amsterdam was a small world in which lives and fates crossed relentlessly. Nothing illustrated that more than the web of interrelationships among the people connected to the greengrocer and to the Annex. There were a number of potential suspects in Van Hoeve's inner circle who might have passed along information about the hiders.

MAX MEILER

Max Meiler was the contact person who placed the Weiszes in hiding at the Van Hoeves'. He was deeply anti-Nazi and as early as Kristallnacht, November 9, 1938, used his brother's summerhouse close to Venlo, near the German border, to shelter Jewish refugees.[7]

From the beginning of the war, Meiler falsified identity cards (Persoonsbewijzen, or PBs) and ration cards and was soon helping Jewish people find hiding places. As of 1942, he regularly traveled to Venlo carrying the underground newspaper *Vrij Nederland* and photos of the royal family, which in itself was an act of resistance.[8]

On May 17, 1944, eight days before Van Hoeve's home and shop were raided, Meiler was arrested on the train between Utrecht and Rotterdam. He was carrying false identity papers.

In his memoir about the war, now housed at the Anne Frank Stichting, Van Hoeve described how he had encountered Meiler in Camp Vught in mid-July. Meiler was shocked to run into Van Hoeve and pleaded with him not to call him by his real name.[9] He was using an alias to hide his Jewish identity. They met again at the Heinkel factories near Berlin at the end of September or early October. Once a large, handsome man, Meiler now looked totally broken.[10] All he told Van Hoeve was that the SS had found out that he was a Jew. He died in Neuengamme concentration camp in northern Germany on March 12, 1945.

Is it possible that Meiler broke under interrogation, perhaps at Camp Vught? It's surely conceivable that Van Hoeve told him about Prinsengracht 263. They were both engaged in resistance work; Meiler may have seen Van Hoeve's delivery lists or even been involved in determining the addresses. Could Meiler have revealed the Annex address to the SS? The team thought that was a working hypothesis until they discovered that the timing was off.

Van Hoeve was arrested on May 25 and sent to Amstelveenseweg prison for six weeks before being transferred to Camp Vught around mid-July. When he met Meiler in Camp Vught, Meiler was still passing as an Aryan and would have had no need to hand over names to the SS. But something must have happened to him on August 12, since there is a record of his admission to the camp hospital.[11] Perhaps he was beaten by a *kapo* and that was when his Jewish identity was discovered. However, the raid on the Annex had occurred eight days before his hospitalization, meaning that it's unlikely that he was beaten into revealing the Prinsengracht 263 address.

RICHARD AND RUTH WEISZ

After their arrest on May 25, 1944, the Weiszes were transported to Westerbork transit camp. Jews who'd been arrested in hiding were considered criminals, were assigned to Barrack 67, the penal barrack, and carried an *S* (penal case) on their identification card.[12] It was the lowest designation possible, meaning that the prisoner must undertake forced labor and would be transported to the east sooner than later. Inmates did everything they could to lose their *S* status, hoping it would save them from deportation.

Pieter and Monique visited Camp Westerbork in the north of the Netherlands on October 10, 2018; it's now a memorial museum. Guido Abuys, the head curator of the camp archives, offered to help them in their search for information about the Weiszes. Abuys went into the archives and was gone for some time. When he returned, he looked puzzled. He was carrying the Weiszes' camp ID cards, which showed something quite rare. The barrack number on the cards looked as if it had been tampered with: the "67" (the penal barrack) had been changed to "87" (the hospital barrack). More significantly, somehow (it is not clear how), between June 11 and June 29, Richard and Ruth Weisz had managed to have the *S* removed from their camp cards. That meant that they had lost their "penal" status and would thereafter be designated as "normal" prisoners, which had brought about a dramatic change in their circumstances.[13]

Adding to the puzzle, Richard Weisz sent two letters to the greengrocer's wife, Mrs. Van Hoeve, requesting that she send clean sheets and clothes. The first letter is stamped "Barrack 67," the second "Barrack 85." Did that mean they were relocated to Barrack 85?[14]

To make that move, the Weiszes would have to have done something extraordinary. Or perhaps someone with influence had interceded on their behalf. Barrack 85, known as the Barneveld Barrack, was the most elite barrack in Westerbork. It was assigned to a privileged group of high-ranking, mostly upper- and middle-class, Dutch Jews considered invaluable to the state, whose status was such that they could not be deported to the east. They were initially housed in a castle near the town of Barneveld in the eastern Netherlands, but on September 29, 1943, they were all deported to Camp Westerbork. Even there they retained some of their privileges.[15]

Of course, it's possible that the Weiszes were never assigned to Barrack 85 and someone else mailed the second letter on Richard Weisz's behalf. Somehow, though, the Weiszes managed to change their penal status. The Cold Case Team knew that "penal" prisoners could change their status for a significant fee (one survivor of Westerbork had paid a fee of 80,000 guilders, the equivalent of $545,000 today). The Weiszes, however, did not seem to have that kind of money, which suggests that they might have paid with a different currency: information.

In handwriting on the Weiszes' identity cards, the date of their deportation is noted along with the added information "Normal case." Despite having "normal" and not "penal" status, on September 3, 1944, the Weiszes were deported to Auschwitz on the same transport as Anne Frank and her family. Both died in the Eastern European camps. It is not known if they were together or separated and exactly when they perished.[16]

LEOPOLD DE JONG

Leopold de Jong's presence in Westerbork is a long story with a curious history. It starts with the man who arrested Van Hoeve and the Weiszes: Pieter Schaap.

Pieter Schaap was the Dutch agent of the SD who led

the raid on Van Hoeve's grocery shop on Leliegracht, around the corner from the secret Annex. He was also the handler of the V-Frau Ans van Dijk and the man behind the betrayal and arrest of Erich Geiringer, the first husband of Fritzi Geiringer, Otto Frank's second wife. According to his boss, Abraham Kaper, desk sergeant at the Bureau of Jewish Affairs, Schaap was one of the men who brought in the most Jews. "And I should know," he added, "since I was the one paying them."[17]

Schaap was best known for his modus operandi: pressuring Jewish people to act as V-Men and V-Women. After a raid, he would focus on a Jewish prisoner and threaten to send him or her and family to the camps or worse. Then he offered an out if he or she would work for him as an informant. Among his most infamous informants was Leopold de Jong. In the case of De Jong, Schaap had a double advantage: he exploited not only De Jong as a V-Man but also De Jong's wife, Frieda Pleij.[18]

In the early days of the occupation, De Jong (who was Jewish) and Pleij (who was not) had people in hiding in their house in Heemstede. They were both known to have lovers. De Jong had relationships with some of the Jewish girls and young women who were in hiding at their home (some of whose families he later betrayed), and Pleij was involved with a man named Herman Mol, who guarded her house when she was in prison after the war. That she also had a relationship with Pieter Schaap was common knowledge at the SD.[19] Pleij said she had been with him only out of fear; he said that she had been his *Friedl* and he had wanted to marry her, even though he was already married.[20]

Pleij later claimed that she had delivered food coupons for the resistance. Her CABR file confirms that she received food stamps through a middleman who had connections with the resistance. Evidently, she then sold the food stamps on the black market.

In searching through Pleij's CABR files, Cold Case Team researcher Christine Hoste discovered a bank statement indicating a large deposit of 4,110.10 guilders (the equivalent of $28,000 today) made on August 5, 1944—one day after the raid on the Annex. Such a large sum; such a suspicious date! How to account for it? Had Pieter Schaap taken part in the raid and this was money he'd stolen from the Annex and passed to his lover, Pleij, to deposit? For Christine it was a eureka moment. But further examination of bank records made it clear that Pleij received such payments on a regular basis.[21] Selling food stamps on the black market was obviously a lucrative scam.

In the summer of 1944, Leopold de Jong began to

panic. It seemed to him that too many people knew about his connection to Schaap through his wife and might suspect him of being a Jewish informant. Schaap ordered de Jong to go to Westerbork, where he could act as a cell spy, or prison informant.[22] De Jong entered Westerbork on July 1.[23] On the transport list, it is stated that his status as a Jew was still under investigation, which of course was a subterfuge.[24] He was assigned to the Barneveld Barrack. Camp records indicate that on one occasion he requested to go to the town of Groningen to help Pieter Schaap track down a resistance leader named Schalken.

The team couldn't ignore the obvious question: Did Leopold de Jong, in his role as prison informant, somehow learn from the Weiszes about Jews in hiding at Prinsengracht 263?

Whether or not the Weiszes knew about the secret Annex, it's clear that the greengrocer Hendrik van Hoeve knew; he was the one who commented to Jan Gies, after the warehouse break-in in April 1944, that he'd thought better of contacting the police.[25] But Richard Weisz had been a greengrocer before he went into hiding. It could very well be that he helped Van Hoeve with the preparation of deliveries before he made his rounds and thus learned that Prinsengracht 263 was one of the addresses on the list.

Van Hoeve said his grocery store had acted like a *doorganghuis* (transit house) for people in hiding. There might have been an opportunity to hear rumors of *onderduikers* in the secret Annex. In that environment, with so many pressures and fears, people slipped and traded information without always realizing it.

Any information sharing could have come about by accident if, say, the Weiszes, who had managed to lose their penal status, met Leopold de Jong in Barrack 85 or elsewhere. They had no reason to suspect he was a V-Man. Like them, he was Jewish; they probably thought they could trust him. As a V-Man he would have cultivated their trust, much the same way Ans van Dijk did with hiders. Perhaps they shared their suspicion that there were Jews in hiding in the Annex. Thinking they were celebrating the Franks' ingenuity in staying hidden, they might have bragged about them. De Jong would, of course, have tipped off Schaap.

In April 1945, De Jong went to meet Schaap in Groningen. He was hoping to ask for his help in escaping to Switzerland. Instead, Schaap, accompanied by an SD man named Geert van Bruggen, lured him to an empty house and shot him in the back. Bruggen later testified, "I saw the Jew in a puddle of blood lying in front of the stairs next to the kitchen. I did not see any sign of life in the Jew."[26] De Jong's file in Camp Westerbork recorded him as having gone AWOL on April 9.

After Dolle Dinsdag (Mad Tuesday) and the wild rumors that the Allied forces were about to liberate the rest of the Netherlands, most SD agents and Nazi collaborators fled from Amsterdam. After the rumors proved false and the panic subsided, Schaap stayed on in Groningen and, together with many of his cronies, established a reign of terror there. They hunted down resistance workers and engaged in multiple summary executions and horrific acts of torture. When liberation finally came in early May, Schaap tried to flee, taking the name "De Jong" to hide his identity.

In his postwar interrogation, Pieter Schaap confirmed that De Jong worked for him as a V-Man and was successful in Westerbork, delivering several addresses where Jews were hiding. According to Schaap, one of the addresses he delivered was that of the "greengrocer on the Leliegracht" where two Jews were hiding. That was Van Hoeve's address. However, that would not have been possible since the raid on the greengrocery was carried out on May 25 and De Jong did not enter Westerbork until July 1. Perhaps Schaap was mixing up the raid on Leliegracht and the raid on Prinsengracht 263.

Schaap was executed by firing squad on June 29, 1949, in the town of Groningen.

Both the excitement and the frustration of a cold case investigation were never clearer than in this instance. When the Cold Case Team began looking for Frieda Pleij, for example, they believed that she was dead. However, when the researchers checked the archives, they learned that she was not registered as deceased. The archives are usually fairly reliable and up to date, so it seemed for a moment that Pleij might still be alive. As she was born in 1911, that would mean she'd have reached the respectable age of 108 years. Eventually they discovered that she had actually lived to be 104 and had died in Düren, Germany, on December 15, 2014.

In early February 2019, Pieter drove 226 miles to the German town of Bad Arolsen, which is renowned for two things: the impressive Arolsen castle at its heart and the International Tracing Service (ITS), now known as the Arolsen Archives. The archives are a center of documentation, information, and research on Nazi persecution and the Holocaust. The collection has more than 30 million documents, from original concentration camp records to accounts of forced labor, transportation lists, records of death, health and social insurance documents, labor passports, and more. It also stores all letters and requests from people who want to know more about the fate of their next of kin and loved ones. Bad Arolsen belongs to UNESCO's Memory of the World Programme.

When Pieter arrived, he was surprised to find that the archives were stored in a nondescript storage facility in an industrial area on the outskirts of town. Upon entering, he was handed a mandatory helmet and protective overshoes, gear more appropriate for a factory than an archive. Clearly, the archives did not have the funds for a more suitable building. Such is the world's care for the Memory of the World, he thought.

The enormity of the collection was overwhelming, but he was able to retrieve digital scans of the Camp Westerbork archive and several relevant transportation lists to and from Westerbork. On that trip he also found out that someone made inquiries into the whereabouts of Ruth Weisz after the war. With the assistance of the archivists, he discovered that a Ruth Weisz-Neuman survived the war and boarded a ship in Shanghai bound for the United States. She was registered as living in an area near Chicago. That was, of course, thrilling, since it might mean that the Cold Case Team had found a living witness. Unfortunately, Pieter discovered that it was a different Ruth Weisz. In the end, he learned that the Ruth Weisz they were looking for had been sent to

Auschwitz and died in February 1945, possibly in Flossenbürg concentration camp.

The greengrocer, Hendrik van Hoeve, survived a number of camps and was eventually liberated. Thinking he might have information about his father's wartime experience, Monique decided to search for Van Hoeve's son, Stef, to ask about his father. She was able to locate Stef in Amsterdam and interviewed him at his home. He said his father had never spoken about the betrayal of the Annex and had been traumatized by the war, which he was continually forced to confront. After the war he was called on to answer questions about camp prisoners who were still missing.[27] He was also a witness at the trial of Johannes Gerard Koning, one of the Amsterdam policemen who'd arrested him and the Weiszes.[28] In the 1950s, he played himself in the film adaptation of *The Diary of Anne Frank.*[29] Stef said his father had been haunted by his camp experiences his entire life, telling one newspaper reporter in 1972, "While inside the camps I thought of nothing but the fact that I wanted to see the liberation. Then after the liberation I thought: now I want to become seventy; out of anger alone I must! I am seventy-seven, and I still think: they won't catch me!"[30]

34
The Jewish Council

Shortly after the German occupation in May 1940, the Jewish community felt it needed a representative body in order to somehow arm itself against any anti-Jewish measures that they rightly feared. It established the Jewish Coordination Commission (Joodse Coördinatie Commissie; JCC), which was meant to function as an overarching organization that would represent the community as a whole. The commission advised, organized cultural activities, and sometimes provided financial assistance. However, it refused to engage directly or negotiate in any way with the German occupier. Doing so, they believed, was not up to them but solely up to the rightful Dutch government of which they were citizens.

The Nazis wanted to isolate the Jews from the rest

of society, but in order to do that, they needed direct access to the Jewish community. They mandated the establishment of an alternative body, the Jewish Council (Joodse Raad). The council, led by the joint chairs, David Cohen, a well-known academic, and Abraham Asscher, the director of a diamond factory, included such leading citizens as the chief rabbi of Amsterdam, Lodewijk Sarlouis, and the prominent notary Arnold van den Bergh. As decrees forbidding Jews from participation in Dutch society accumulated, the council took over more and more aspects of Jewish life, providing employment, accommodations, food, and special support for the elderly and the infirm.[1] At its height, the council had 17,500 members.

Beginning in July 1942, the council was ordered to help organize the selection of Jewish deportees from the Netherlands to Camp Westerbork and on to the internment camps in the east. Then, on July 30, the Germans authorized the general secretary of the Jewish Council, M. H. Bolle, to give safe-conduct passes, or *Sperres*, to the council's own staff and other "indispensable" people. A stamp on their ID card read "Exempt from labor service until further notice."[2]

That turned out to be a cunningly conceived strategy to divide people and create chaos so that the Jews would focus their attention on the desperate hustle for exemptions. An eyewitness related that on the day the first *Sperres* were issued, people broke down the doors of the Jewish Council office and attacked staff.[3] In fact, the *Sperres* were a delusion; they only delayed the inevitable. In the end, the Germans simply deleted the words "until further notice" and deported people anyway. "Further notice" had arrived.

***Sperres* were** personal. Each *Sperre* had an individual number and fell into a specific range, from 10,000 to 120,000, that corresponded to the type of exemption that was granted. (The goal was to get as close to 120,000 as possible.) The bureaucratic complexity was astonishing. The Nazis considered various permutations, giving different levels of *Sperres* to "foreign" Jews; to Christian Jews—those born Jewish but baptized before January 1, 1941 (only 1,575 Catholic and Protestant Jews were protected that way); and to Jews in mixed marriages, who were invited to choose between deportation and sterilization. (That didn't work; many doctors provided a phony certificate of the operation or refused to do it; an estimated eight thousand to nine thousand Jews in mixed marriages survived the war.)[4] There were also "exchange Jews," who'd been able to buy citizenship in a South American country and were considered candidates for exchange with German prisoners of war. The parents of Anne Frank's schoolmate and close friend Hanneli Goslar, who was also interned in Bergen-Belsen, were able to buy Paraguayan passports through an uncle in neutral Switzerland. Though Hanneli and her younger sister were never exchanged, they were allowed to keep their own clothing in the bitter north German winter and received the occasional Red Cross package of food. Probably because of those "privileges," Hanneli and her sister survived.[5]

Also up for exchange were so-called Palestine Jews, who had relatives in the British Protectorate of Palestine. At the end of 1943, 1,297 Jews held Palestine certificates and were marked for exchange. In January 1944, they were sent to Bergen-Belsen.[6] About 221 people made it to Palestine via Turkey that July. Most of the rest did not survive the camp.

The categories went on and on and were based on a diabolical and ultimately meaningless series of distinctions. Most *Sperres*, including those held by members of the Jewish Council, did provide some protection but only for a limited period of time.

Still, far and away the most desirable and useful exemption was known as Calmeyer status; the *J* was permanently removed from the identity cards of those who were approved for Calmeyer status, and they were no longer considered Jewish, which meant that they could avoid deportation indefinitely.

The Germans defined a Jew as anyone who had one Jewish grandparent by race or belonged to a Jewish religious community (see the table on page 233). Doubtful cases in which the definition was challenged were referred to the Reich Commission in The Hague, which passed them on to the General Committee for Administration and Justice (*sic*), and ultimately to the Nazi-controlled Internal Administration Department, whose chief adjudicator was a German named Dr. Hans Georg Calmeyer.

The Calmeyer list included people who claimed not to be Jewish or to be only partially Jewish. They based their requests for a revision of their status on anthropological and ancestral documents or on evidence that they had never held membership in a Jewish religious community. The process necessitated the assistance of a lawyer, the creation of a genealogical record, a notary statement, and, where necessary, the forging of documents, since most applications were from people who were, in fact, Jewish by birth. All of that required substantial money. During the research phase of the investigation of heritage, applicants were exempt from deportation.

Calmeyer's office was a department of the German authority, but it seems that he and his staff were not overly scrupulous in determining the provenance or validity of documents and accepted dubious birth and baptismal certificates, divorce papers, and letters claiming that children had been born out of wedlock and therefore were not Jewish. Calmeyer was regarded as "totally incorruptible," "neither a Nazi, nor an avowed anti-Nazi," yet he often went to extreme lengths in order to make a case for an applicant, and some members of his office staff were secretly sympathetic to the Jews.[7] It is estimated that Calmeyer saved at least 2,899 people, or three-quarters of the cases sent to him.

That was the bureaucracy of the absurd. The Nazi sense of order imposed a level of complexity and pseudolegality on something very simple: how and when to send hundreds of thousands of people to their deaths.

After the war, many people accused the Jewish Council of cooperation, indeed almost collaboration, with the Germans, insisting that it protected the elite at the expense of poor and working-class Jews. The council picked the people to be deported, and it picked the people to be exempted from deportation. However, the council's supporters claimed that at least they gave Jews a modicum of control over their lives and a way to negotiate with the Germans.

But the truth was that there had always been a deep division in the Jewish community over tactics. At the beginning of the occupation, the JCC and the Jewish Council coexisted for several months, but there was strong friction between the two organizations. The JCC accused the Jewish Council of being an instrument of the Germans, while the Jewish Council believed that the JCC had no power whatsoever, indeed had abdicated power, because it did not wish to negotiate with the Germans. The Jewish Council members insisted that if they entered into a dialogue with the occupiers, they might gain some influence and could possibly prevent, mitigate, or delay some of the Germans' oppressive measures and somehow retain something of their dignity. They feared that if they ignored or even revolted against the rules the Germans were introducing, their fate would be much harsher. In October 1941, the German authorities disbanded the JCC.

In retrospect, much of the surviving Jewish community in the Netherlands concluded that the Jewish Council had been a weapon in the hands of the Nazis. It had had hardly any influence and delayed nothing. But of course, such a judgment is easy in retrospect.

There was no blueprint in the Netherlands for survival under an occupying enemy regime. In the end, Cochairman David Cohen admitted that he "had misjudged the unprecedented, murderous intentions of the Nazis."[8]

35
A Second Look

The Cold Case Team regularly worked on several scenarios at one time, so while Monique was running names through the AI to establish connections to Westerbork, Pieter and several young historians were in the archives searching the files of persons related to their own scenarios. Vince was back in the office, going through the forty-page summary Detective Van Helden made of his 1963–64 investigation when something jumped out at him. Van Helden mentioned that Otto Frank had told him he'd received a note shortly after the liberation denouncing a betrayer. It was unsigned. Apparently, Otto told him he'd made a copy of the note and given the original to a board member of the Anne Frank House. In his summary, Van Helden had written out the text of the anonymous note as follows:

> *Your hideout in Amsterdam was reported at the time to the Jüdische Auswanderung [Jewish Emigration] in Amsterdam, Euterpestraat by A. van den Bergh, a resident at the time at Vondelpark, O Nassaulaan. At the J.A. was a whole list of addresses he submitted.*[1]

Vince had known about the note from prior readings of the file, but the Cold Case Team had not yet made it a priority in the investigation.[2] The A. van den Bergh mentioned in the note was a member of the Jewish Council, which was abolished in September 1943, virtually all of its members shipped off to various concentration camps. Even if Van den Bergh had information about the Annex, he would not have been likely to wait a year to pass it on, and, further, if he'd somehow passed it on before he had been deported, it's not likely that the SD would have waited eleven months before acting on the tip. Then a search of the Bad Arolsen (ITS) terminal at the United States Holocaust Memorial Museum revealed that neither Van den Bergh nor any of his immediate family were listed in any of the concentration camps' archives. They were never deported or interned in a camp. If Van den Bergh was still living at his old address in Amsterdam, might he have had the opportunity to pass on the list of addresses referred to in the note?

Vince decided that the team needed to pursue both the information in the anonymous note and the provenance of the note itself. Was the text Van Helden wrote out in his report the complete note? Where was the original note or at least the copy Otto said he had made? It certainly wasn't in the full police file. As for Van den Bergh, Vince fed his name into the AI program, which connected him to a woman who'd been employed as a secretary for the Jewish Council: Mirjam Bolle. She was 101 years old and living in Israel.

Bolle had written a book titled *Letters Never Sent*, published in English by Yad Vashem in 2014; part of it described her time with the Jewish Council. After he learned of her background, Vince said he thought that if he could interview her, she might offer a unique perspective on how the council functioned. He also wanted to find out more about Van den Bergh, whom, presumably, she'd known personally. Was Van den Bergh very active on the Jewish Council? Did she know what happened to him, which concentration camp he was sent to, whether he survived the war?

Starting in 1938, Bolle, at the time Mirjam Levie, was employed by the Committee for Jewish Refugees.

After the Nazi occupation, the committee was incorporated into the Jewish Council and she became a member of the new staff, based partly on her ability to read and write German. Like many of the employees of the council, she ended up in Camp Westerbork and eventually in Bergen-Belsen. She was luckier than Anne and Margot. In June 1944, she was one of the 550 prisoners selected for the onetime prisoner swap of Palestine Jews and was thus gone before the Frank sisters arrived in the camp.

During the war Mirjam wrote letters to her fiancé, Leo Bolle, who'd emigrated to Palestine in 1938. She never sent them, but she was able to hide the letters she'd written in a warehouse in Amsterdam; they were found in 1947 and returned to her. In the letters Mirjam recalled the terrible days and nights within the Jewish Council when the deportation lists were drawn up; the panic, despair, and arguments among members of the council's staff; and the human suffering that underscored the impossibility of their task. She wrote about the utter chaos in the Expositur, the office responsible for issuing the *Sperres*, and the intimidating visits of the SD leader Aus der Fünten. She stated that the oversight of the *Sperres* was a very dark chapter: "The Germans threw us a bone and watched with great pleasure how the Jews fought over it among one another."

> *I ended up in the house alone, I cried tremendously, because I knew it was going wrong for us and because I was appalled that the JC [Jewish Council] was used for this butcher's job once again, instead of saying: it is enough . . . I was . . . crying from anger and rage, but I couldn't do anything about it.*[3]

Through a contact in Israel the Cold Case Team was able to obtain a telephone number for Mirjam, and Thijs and Vince called her. She apologized for not speaking English very well, even though her command of the language was more than adequate. Her voice was soft yet surprisingly strong for someone her age.

Mirjam told them that her role as a secretary had been quite limited in that she took dictation, sent letters, and sat in on discussions when the first mention of Nazi concentration camps was made. Thijs and Vince asked Mirjam if she recalled the Jewish Council member Arnold van den Bergh. When she answered in the affirmative, the men looked at each other in anticipation. At first she couldn't remember what he had done on the council because she had not worked for him directly. Only when Vince mentioned that Van den Bergh was a notary did she seem to recall that fact. She did not remember him as being very vocal in the meetings, unlike the cochairmen, Asscher and Cohen.

She called Van den Bergh "reserved" and "unassuming." She asked if they could wait a moment while she retrieved copies of minutes that she still kept from the Jewish Council meetings. They could hear her shuffling papers. Then she came back to the phone and said she could confirm that he'd attended some of the meetings.

Mirjam did not know if Van den Bergh had ever been a prisoner at Camp Westerbork. She did not recall having seen him there before she was put on the train to Bergen-Belsen. Similarly, she did not know if he had ever been in a German concentration camp. Unfortunately, she could not add more to the story since she had not returned to Amsterdam after the war.

If Thijs and Vince wanted to know more about Van den Bergh, they would have to look elsewhere.

36
The Dutch Notary

Arnold van den Bergh was born in 1886 in the Dutch town of Oss, located a little over sixty miles southeast of Amsterdam. He married Auguste Kan, and together they had three daughters, twins Emma and Esther, and a third, Anne-Marie, who happened to be the same age as Anne Frank. Van den Bergh was a notary by profession, one of only seven Jewish notaries operating in Amsterdam prior to the war. He owned one of the largest and most successful notary businesses in the city; his name regularly appeared in newspaper notices involving the sale and transfer of properties. He was wealthy and respected in the Amsterdam Jewish community and was a member of the Committee for Jewish Refugees, a charitable organization headed by David Cohen.

A notary in the Netherlands is quite different from the same functionary in North America or, indeed, in some other European countries. A Dutch notary is an impartial official who is under a strict oath of secrecy, is authorized to draw up authentic documents, called notarial acts, between parties, and ensures that these documents are securely handled and stored. So strict is the oath of secrecy that even a judge is unable to force a notary to reveal the details of his transactions. Notaries are required to be present at and validate transactions related to families (marriage, divorces, wills, and so on), the incorporation of businesses, and transactions of property (mortgages, sales of homes, and so on). A notary is required to ensure that all parties are willing and able to make a sale or transaction legitimate. Being a notary is an esteemed position, and Van den Bergh was at the top of his profession.

As the writer of the anonymous note was clearly aware, since the note included the address, Van den Bergh resided in an elegant villa on Oranje Nassaulaan, a street adjacent to the famous 120-acre Vondelpark with its rose garden and Blue Tea House. He seemed to be a quiet but confident man. His wife loved to entertain guests at their home, and he had a passion for fine seventeenth- and eighteenth-century paintings, a luxury that his income afforded him. Not surprisingly, the team discovered that Van den Bergh had been registered as the notary for Goudstikker N.V., a famous Amsterdam art house that dealt in priceless paintings and artworks.

At the beginning of the occupation and prior to the Nazis' strangling restrictions against the Jewish population, it was business as usual for Van den Bergh, much as Otto Frank's business was for him. The Cold Case Team located records that showed Van den Bergh still officiating at various transactions in 1940. Several art sales drew the team's particular scrutiny, not so much for what had been sold as for the prominent Nazis, such as Hermann Göring, who bought the works.

Van den Bergh's invitation to become a founding member of the Jewish Council came in early February 1941, probably from David Cohen. Van den Bergh was appointed to the council's Commission of Five, a committee concerned with the council's internal organization. In addition to serving as the council's notary, he attended weekly meetings of its Emigration Department, the group with the unenviable task of compiling the names of Jews who would be placed on the deportation lists. At the NIOD Institute for War, Holocaust and Genocide Studies, the Cold Case Team was able to review the preserved minutes of the Jewish Council, which showed that Amsterdam SD leaders Willy Lages and Ferdinand Aus der Fünten had constant interactions with the council, sometimes even attending its meetings.[1]

Ten months into the occupation, on February 21, 1941, the Nazis decreed that all Jewish notaries must surrender their public functions to non-Jewish notaries. But it was not unusual for months to go by before a replacement was named.[2] In Van den Bergh's case, it wasn't until January 1943, almost two years later, that he was informed that he would be replaced by an Aryan notary.

Van den Bergh had begun to understand the terrible threat the Nazis posed to his own and his family's safety. When the Cold Case Team checked the NIOD files, they discovered that his name and the names of his wife and three daughters appeared on the list of persons who held the exclusive 120,000 *Sperre* (approximately 1,500 people held it); it was supposed to offer the most protection. The elite of the Jewish Council and all other Jews whom the Germans found it expedient to protect held this protection, which shielded them from deportation "until further notice." According to the NIOD files, Van den Bergh applied for (in effect bought) the *Sperres* for himself and his family in July 1943. With the coveted *Stempel* (stamp) on his ID, he was able to live openly in Amsterdam. In effect, he was "hiding in plain sight." Interrogated after the war, a man named Hans Tietje claimed to have assisted Van den Bergh to obtain the *Sperres*.[3]

Hans Tietje was a German businessman who'd moved to the Netherlands to direct a firm producing tin. He'd climbed from civil servant to millionaire, art collector, and Wehrmacht supplier and was married to a Jewish woman. His friends were some of the most powerful people in the Netherlands, including Willy Lages, Ferdinand aus der Fünten, and the businessman and art dealer Alois Miedl. During the postwar investigation by the BNV into his collaboration, Tietje claimed that he had maintained high-level contacts with German officials only to help Jews. He said that more than a hundred Jews were not deported because of his close relationship with Lages and insisted that he was never paid for the work he did.

Vince and the Cold Case Team saw things differently. Tietje was by no means a "Schindler's list" character, although he tried to portray himself as such. He did save some Jews, but most were the children of influential industrialists who would be able to provide him with protection after the Germans lost the war, which he was convinced would happen. On the other hand, when twelve workers from one of his factories were imprisoned, he did not use his influence to free them. And he was unable (or unwilling) to save his own brother-in-law and his family, who were deported and perished in the east.[4] Tietje was essentially a war profiteer who played both sides of the fence. He dealt in stolen art coerced from Jews and sold them 120,000 *Sperres.* Sometimes they were a con and people were deported anyway. But that was the kind of man with whom Van den Bergh, by necessity, found himself working.

On August 31, 1943, a notary named J.W.A. Schepers was officially appointed to take over Van den Bergh's notary account.[5] Pieter found a CABR file in the National Archives under Schepers's name, meaning that after the war he was investigated as a collaborator. The file revealed some fascinating information. Soon after Schepers took control of Van den Bergh's business, he discovered that it was impossible to run the office because of what he called a "Jew trick": before he had left his business, Van den Bergh had cunningly assigned all notarial files to one of his employees, who had then "conveniently" taken ill. Another employee, who had been assigned the office's administrative duties, did not possess the legal authority to access the files or transfer them to Schepers. Without access to the files, Schepers was unable to conduct business, though he was still saddled with office expenses. Of course, the pro-Nazi Schepers turned his fury against Van den Bergh.

In his book *Cold Mist: The Dutch Notaries and the Heritage of the War*, Raymund Schütz described how Schepers set out to destroy Van den Bergh. He turned to the Lippmann-Rosenthal bank (LIRO), which had been established by the German occupiers to register and loot Jewish property. In a letter dated October 15, 1943, he complained that Van den Bergh was still living in his stately home at Oranje Nassaulaan 60 and did not wear the required yellow star.

A researcher for the Cold Case Team, Anna Foulidis, rooting through the Calmeyer archive, discovered how Van den Bergh managed that. The previous month, on September 2, he had received Calmeyer status, which meant that he was no longer considered to be Jewish or required to wear the yellow star. He had obviously mistrusted the security of the 120,000 *Sperres* and had traded up. Now that he was no longer a Jew, he was no longer a member of the Jewish Council, and he wouldn't be deported with other council members. In fact, he escaped deportation by a matter of weeks.

It had been a long process. The records showed that Van den Bergh applied for Calmeyer status one and a half years earlier, in the spring of 1942. He was challenging his identity as a Jew. If he could prove he had just one Jewish parent, by the Nazi system of classification he could be declared as "partly belonging to the German race."

For the Nazis an essential question was: Who was a Jew and who was not? According to Nazi race laws, one's Jewishness was determined by a complex table like the one on page 355, which was given to local policemen to use when questioning someone who was thought to be Jewish.[6]

The Calmeyer office declared that Van den Bergh had had only one Jewish grandparent and was therefore Mischling second degree (zweiten Grades).[7] This meant that he belonged to the German race and was approved to have German citizenship. His daughters were also Mischling second degree, and because he was now considered a non-Jew, his Jewish wife, Auguste, was protected by their mixed marriage. The ruling allowed him to have the *J* removed from his registration card. It also meant that, now being a non-Jew, he had to resign from the Jewish Council in early September, which, as it turned out, was fortunate timing for him.

Van den Bergh's receiving Calmeyer status was quite unbelievable, considering that it took place in the middle of a war. The process took almost eighteen months, although while his application was being considered, he was exempt from deportation. First, a letter was sent to the offices of Drs. J. & E. Henggeler, Zurich, Swit-

CLASSIFICATION	TRANSLATION	HERITAGE	DEFINITION
Deutschblütiger	German-blooded	German	Belongs to the German race and nation; approved to have Reich citizenship
Deutschblütiger	German-blooded	⅛ Jewish	Considered as belonging to the German race and nation; approved to have Reich citizenship
Mischling zweiten Grades	Mixed race (second degree)	¼ Jewish	Only partly belongs to the German race and nation; approved to have Reich citizenship
Mischling ersten Grades	Mixed race (first degree)	⅜ or ½ Jewish	Only partly belongs to the German race and nation; approved to have Reich citizenship
Jude	Jew	¾ Jewish	Belongs to the Jewish race and community; not approved to have Reich citizenship
Jude	Jew	Jewish	Belongs to the Jewish race and community; not approved to have Reich citizenship

zerland, who forwarded a search request to a society of genealogists in London on March 7, 1942.[8] The society was required to locate church records in an effort to prove that one or more of Van den Bergh's parents or grandparents were not Jewish. The agency received the request on August 6, 1942, but did not reply until January 12, 1943. It apologized for the delay, explaining that the records that needed to be located were stored in bomb shelters.[9] It is uncertain if any of the searches and results were authentic or all were clever forgeries.

When Schepers discovered that Van den Bergh had secured Calmeyer status, he was apoplectic. Insisting that Van den Bergh had always ostentatiously advertised himself as a Jewish notary before the war, he took his complaint directly to the SS and to the Calmeyer office in The Hague, demanding that they conduct an investigation.[10] Unfortunately for Van den Bergh, Schepers was successful. The Cold Case Team concluded from Schepers's CABR file that he could leverage more pressure with high-ranking Nazi factions in The Hague than Van den Bergh could.

The Cold Case Team located a letter, dated January 4, 1944, addressed to Van den Bergh in which two attorneys who worked in the Calmeyer office warned him that he was at risk of being arrested.[11] Van den Bergh immediately vacated his villa and formally registered at a small house at Nieuwendammerdijk 61 in Amsterdam-Noord owned by Albertus Salle, who had been a clerk in his old notary office.[12] Pieter was able to locate and interview Salle's daughter, Regina Salle, who had no memory of people other than her family having lived in the house during that time period, indicating that the address was probably a cover.[13]

Pieter spent some time at the Amsterdam City Archives and learned from archivist Peter Kroesen that Van den Bergh would have had to physically present himself at the Amsterdam city registry in order to change his address. Evidently, he was not yet afraid to be seen walking about on city streets.[14] But he understood that Schepers's constant harassment of the authorities regarding his "non-Jewish" status was becoming increasingly dangerous for him and his family.

Forced to take notice of Schepers's complaints, on January 22, 1944, the Calmeyer office issued a formal decision that Van den Bergh had possibly used false evidence to claim his "Aryan" status and that his bank accounts should be blocked.[15] The surreal absurdity of those bureaucratic musical chairs, when a man's life and the lives of his family were at stake, is a brutal example of the Nazi method of murder by small bureaucratic cuts.

Curiously, the Cold Case Team found Van den

Bergh's name referred to in the collaboration file of the notorious Jew hunter and IV B4 squad member Eduard Moesbergen,[16] who was with the Henneicke Column until it was dissolved. (He then worked for Sergeant Abraham Kaper at the Bureau of Jewish Affairs. Kaper described Moesbergen as one of his most prolific Jew hunters.) Moesbergen's CABR file contained two witness statements, from a V-Man and a V-Woman working for him, who claimed that Moesbergen would often carry lists of addresses where Jews were thought to be hiding. In the summer of 1944, he was apparently methodically raiding the addresses on the list one after the other.[17]

In his postwar interrogation, Moesbergen claimed to have learned that Arnold van den Bergh had lost his Calmeyer status, and had gone to his residence at Oranje Nassaulaan 60 shortly afterward only to discover that he was no longer there. When Moesbergen returned a few days later, it was clear that Van den Bergh had fled. Looking to lessen his sentence for his own recent collaboration conviction, Moesbergen claimed that he had wanted to warn Van den Bergh to go into hiding, something that the CABR file reports did not suggest.[18]

The Cold Case Team wondered whether Moesbergen actually intended to warn Van den Bergh or meant to arrest him for the *Kopgeld* bounty. After the war,

Moesbergen would not have admitted that his purpose in going to Van den Bergh's residence was to arrest him. There is no record of Van den Bergh's ever having been consulted about the truth of Moesbergen's testimony.

But then the unexpected happened. By serendipity, Thijs came across a man who insisted, with convincing documentation, that his grandparents successfully hid Van den Bergh's daughter Anne-Marie during the war. According to that man's grandparents, Arnold van den Bergh placed his daughter in hiding with the help of the resistance. One way or another, it seems, either through his relationship with powerful Nazis, who helped him get Calmeyer status, or through the resistance, which helped hide his children, Van den Bergh endeavored to save his family's lives.

Van den Bergh's case was exceptional. On the one hand, he was able to ask the resistance to hide his children; on the other, he had enough powerful contacts in the Nazi hierarchy to secure Calmeyer status and then to be warned in time when that status was withdrawn. This, to the team, was suspicious.

37
Experts at Work

Vince clearly remembers the moment that shifted everything in the ongoing cold case investigation. He was rereading the anonymous note for the hundredth time. It said, "Your hideout in Amsterdam was reported at the time to the Jüdische Auswanderung in Amsterdam, Euterpestraat, by A. van den Bergh."

He suddenly realized that it didn't say that Otto Frank's *name* was passed on; it mentioned only the address. Whoever wrote the note might not even have known who was hiding at Prinsengracht 263. Furthermore, the note said, "At J.A. was a whole list of addresses he submitted."

Suddenly Vince began to see things differently. If A. van den Bergh indeed passed on a list of addresses, not names, somehow it made the crime of betrayal, if it *was* betrayal, seem less personal. At the very least, he did not have to feel he was betraying someone he might have known.

In the forty-page report of his investigation, Detective Van Helden had transcribed the anonymous note, but Vince wanted to know if it was the exact wording or a summary. Was there more to the note? Who was the board member of the Anne Frank House to whom Otto said he'd given the original note? Where was the copy he'd made? Just as Abraham Kaper had kept important files at home, Vince was now betting that Van Helden would have done the same. The Cold Case Team set out to locate Van Helden's relatives and, with a bit of searching, was able to find his son, Maarten.

When Vince first emailed him, Maarten van Helden did not seem much interested in talking about his father. He claimed that he did not know very much about his work and would be of little help in the investigation. But when Vince asked him if he happened to have any papers that his father had left behind, Maarten said he did. About eight years after his father's death, he said, he'd come across a number of files relating to the 1963–64 investigation.

Maarten van Helden emailed the Cold Case Team scanned copies of some of the documents he'd located. As he was going through the records, Vince came across a small typewritten note that also contained ink handwriting. The contents and size matched Van Helden's description of the anonymous note. That couldn't be the original, Vince thought, not with handwritten comments on it. Could it be the copy that Otto himself had made?

Immediately after the Christmas holidays, Vince set up a meeting with Maarten van Helden. As he walked into Van Helden's living room, his eyes were drawn to a large stack of papers sitting on the coffee table. He felt a kind of shock. Vince turned to the elderly man, who was extending his hand in greeting. His wife of forty-five years stepped forward and introduced herself as Els. Maarten began talking about his father.

Arend van Helden was eighteen when he joined the army and rose to the rank of sergeant in the military police. After the German invasion in 1940, he was captured and imprisoned in The Hague. After he was released, the Germans allowed him to continue as a policeman, an oversight on their part since he was soon working for the resistance.

Arend used his position to help people in hiding by providing them with food. Because meat was scarce during the war, a policeman needed to be present when pigs or cows were slaughtered to ensure that there was no theft. Since there were always scraps of meat left behind, Arend would gather them and deliver them to homes where he knew people were hiding.

Maarten became the archivist of the war stories his father told him. One story involved his father's capture of a man he had been ordered to transport to Camp Amersfoort. The prisoner pleaded to be released for one hour so that he could warn others of a pending roundup. He gave his word that he would then turn himself in. Maarten's father complied with his request, and the man kept his word and returned for transport. Another story was about a confrontation between his father and a Nazi officer. In September 1944, Arend was involved in the investigation of the black-market activities of a particular SS officer in the town of Elst. He picked up the officer for questioning. As they were driving, the officer ordered Arend to hand over his pistol. He complied, and the SS officer made him pull off the road. He was preparing to shoot Arend but heard the sound of approaching footsteps. When he lowered the gun, Arend took off like a deer, running through ditches and meadows to escape.

After the war Arend van Helden remained a policeman and was eventually promoted to the rank of inspector in the Amsterdam police force. Maarten was twenty years old in 1963 when his father was assigned to the investigation of the Annex raid. When the elder

Van Helden was frustrated or blocked at work, he occasionally brought up the case at home. Maarten recalled that his father had traveled to Vienna to meet Simon Wiesenthal and during that same trip had gone on to Basel to interview Otto Frank.

When the two men turned their attention to the stack of papers on the table, Vince recalled that he tried to hide his excitement. Here were dozens of originals and carbon copies of almost every page from the 1963–64 investigation, including the original Criminal Investigation Department file folder cover. He said his hands began to shake.

At the bottom of the stack of papers, he found what he was looking for: an approximately five-and-a-half-by-nine-inch page of bonded stationery, slightly yellow in color, with a typewritten message below which were handwritten sentences in ink. The note appeared to be original and not photocopied or reproduced. The ink handwriting also appeared to be original. No wonder the copy of the anonymous note was not to be found among Van Helden's papers filed with the State Department of Criminal Investigation—because it had been here all these years in his private collection!

At the top of the note was typed the German word *Abschrift* (copy). That would support the theory that it was the copy Otto had made. Otto's native language was German, and it would have been natural for him to use the German word for "copy." The remainder of the typewritten text was in Dutch. There was handwriting on the note, and Maarten identified it as his father's. He agreed to lend the Cold Case Team the *Abschrift* note, as Vince came to call it, for forensic testing. Vince wanted to confirm that the note was typed by Otto Frank and that the handwriting was indeed Van Helden's.

Vince decided to contact one of his former colleagues from the FBI laboratory, and together they worked through all available tests that might help extract the maximum information. Unfortunately, many of them would have destructive side effects, and Vince hesitated to conduct any test that could alter the note. Testing for fingerprints was a possibility, but because the dusting or cyanoacrylate (superglue) process can cause extreme discoloration, it was ruled out. He then turned to forensic expert Detective Carina van Leeuwen. Together they concluded that the examination of the note would require a two-pronged approach: a scientific examination and a linguistic analysis.

Not trusting the mail with such a potentially historic document, Maarten drove to Amsterdam with his sister and personally handed the note to Vince and

Brendan. They were asked if they recognized the cursive handwriting on the note to be that of their father. Both agreed that it was.

For a scientific opinion, Vince contacted a Dutch handwriting expert, Wil Fagel, now retired from the Netherlands Forensic Institute. He asked them to obtain exemplars, copies of the detective's handwriting, from Maarten, who still had several of his father's handwritten letters. Fagel compared that handwriting to the *Abschrift* note and concluded that the handwriting on both was the same.[1] (By coincidence, Fagel's department at the Netherlands Forensic Institute examined Anne Frank's diary for authentication of her handwriting in the mid-1980s. The results of the examination were published in the NIOD critical edition of the diary and refuted all claims that the diary was not written by Anne Frank.)[2]

It was essential to determine when the *Abschrift* note was written. Radiocarbon dating would probably determine how old the paper was, though not the writing on it, but it would require cutting off a piece of the note. Vince noticed that there were two punch holes on the left side of the note, one of which actually cut through a portion of the handwriting. He phoned Maarten van Helden, who explained that he'd punched holes in all the documents to store them in a binder.

Vince wondered if the hole-punch device he'd used had a compartment to catch the punched-out rounds. Had Maarten ever emptied the compartment? No? Soon the office mail room delivered a bulging envelope. When it was opened, about a thousand punched-out rounds spilled out.

Vince and Brendan examined all of them on a retina screen. After several hours they were able to select fifteen possible matches on the basis of color but could not find any punched-out rounds with the ink handwriting, nor could they say definitively that any of them exactly fit the holes in the note.

Meanwhile, Vince and Brendan hoped that an examination of the note's typeface might confirm its author and date. They contacted the international typeface expert Bernhard Haas, the son of the author of the Haas Atlas, the definitive guide to identifying typefaces. In typewriter terminology, document typeface describes the image left on paper after the striker bar has hit the ink ribbon. (In the age of computers and inkjet printers, typeface examination is a lost art, and the team was lucky to find Haas.) They briefed Haas on the investigation and informed him that they suspected the *Abschrift* note might have been produced by Otto Frank. Haas said that he would need either the typewriter Otto used or several original documents that

Otto was known to have typed on his typewriter. The team did not hold out hope of obtaining Otto's typewriter, since it was likely under the control of the Anne Frank Fonds in Basel, Switzerland, a group that had been unhelpful so far. The obvious solution was to turn to one of Otto's regular correspondents.

As an American teenager in the late 1950s, Cara Wilson-Granat was so inspired by Anne Frank's diary that she wrote to Otto Frank. She even auditioned to play Anne in the 1959 Academy Award–winning movie *The Diary of Anne Frank* by George Stevens, a role that was landed by Millie Perkins. Her correspondence with Otto and their friendship lasted more than two decades. In 2001, she published the letters in *Dear Cara: Letters from Otto Frank.*

Vince had previously spoken with Wilson-Granat about her correspondence and personal conversations with Otto and knew that she had kept his original letters. He phoned her and explained that the Cold Case Team had come into possession of a document that was possibly typed by Otto. Would she send a few of her letters so that they could be compared? She said she would, happily.

When Vince was inquiring about overnight shipping of the letters to the Amsterdam office, the shipper asked the value of the package's contents. When he was told it was priceless, he answered, sorry, that was not one of the options. The CCT then consulted a document expert who suggested an estimated value, and the package was on its way. That night Vince spent the entire evening tracking the shipment, and the next morning he saw that it had arrived at Amsterdam's Schiphol Airport. His heart sank when at 8:15 a.m. he received a text that the shipment would be delayed until the next day, although the online tracking still showed that it would be delivered before 10:30 a.m. that day. He was in a bit of a panic, imagining having to call Cara to tell her that the letters had been lost or damaged. But at 9:00 a.m., the delivery truck showed up at the office, and the driver walked in and asked for a signature. Vince thought: If only he knew what was inside!

Vince and Brendan then set out on the six-hour train ride to Winnenden, a small town in the southwest of Germany where Bernhard Haas lived. They carried the note and several of Cara's original letters. In retirement, Haas had turned the upper floor of his house into his office, decorated with a collection of antique typewriters. The tools of his trade were spread out over a large glass examination desk: a stereo microscope, spacing templates, special lights, and a magnifying glass.

The assessment took several hours. In order to examine the typeface of the *Abschrift* note, Haas carefully slid the note out of its protective evidence sleeve. Moving it under the stereo microscope, he turned on special lighting that would show even the finest of details. He jotted down some observations and mumbled in German as he carefully studied the typeface. He began measuring the letters, the distance between letters, and the spacing between the lines of text with a special template. He then spun around in his chair, grabbed the encyclopedia of typefaces that his father had authored from the shelf, and told Vince and Brendan that the note was an original typed document and not a copy. The typewriter used to write the note had had type defects in the letters *h* (at the head stroke), *n* (at the right foot), *a* (at the lower tick), and *A* (at the right side). He identified the type set as having been manufactured by Ransmayer & Rodrian in Berlin, Germany, somewhere between 1930 and 1951.

Haas explained that the next step was to compare the note to Wilson-Granat's original letters. Brendan and Vince waited nervously while he muttered in German. Finally, he pushed himself back from the desk and announced that he was able to conclude with the highest forensic certainty that the note and the letters were created with the same typewriter.[3] He then added something that the two investigators didn't expect: based on the progression of certain typeface letter degradations in the Wilson-Granat letters, he concluded that the note was produced several years prior to the date of the earliest letter, 1959. (That meant that the typeface on the note was cleaner; type gets progressively dirtier as a typewriter is used.) That would confirm Otto's statement to Detective Van Helden that he'd made a copy of the note prior to providing the original to a board member of the recently formed Anne Frank House in May 1957.

On the train ride back to Amsterdam Vince and Brendan felt a sense of satisfaction. They had proven that the note they were carrying was not just the single piece of hard physical evidence relating to the Annex betrayal; it was a piece of evidence that originated with Otto Frank.

The next task was to investigate the content of Detective Van Helden's handwriting that appeared below the typewritten portion of the note. Between what Van Helden's children thought their father had written and a consensus of the Dutch researchers, this is how it translated:

The original is in the possession of
or
The original is in depot 23 [handwriting unclear, but this latter is the more likely reading]
Notary v.d. Hasselt, 702 Keizersgracht (230047) (234602)
By mail receiving in Basel whether or not via Foundation
Personal details
Likely
Already more years
Given to me on 16/12-63—
Mr. Heldring,

1 has been a member of Jewish council among others society of nursing & care
2.Department Lijnbaansgracht (???? & ????)

These were Detective Van Helden's jottings to himself. The first sentence clearly states that the original note was in the possession of a notary named Van Hasselt at Keizersgracht 702, followed by two six-digit numbers. A search of the 1963 Amsterdam telephone directory confirmed that those were the address and phone numbers of Notary J. V. van Hasselt.

The words following this are not as clear but mention Basel, where Otto was living in 1963. The team interpreted the next full sentence, "Given to me on 16/12-63," to mean that Detective Van Helden received the copy of the note on December 16, 1963, approximately two weeks after he interviewed Otto.

The team believed that "Heldring" referred to Herman Heldring, an original board member of the Anne Frank Stichting. The last portion of the note, "has been a member of Jewish council among others society of nursing & care," appeared to be about Van den Bergh and the organization he joined after the liberation. The "Department Lijnbaansgracht" was the street location where the Jewish Council's Central Information Office was located during the war. The translator has used "????" to indicate that two words, separated by &, followed but they are completely unintelligible.

The Cold Case Team members were now certain that they had the copy that Otto had made of the original note, but they were left with some puzzling questions: Who was this notary, Van Hasselt? Why did he end up with the original note? And why hadn't they heard of him before?

38
A Note Between Friends

Jakob van Hasselt was about to become an important figure in the investigation. It turned out that he knew Arnold van den Bergh quite well. Before the war, they were two of only seven Jewish notaries in Amsterdam, and they conducted many business transactions together.[1] During the war their lives went in different directions: Van Hasselt was asked to be a member of the Jewish Council but declined. Van den Bergh accepted. Van Hasselt and his family went into hiding; he and his wife eventually made it to Belgium, while his two daughters remained behind in the Netherlands.*

---

* Families' separating while in hiding was very common; it was less of a burden on the people providing shelter to care for one or two people rather than an entire family.

After the war, their lives intersected again. Van Hasselt returned to Amsterdam and became deeply involved in Jewish relief work, appointing Van den Bergh to a board position on the Jewish Social Work organization (Joods Maatschappelijk Werk).

Van Hasselt was also very close to Otto Frank. He was the notary who established the Anne Frank Stichting, the foundation originally formed in May 1957 to protect Prinsengracht 263 from demolition. He served as a founding board member along with Otto, Johannes Kleiman, and several others. Van Hasselt also prepared the prenuptial agreement for Otto and his second wife, Fritzi, before their November 1953 marriage.[2] He even supported Otto when people began questioning the authenticity of Anne's diary; in 1954, he notarized a statement that he'd examined the diary and declared it to be authentic.[3]

Otto and Van Hasselt had something else in common: Van Hasselt also lost his two young daughters (ages six and nine) in the Holocaust. The callousness of what happened is shocking. To avoid paying a fine for violating the blackout curtains order, a woman reported an elderly Jewish woman in hiding who happened to be the grandmother of the two Van Hasselt girls. When the grandmother was taken, the arrest team found letters from her granddaughters with the return address of the place they were hiding on the envelope.[4]

The two men's tragic loss bonded them in a way that no one but a person who'd experienced such loss could know. Otto and Van Hasselt must certainly have discussed the contents of the anonymous note, but they seemed unsure as to what to do with it. Otto clearly felt the note was important enough to copy it and give the original to his friend, presumably for safekeeping.[5]

The name Van Hasselt came up in many documents the Cold Case Team found through the Statements Project, including a March 1958 letter from Kleiman to Otto Frank. In the letter, Kleiman referred to the anonymous note, saying:

> *I have read the anonymous letter that was sent to me by notary van Hasselt. The latter knew notary van den Bergh, who lived nearby, but the latter has long since passed. He did not know any better than that the latter was "good" at that time. Dr. de Jong would inform the justice department, but both gentlemen found it better not to ascribe too much value to such anonymous notes. Question 1 arises immediately, why does such a person only now come forward with such*

an accusation? Dr. de Jong will report to me further when he finds out something.[6]

Kleiman's letter verified two things: one, that the original note was given to Notary Van Hasselt (as Detective Van Helden's handwritten notes on the *Abschrift* copy suggested) and two, that Van den Bergh and Van Hasselt knew each other and were colleagues. It also suggested that Kleiman was indeed confused (or misled?) about when the original note was sent, since he wrote, "Why does such a person only now come forward?" He seemed unaware that Otto had received the note shortly after the liberation, some thirteen years earlier. Kleiman was one of Otto's most trusted friends. There is evidence that in the immediate years after the war, Miep, Bep, Kugler, and Kleiman often mulled over who had betrayed them, but on the basis of all the statements the Cold Case Team sifted through, it seems that among them, Van den Bergh's name had never come up.

Kleiman's letter to Otto made it clear that Notary Van Hasselt told him that Van den Bergh was dead, but the notary's comment about Van den Bergh, "He did not know any better than that the man was 'good' at that time," is a remarkably guarded statement.

When Kleiman contacted Dr. Loe de Jong, a Dutch historian who was the director of RIOD (later renamed NIOD), asking him what to do with the note, De Jong first recommended informing the Justice Department, but then he and Van Hasselt decided that the note shouldn't be given too much credence. There is no evidence that the note was ever passed on to the RIOD archives, nor was its existence ever reported to the Justice Department.

Contrary to what he told Detective Van Helden, Otto had indeed done some investigation into Van den Bergh. When he visited the Dutch policeman Gezinus Gringhuis in prison on December 6, 1945, he specifically asked him about Van den Bergh and the anonymous note. Gringhuis supposedly replied, "There was no reason to suspect the man's integrity."[7] It's hardly likely that Otto accepted Gringhuis's word as to Van den Bergh's character. But it is clear that only a few months after receiving the anonymous note on his return from Auschwitz, Otto was taking it seriously.

What is most interesting is that in his visit to the prison, Otto didn't take either Kugler or Kleiman with him but rather (as his agenda indicated) "Ab." Abraham "Ab" Cauvern was a close friend who eventually helped Otto edit Anne's diary and in 1947 invited him, Miep, and Jan Gies to share his large apartment after the death of his wife. Though Cauvern obviously knew about the anonymous note, Kleiman and Kugler remained unaware of its existence. Why Otto kept the anonymous note secret from them and only in 1963 gave the copy he'd made to Detective Van Helden is a mystery at the center of the cold case investigation.

39
The Typist

Now the Cold Case Team turned their attention to the question of who sent the anonymous note. The most obvious suspect was J.W.A. Schepers, the pro-Nazi notary who took over Van den Bergh's office. He loathed Van den Bergh and certainly was engaged in a vendetta against him. Even after the war, it's unlikely that his anger would have cooled. So why not take the next step and slander the man by accusing him of betraying a fellow Jew?

But Schepers would not have had the opportunity to deliver the note, since he'd been sent to prison as a collaborator on June 2, 1945, one day before Otto returned from Auschwitz. Prisoners were permitted to send letters but only handwritten on prison letterhead.

If the original note had been on prison letterhead, Otto would surely have mentioned it to Detective Van Helden or Kleiman would have commented on it in his letter to Otto—assuming, of course, that Schepers even knew who Otto Frank was, which was not necessarily the case. Besides, as the team learned from his letters about Van den Bergh before the war, Schepers had no scruples about signing his name to nasty accusations and sending them to the appropriate authorities.

The author of the note had to have known Van den Bergh, and he or she must also have been privy to some sort of inside information. Perhaps the anonymous writer worked for the SD, since the note mentioned that many other addresses were passed to the SD office on Euterpestraat. Only someone who worked there could have possessed such information.

The Cold Case Team turned to the Dutch forensic linguist Dr. Fleur van der Houwen of the Free University of Amsterdam, who has twenty years of experience in the field. After examining the anonymous author's choice of words and sentence structure, she provided the following assessment:[1]

1. *The text was written at an advanced level of the Dutch language.*

2. *The formal choice of words and sentence structure indicated that the writer was Dutch and not German.*

3. *Most likely an adult.*

4. *Possibly worked in some sort of government office.*

From this analysis and other assimilated knowledge, the team concluded that the author of the note was:

1. *Dutch.*

2. *An employee of, or somehow connected to, the Amsterdam SD at the Zentralstelle office in Euterpestraat.*

3. *Possibly working directly with or for leading officers dealing with highly classified material. One can assume that only trusted Nazi employees, SD men, Dutch detectives who worked for the SD, and V-persons were able to see or be aware of the kinds of lists mentioned in the note.*

4. *Eager to unburden him- or herself of painful information.*

5. *Someone who knew or knew about Arnold van den Bergh, since his private address was mentioned in the note.*

Looking for a Dutch insider at the Zentralstelle who might fit the operational profile, the Cold Case Team came up with the name of Cornelia Wilhelmina Theresia "Thea" Hoogensteijn. The team had earlier come across her name in the telephone directory of the Amsterdam SD, where she was listed as secretary to Willy Lages and Julius Dettmann.

Born in Germany in 1918, Hoogensteijn moved with her Dutch Catholic family back to the Netherlands when she was nine. By age twenty-four, proficient in both German and Dutch, she got a job as typist at the Zentralstelle. At first, she was translating the Nazis' anti-Jewish provisions into Dutch, registering Jews during the *Razzias*, and typing the reports of the interrogations of political prisoners at SD headquarters.[2]

At face value, her employment at SD headquarters gave the appearance that she was a supporter of the Nazi occupation, but the Cold Case Team discovered that she was on good terms with two Amsterdam policemen who were working for the resistance: Arend Japin and Piet Elias. They would later testify that she was helpful to them and instrumental in securing the release of twenty students arrested to be sent to forced labor in 1943. Psychologically, working as a quasi double agent eventually became too much for her. Appalled by the gross abuse of prisoners at the headquarters, she resigned in early 1944.[3] However, the resistance considered her a valuable asset and pressured her to return to work. That June, she was promoted to personal secretary to the dreaded SD chief, Willy Lages. And as the SD telephone directory makes clear, she also became secretary to Dettmann, which means that she very likely could have known about a list made and delivered to the SD by Van den Bergh, as the note suggests.

By the end of 1944, however, the SD began to suspect her of connections to the resistance. Lages typed on her typewriter, "Thea, you are a traitor."[4] In January 1945, she was arrested on suspicion of spying, but without hard proof, she was released after three days. With her cover blown, she immediately went into hiding, with a letter from a member of the resistance vouching for her.

Attempting to cross into the liberated south, Hoogensteijn and her lover, Henk Klijn, were arrested on March 11 and sent to a prison camp near the city of Tilburg. The intelligence officer from the 15th Scottish Division who interrogated her had obviously learned of her past employment with the Amsterdam SD. (It seems that her letter of reference from the resistance carried no weight.) After the liberation on May 5, she was transferred to Fort Ruigenhoek internment camp near Utrecht, where she was held along with more than one thousand other women, mostly wives of NSB members. Devastated, she isolated herself from the rest of the prisoners, refused to eat, and attempted suicide. She was then sent to a mental institution in Utrecht. By the end of August, she was admitted to the Valerius Clinic, a psychiatric hospital in Amsterdam, where she was diagnosed as suffering from hysterical psychosis, and at the end of November, she was given the first of fifteen shock therapy treatments.[5]

She was finally released on May 21, 1946, but the war had destroyed her life. No longer welcome in her family, who saw her as a *moffenhoer* (whore of the Germans), she emigrated to Sweden in 1947 and eventually to Venezuela. It wasn't until 1960, when a full-page article appeared in a Dutch newspaper with the title "At the SD in the Euterpestraat, Thea Saved Many Lives," that she was finally praised as a forgotten resistance heroine.[6]

It is unlikely but not impossible that Hoogensteijn wrote the anonymous note. Had she written it before she was arrested on March 15 and sent it to the Prinsengracht 263 address (she did not have Otto's name), Kleiman or Kugler would have opened the letter. However, they did not know anything about an anonymous note. Writing it later from one of the internment camps, she would probably have had to use special stationery, and Otto would have mentioned it. By the end of August, it would seem, she was in no state to write such a letter. Unfortunately, although Otto told Detective Van Helden that he had received the note shortly after liberation, he did not disclose the exact date. In the end the team concluded that the note, if not written by Thea, was very likely written by someone with inside knowledge of the workings of the SD. But just as they were preparing to investigate further theories of its authorship, they became distracted by something that would turn out to be even more important: reasons to believe in its *contents*.

40
The Granddaughter

For his part, Thijs was pursuing the man whose grandparents had successfully hidden Anne-Marie van den Bergh during the war. When Thijs spoke with him by phone, he was friendly and offered to provide an introduction to Van den Bergh's granddaughter, with whom he'd kept in close contact. (To protect her privacy, we have not identified him and have followed her wishes by referring to her as Esther Kizio, the pseudonym she requested.)

On February 13, 2018, the man sent a letter to Esther to introduce Thijs. He asked whether she would like to participate in the cold case investigation and reminded her that at the end of the war, her grandparents, Arnold and his wife, together with their three children, moved to Minervalaan 72-3. It was a couple of miles from Merwedeplein, where the Frank family lived before going into hiding. On March 6, she answered. Somewhat warily, she agreed to a meeting.

Thijs described for me his drive on March 15 to Esther's town, which is close to the North Sea coast outside Amsterdam. He said he felt very tense, knowing what was at stake. Before he left, he'd reread the 1963 police report and the note naming Arnold van den Bergh as the betrayer. Thijs could feel Esther's reluctance; suddenly a stranger comes along who wants to talk to you about your grandfather, who, she probably knows, was on the Jewish Council, whose members were so vilified after the war.

He parked his car and rang the bell. A woman in her fifties opened the door and welcomed him. She was all warmth. While talking, she led him through a living room to the garden side of the house and the kitchen. She offered him tea. And biscuits. Ginger biscuits.

That turned out to be the first of several interviews. Esther was quite forthcoming. Though she'd never met her grandfather, who had died before she was born, she had plenty of family stories about the past.[1]

Esther recalled that she was nine or ten years old when her mother first spoke to her about the war. Anne-Marie told her that after the Nazi invasion, the family was protected from deportation because of her father's position on the Jewish Council.[2] However, sometime in 1943, things changed; suddenly they were at risk. (That likely occurred when the Jewish Council was abolished in late September of that year.) The family felt terrible anxiety and always had bags packed, ready to flee, to leave everything behind. Anne-Marie told Esther that that was when her grandfather turned to the resistance for help in hiding his three daughters.

The resistance always advised that it was safer for a family to split up than to go into hiding together, and Esther remembered her mother saying that she was asked if she wanted to stay with the family and she had said no. Anne-Marie had a poor relationship with her mother, whom she described as cold and socially ambitious. On the other hand, she loved her father deeply. They shared a bond rooted in their love of art and literature. As Esther put it, for Anne-Marie the death of her father was "the biggest disaster of her life. She didn't really care about the rest."[3]

The resistance placed Anne-Marie's twin sisters on a farm outside the northern town of Scharwoude with a family named De Bruin. Anne-Marie went into hiding in Amsterdam, but the experience was dreadful. The family forced her to work, and she was given very little to eat. At one point she was so hungry that she stole food, which led to a terrible fight. Esther also understood that Anne-Marie was sexually abused, though the words were never spoken.

After Anne-Marie complained to a resistance worker who'd come to check on her, she was moved to a new location in the south of the Netherlands. The resistance worker accompanied her partway on the train journey. While waiting alone on a train station platform for the final leg of her trip, she was noticed by a Dutch man whom she remembered as wearing a German-style hat with a feather on it. With her dark hair and eyes, she must have looked Jewish to him. The man tipped off the police that there was a Jewish girl at the station.

The police picked her up, took her to a jail in Scheveningen, and placed her in a cell with other Jews. During several interrogations, she repeated the story the resistance had trained her to say if she was ever stopped. Years later, she told her daughter that she had retained her composure by staring at the photo of a happy family displayed in the office of the man who was so aggressively interrogating her.

Anne-Marie finally provided the name Alois Miedl to her interrogator, a name her father had told her to use if she was ever in trouble. Miedl was a German business associate of Van den Bergh who was involved in the acquisition of antique paintings. At the end of two weeks, Anne-Marie was the only person left in the cell. All the others had been deported.

She was released without explanation and continued her train journey to the small town of Sprundel, where she was met by a Professor Ruijgrok, who took her to the Bastiaensen family, who'd agreed to hide her. They were Catholic and very welcoming. But children in hiding could not expect stability. Anne-Marie was suddenly moved again after word came that German soldiers were to be lodged with the family. The resistance then placed her with the Sadee family in the city of Breda, where she stayed for about six weeks before rejoining the Bastiaensens after the Germans vacated their house. She stayed with them until the liberation.

Esther said that her mother didn't want to leave the Bastiaensens after the war ended. She'd come to think of their children as her stepsisters and stepbrothers and even wanted to become Catholic. Eventually the Bastiaensens were able to convince her to rejoin her own family in Amsterdam, but she kept in contact with members of the family long after the war.

This is Esther's version of her mother's story, and it closely matches the information the Cold Case Team uncovered in her grandfather's file.[4] In his testimony to the Dutch authorities, Van den Bergh said that his daughter was arrested in Rotterdam on her way to her hiding address. He said that she was imprisoned for nine days and was released because her identity papers did not carry the letter *J*. However, he did not mention that he had told his daughter to use the name Alois Miedl if she got into trouble.[5] Perhaps he understood that in the postwar era, indicating that he'd had a strong relationship with a well-known Nazi would not reflect well on him.

When the Cold Case Team asked Esther if she knew more about Miedl, she recalled that he was an art collector and had a Jewish wife. Esther's grandfather collected seventeenth- and eighteenth-century paintings by famous artists, and he and Miedl would go to art auctions together. She also recalled that Miedl was the person who purchased the Goudstikker art collection around the time of the German invasion. He then sold the collection to Hitler's close henchman Hermann Göring. Esther did remember once seeing a wartime photo on the internet of Göring leaving Miedl's office. However, she seemed unaware that her grandfather was the notary who officiated over Göring's purchase of the collection.

Esther used to visit her grandmother and aunts regularly. She remembered that when she opened the door to her grandmother's house, it felt like walking into the Rijksmuseum. The walls were covered in paintings from the school of Jan Steen and others. After her grandmother died in 1968, Esther had the task of going through their Amsterdam home. She found many documents, but her grandfather's collection of valuable paintings seemed to have disappeared (she is still trying to trace them). She told Thijs that there was a suitcase full of documents that had sat in her grandfather's house for forty years. But as had happened in Abraham Kaper's house, there was an accident and everything was destroyed in a house fire caused by a gas leak.

Esther was eventually invited to the Cold Case Team's office in Amsterdam-Noord, where Vince and Brendan interviewed her.[6] Finally, they showed her the anonymous note that identified her grandfather as the betrayer of the Frank family. She was visibly shocked. "What would motivate someone to send such a note?" she asked.

She told them that after the war there was a great deal of anger directed against the Jewish Council. She said that her grandmother rarely spoke about the war and there were never any accusations about her grandfather within the family. But she also said she'd personally received verbally abusive anonymous phone calls about the Jewish Council well after her grandfather's death.

"Why would someone betray others like this?" she wondered aloud again. Her grandfather must have been forced to cooperate with the Germans, but she could not imagine him betraying Otto Frank. Reading the note carefully, she realized that it referred to lists, not specific people. Yes, she could imagine this. If indeed her grandfather gave up the Prinsengracht 263 address, it was probably just an address on an impersonal list; he didn't know who was living there. If in fact he had done it, she said finally, she knew it could have been for only one reason: because he was forced, because he had to save his family's lives.

41
The Goudstikker Affair

Esther's comments about her grandfather's connection to the Goudstikker affair, the most famous art collection "acquisition" in World War II, coincided with what the Cold Case Team had discovered. Her account also contributed to the growing sense that Van den Bergh might well have been involved in the Franks' betrayal.[1]

Jacques Goudstikker was one of the wealthiest Dutch art dealers of seventeenth- and eighteenth-century Old Masters in Europe in the 1920s and 1930s. As he was a Jew, in the summer of 1940, he was forced to sell his famous collection, which included more than a thousand works of art, as well as real estate, at a greatly reduced price to Alois Miedl,[2] a German-born naturalized Dutchman and art collector who'd moved to the Netherlands to work as a banker. What many people didn't know was that Miedl also worked for the Abwehr, German military intelligence, and was therefore very well connected within the circle of Nazi SD officers in the Netherlands, including Ferdinand aus der Fünten, the head of the Zentralstelle, and Willy Lages, the head of the SD in Amsterdam. In fact, Lages's wife lived at Nijenrode Castle, one of the elegant properties Miedl acquired along with Goudstikker's art assets. Miedl and his wife, who was Jewish, often hosted lavish parties attended by the who's who of the SD, as well as highly placed German officials in the civil administration. Miedl had deep connections in Germany as well. He was a close friend of Heinrich Hoffmann, Adolf Hitler's personal photographer.[3] He was reported to have spent several days with Hitler at Berchtesgaden.[4]

The Goudstikker sale, set up almost immediately after the German invasion in 1940, was a shadow transaction on behalf of Field Marshal Hermann Göring, the number two man in the German Reich. To keep their own hands clean, Hitler and Göring used surrogates to locate collections and negotiate transactions to satisfy their taste for rare works of art, and it is clear that Göring or his art agents had the notable Goudstikker collection on his wish list of acquisitions. One condition that Goudstikker demanded before he agreed to the forced sale to Miedl was that Miedl protect his elderly Jewish mother.

As the German forces approached Amsterdam on May 13, 1940, the Goudstikkers, who had missed their chance to leave Amsterdam for the United States, fled, without visas, for England, finding passage on the SS *Bodegraven*, in part because a soldier on guard recognized Goudstikker's wife, a well-known opera singer. But Goudstikker never made it to England alive. During the overnight sailing, he mysteriously fell through an open hatch into the ship's cargo hold, fatally breaking his neck.[5]

Even after his death, Goudstikker's "art house" continued to thrive under the occupation as large numbers of Germans with unlimited money flooded the country. After his first visit at the end of May 1940, Hermann Göring came several more times, using his private train or plane and taking over the Hotel Astoria in Amsterdam. There is a famous photo of Göring exiting the Goudstikker gallery on the Herengracht during one of his trips to inspect the paintings he wanted to purchase. (It was that photo that Van den Bergh's granddaughter recognized.) During his postwar interrogation on August 30, 1946, a little more than six weeks before his suicide, Göring claimed to have met with Goudstikker's notary. Whether that was on his first visit or later, he did not specify, nor did he name the notary, but it was clearly Van den Bergh.[6] The field marshal held leverage over Miedl because of Miedl's Jewish wife, whom he, being a conservative Catholic, refused to divorce. Miedl continued to pacify Göring by supplying him with valuable paintings and gifts.

In the sham transaction, Alois Miedl acquired the real estate and the company name Goudstikker N.V., while Göring acquired most of the paintings, including a Rembrandt (which he gifted to Hitler), a Frans Hals, and a Ruysdael. Arnold van den Bergh officiated over the transaction as the Goudstikker notary and wrote the deeds of sale for the art collection, even though, as the Cold Case Team later learned, a notary was technically not required for such a sale.* The payment of 2 million guilders ($10 million today) was tendered in 1,000-guilder bills that Van den Bergh purportedly had to count by hand. (The original agreement called for the transaction to be handled via bank check, but there seems to have been great urgency to complete the sale and the conversion to a check never took place.)

---

* The Dutch notary Corneils M. Cappon confirmed that a notary was required only for the sale of property.

After the sale to Göring, which was clearly illegal since it was a coerced sale, everyone in Goudstikker N.V. received a bonus. Van den Bergh received 10 percent of the 2 million guilders. The appraiser and restorer, J. Dik, Sr., and the administrator, A. A. ten Broek, each received 180,000 guilders. Even the lower-level personnel, such as the gardeners, were given bonuses. Privately, they called the sale "the golden shower."[7]

The Cold Case Team determined that Van den Bergh himself was a prolific art collector and sold artworks directly to the Reich Chancellery, one of which ended up in Hitler's personal collection.[8] He was paid handsomely, but even more important than the money was the fact that his role at Goudstikker N.V. and his association with Miedl provided him with many contacts within the SS and the Nazi administration who could ensure his safety.

Evidently at Miedl's request,[9] in September 1943 Van den Bergh opened the doors of his villa at Oranje Nassaulaan to Goudstikker's mother, Emilie Goudstikker, and she remained there until the end of the war. A check of her Jewish Council card indicated that Miedl managed to have her card "cleaned": there was no identification number, no *Sperre* number, and no mandatory *J*.[10] That was impressive; the man obviously had real power. Van den Bergh was clearly counting on Miedl to return the favor by using his influence with the Nazi administration to protect him and his family.

Van den Bergh was a clever man. He'd tried several strategies to save his family. He applied for and received several *Sperres* and even a Calmeyer exemption—until the Dutch notary J.W.A. Schepers challenged it. He had the resistance hide his children. He clearly recognized that survival was a matter of whom you knew. Through his relationship with Miedl he enjoyed the (indirect) protection of Ferdinand aus der Fünten and Willy Lages. But even though he had connections at the highest levels of the Nazi world, Van den Bergh was not naive enough to trust a Nazi. His duties as notary for Goudstikker N.V. ended on February 28, 1944. After this he must have been making plans to find refuge. The Cold Case Team knew that Van den Bergh and his wife were never deported, were never listed as being in any concentration camp, and survived the war. What did Van den Bergh do to secure their survival?

By 1944, it was becoming clear that the Germans were going to lose the war. Hermann Göring's influence was on the wane; Hitler was furious that Göring's Luftwaffe was unable to stop the Allied bombings of German cities. Miedl saw the writing on the wall. No longer able to count on Göring's protection, he decided to move his family to Spain, whose caudillo, Francisco Franco, was friendly toward Germans. In his postwar interrogation by a US Army representative, Miedl claimed he entered Spain on July 5, 1944, with three paintings in his personal luggage. The Cold Case Team found a report indicating that he was arrested and briefly held by the Germans in France on August 21, 1944. He probably smuggled his paintings across the frontier into Spain on a number of occasions. He left his business and two mansions to his friend Hans Tietje, the same Tietje who had secured the 120,000 *Sperres* for Van den Bergh and his family. The caretaker, servants, and a neighbor of Miedl's reported to the Dutch resistance that in the months prior to Miedl's departure, many German Army trucks had stopped at his villa and loaded valuables into them for transportation to Germany.[11]

With Miedl's power seriously diminished, Van den Bergh was more exposed than ever. Although the team cannot be certain, it's possible that he and his wife sought sanctuary at one of the two properties Miedl had "bought" from Goudstikker and for which Van den Bergh had served as notary. The Cold Case Team checked to see if the couple stayed at the Oostermeer estate just outside Amsterdam. They discovered that there were many people in hiding there at the end of the war, but there was no mention of Van den Bergh and his wife, and they therefore ruled that possibility out. However, Castle Nijenrode remained a plausible address for the Van den Berghs.

One former resident, a German friend of Miedl named Henriette von Schirach, the wife of the notorious leader of the Hitler Youth and Reich governor of Vienna Baldur von Schirach, was a close personal friend of Hitler. She described the castle as a very strange place:

> *The same evening, I followed Miedl's advice and moved to his moated castle. In this house you would find anybody that feared persecution in Germany: engineers of the Messerschmittwerke, who were brought here because of Göring and had Jewish wives, actors who had escaped from a Wehrmacht tour in Holland, journalists, impostors, men and women with fake/wrong passports and fake/wrong names.*[12]

If the Van den Berghs were at the castle, sharing space with German fugitives could hardly have felt safe. With Miedl now in Spain and unable to protect him, Van den Bergh might have needed to find some additional insurance—something the SD would value enough that it would provide protection for himself and his family. When IV B4 men made arrests, it was standard MO for them to pressure the arrestees for the addresses of other Jews in hiding. For Van den Bergh, addresses where Jews were purportedly being hidden would have been a valuable commodity.

42
A Bombshell

The Cold Case Team began their search for possible sources of address lists by looking into the workings of the Contact Committee (Contact Commissie) at Camp Westerbork. When prisoners needed specific papers to prove they were eligible for a *Sperre*, they had to go to the Contact Committee. The office was run by two men appointed by the Jewish Council who traveled regularly between Westerbork and Amsterdam to secure necessary documents and intervene on behalf of prisoners. One of the men was Eduard Spier, Van den Bergh's close colleague and friend. Before the war, they shared an office at Westeinde 24. Spier, Van den Bergh, and van Hasselt often did business together; the team found numerous business ads featuring their names in prewar newspapers.[1]

Eduard Spier was also in charge of the Jewish Council's Central Information Office, which worked closely with the Expositur, the liaison office between the Jewish Council and the Zentralstelle, run by Ferdinand aus der Fünten. In other words, Spier had the ear of one of the highest-ranking Nazis in Amsterdam and was in a position to receive information and offer favors. Did he try to help his friend Arnold van den Bergh by providing him with lists of hiders as a bargaining tool to purchase his freedom if he were confronted with arrest?

But the Cold Case Team discovered that in April 1943, the Westerbork camp commander, Albert Konrad Gemmeker, decided that he wanted his own men running the Contact Committee.* He sent Spier to join the Barneveld group in its castle outside the Dutch town of that name. Spier managed only a few months there before the entire Barneveld group was relocated to Camp Westerbork. He was assigned to Barrack 85, where he could well have met Leopold de Jong. But he no longer had the access he once had to the Jewish Council, which had been disbanded, and it seems likely that he was too preoccupied with his own survival to help Van den Bergh.

---

* They were Hans Eckmann, Fritz Grünberg, Walter Heynemann, and Hans Hanauer.

The corruption at Westerbork was extensive. In a notarized deposition, the four prisoners assigned by Gemmeker to take over the Contact Committee from Spier described how, in May 1944, they were called into Gemmeker's office and told to offer prisoners the possibility of buying off their "penal" status with diamonds.[2] In a postwar criminal investigation of the Contact Committee, it was also reported that Gemmeker ordered Contact Committee members to contact Jews in hiding in Amsterdam and elsewhere to offer them the possibility of buying their freedom with money and valuable jewels.[3] The task of the Cold Case Team was to determine how the Contact Committee went about finding the addresses of Jews in hiding in order to offer them Gemmeker's bargain.

Pieter decided to review the CABR files of the cochairs of the Jewish Council, David Cohen and Abraham Asscher, at the National Archives. The two men were arrested on November 6, 1947, on orders of the Special Justice Court in Amsterdam, accused of collaboration with the Germans. They were imprisoned for a month and then released, pending trial.* There

---

* In 1951, the prosecution of Cohen was suspended (Asscher had died in 1950) on the grounds of public interest.

were many witness testimonies as to how the men had curried favor with high-ranking Nazi officials. Asscher was the owner of the Asscher Diamond Company. Hermann Göring's proxy A. J. Herzberg visited the factory numerous times, as did Göring himself at least once. Göring wanted to buy 1 million Reichsmarks' worth of diamonds, likely for his personal use and not for the good of the German nation. It was made clear to Asscher in veiled terms that if he refused to sell, there were other ways to obtain his cooperation.[4]

Witnesses reported that Cohen, and particularly Asscher, visited Willy Lages regularly. Asscher often brought diamond rings and jewelry for Lages and his secretary. According to Lages, who was interrogated in prison, Asscher told him that his first priority was the safety of his family and he needed assurances that if he cooperated, they would be safe. Lages said he replied that they would be permitted to emigrate to another country. That never happened, of course, but Asscher believed him. The Camp Westerbork commander, Gemmeker, who also gave testimony, claimed that Asscher requested that the fiancée of one of his sons, a young woman named Weinrother, be deported to Auschwitz. He didn't want her as a daughter-in-law. Gemmeker said he refused, but other witnesses reported that she was, in fact, deported. The young woman survived the war, and after she returned home the whole story came out.[5]

It was in those files that Pieter uncovered a bombshell in the testimony of Ernst Philip Henn, age thirty-seven, a German who from September 1942 to July 1943 was a translator for Air Force Command Holland (Luftgau-Kommando Holland) in Amsterdam. While he was working at Civilian Affairs, Henn claimed to have overheard a sergeant in the Feldgendarmerie (military police) talking to a court assessor by the name of Willy Stark. The sergeant mentioned that the Jewish Council had a list of more than five hundred addresses of Jews in hiding. His department had requested a list, and the Jewish Council had sent between five hundred and a thousand addresses. He added the nasty comment that the Jewish Council members had probably thought that the more addresses they "betrayed," the more leniently they themselves might be treated.[6]

Henn said that he'd asked a Jewish woman how the Jewish Council was able to get hold of the addresses of hiders. She said that one way was through the mail. All mail from Camp Westerbork and the occasional mail from camps in the east went through the Jewish Council. Trusting the Jewish Council, people wrote to family and friends in hiding, using their hiding addresses.

Henn did stand trial after the war, since he'd worked as an interpreter for the German occupiers, but it's hard to see how that particular statement could have helped him. What is interesting in his testimony is that he mentioned addresses and not names. He must have overheard the conversation before July 1943, when he moved on to another position. So the Cold Case Team had to ask if the information was at all relevant to Arnold Van den Bergh and the possibility of his giving lists of addresses to the SD.

As the team discovered, although the council was dissolved, some of its members were still at large—and many likely still had access to addresses. Rudolf Pollak, for example, was a member of the Jewish Council, and part of his role was to distribute food coupons to prisoners in Westerbork and the Dutch Theater (Hollandsche Schouwburg). He also kept a card catalog with addresses of Jewish hiding places.[7] In March 1944, the SD arrested him, and under pressure, he immediately buckled. He gave up his card catalog and became a V-Man for the SD; he was eventually targeted and killed by the Dutch resistance in November or December 1944.

The team thought it highly probable that Van den Bergh had had a list of addresses for quite some time and kept it as insurance until he needed to use it. Until the summer of 1944, he had secured safety for his family by sending his children into hiding and also by applying for various exemptions. After his Calmeyer status was revoked he turned to his friend Alois Miedl and probably hid on Miedl's property. But after Miedl fled to Spain, Van den Bergh might have figured he needed a different kind of protection. Whatever he did, it worked, since he and his immediate family survived the war. It is always possible that he and his wife went into hiding with the help of the resistance, as did his daughters in 1943, but the Cold Case Team never found a record of his either speaking of going into hiding or specifying a hiding place, though he had opportunities to do so during postwar interrogations of Jewish Council members. The team knew that he was also vague about his friendship with Miedl, a Nazi.[8] Most people who survived in hiding celebrated the brave people who hid them. Even Van den Bergh's granddaughter, when asked, said that her grandparents never spoke of hiding.[9]

After the war, the surviving Jewish community set up Jewish Honor Courts to call to account Jews who they believed had collaborated; the courts carried a moral rather than a legal authority. Having been board members of the Jewish Council, Van den Bergh and four other defendants were called to appear before the Honor Court in Amsterdam. All five chose not to participate.[10] Trying the men in absentia, the court ruled in May 1948 that the five had assisted in a number of anti-Jewish measures, including distributing the Jewish star, unfairly determining the lists of exemptions, and participating in the selection of deportees.[11] Any defense of Van den Bergh was mild—"No particularly ugly facts had arisen about him," said one member—and when he refused to step down from the Jewish Coordination Committee (Joodse Coördinatie Commissie), which helped Jewish survivors returning from the camps, several members resigned. In the end, he lost his right to hold any Jewish office and access to honorary functions in the Jewish community for five years.[12] But there was never any public accusation that he betrayed fellow Jews.

It was around that time that Otto told the Dutch journalist Friso Endt, who worked for *Het Parool*, "We were betrayed by Jews."[13] He used the plural, likely referring to Van den Bergh and the Jewish Council. Clearly the anonymous note identifying Van den Bergh as his betrayer must have been on Otto's mind, but although he surely followed the proceedings, he never spoke up either for or against Van den Bergh, who, shortly after the verdict was handed down, was diagnosed with throat cancer.[14] Van den Bergh traveled to London to seek treatment and died on October 28, 1950.[15]

Van den Bergh's body was returned to the Netherlands for burial. Although his sentence of exclusion from Jewish society had not expired, it didn't seem to matter; he was buried in a Jewish cemetery. The plane carrying his body was delayed by fog so that the funeral took place at an unusual hour, 7:00 p.m., in Muiderberg. A large procession of cars followed the hearse. Emergency lighting was installed at the grave site, and car headlights lit the path. Those who offered eulogies spoke of a good husband and father, a man who gave his time to the community, though one speaker offered apologies on behalf of his association with the deceased for having "come up short on respect and appreciation." Van den Bergh's friend the notary Eduard Spier, who was in the United States, sent word that those who penetrated his "outer closedness" recognized an exceptional colleague and friend.[16]

Perhaps Otto's lack of interest in exposing his betrayer can be put down, in part, to Van den Bergh's death. What would be the point in pursuing a dead man? Otto always said he didn't want to harm the man's children. He also may have concluded that Van den Bergh would become a convenient scapegoat for Jew haters. If it was a Jew and the Jewish Council who betrayed the Jews—not the Nazis and a passive German population; not the Dutch Nazis and an acquiescent Dutch population; not the Western governments, which turned their backs on Jewish refugees—wouldn't he just be playing into the hands of the many anti-Semites who still roamed Europe?

43
A Secret Well Kept

According to Vince, by midsummer of 2019, the Cold Case Team had only four theories about the betrayal that still seemed viable. All others had been eliminated, either because the team found them improbable or, for a few, because there was not enough information to investigate further.

The case against Ans van Dijk was still particularly strong. She was a prolific V-Frau, having betrayed an estimated two hundred people, and was known to work in the Jordaan neighborhood close to where the Annex was located. Although the team had discounted Gerard Kremer's theory that Van Dijk had heard about the Annex from the Wehrmacht secretaries at Westermarkt 2, she was still a viable suspect.

However, after searching Van Dijk's extensive CABR

file, the Cold Case Team discovered that she and her crew of V-people (Branca Simons; her husband, Wim Houthuijs; and Mies de Regt) were not in Amsterdam in August 1944; they had moved to the town of Zeist, near Utrecht, at the end of July to infiltrate a large resistance network there.[1] (When "Zeist" was typed into the AI database in relation to Van Dijk and her whereabouts that August, there were 705 hits, including handwritten notes and even video files attesting to her presence in that city.) On August 18, Van Dijk and her cohorts in Zeist turned over to the SD five of the resistance members they'd been stalking and six Jews in hiding.

There is another consideration: the Cold Case Team knew that Otto went out of his way to protect the identity of the betrayer. It doesn't make sense that he would do so for Van Dijk, who was not only widely despised after the war but had also been indirectly responsible for the capture of his second wife, Fritzi, and her entire family. Why would he hesitate to name her?

The scenario involving Bep's sister Nelly also seemed initially possible. Nelly was a known Nazi sympathizer and had worked for a year on a German air base in France. Her father and sister were among the helpers to the Jews in hiding and privy to the secret of the Annex. The various theories—that she was the anonymous female caller; that she betrayed the people in the Annex out of anger at her father's mistreatment—were only speculation. However, after Bep's son Joop van Wijk and his coauthor, Jeroen de Bruyn, published *Anne Frank: The Untold Story*, in which they advanced the theory that Nelly was the betrayer, the Cold Case Team had reason to pause. Joop said that when he had asked Nelly about the war for the purposes of the book, she had fainted. Did she conveniently faint to evade addressing his questions?

At the end of the book, Joop said that "claiming Nelly was the betrayer is taking it too far. We have no smoking gun." He wrote eloquently of his mother, Bep:

> *She often lived in the past after the war and mulled over the split she found herself in: the loss of her Jewish loved ones from the Annex on the one hand, and her loyalty to her sister who had proven her services to the occupier on the other hand. An occupier that had brutally deported and killed those same loved ones.*[2]

In his interview with the Cold Case Team, Joop made it clear that in his mind, his mother and his aunt were testimony to the brutal paradox of divided loyalties in wartime, reflected within a family. But he would not say, conclusively, that Nelly betrayed the Franks.

In fact, there are two other sources who rule out the possibility that Nelly was the betrayer: Miep and Otto. In a 1994 lecture at the University of Michigan, Miep "slipped" and told a young student that the betrayer had died before 1960—and Nelly was very much alive until 2001. In addition, Otto told a Dutch journalist in the late 1940s that they'd been betrayed by Jews and he did not wish to pursue the culprit because he did not wish to punish the family and children of the man who betrayed them, indicating, among other things, that the betrayer was a man who had children. Nelly was not Jewish and had no children. Even if some of those statements were subterfuges to keep the curious at bay, others were also clearly true, and all of them rule out Nelly.

A third scenario, the one involving the greengrocer, also had sticking power. Van Hoeve was arrested on May 25 for hiding a Jewish couple. Under duress, could he have provided information about the Annex? It's possible, but had he done so, it's unlikely that Dutch detectives would have waited nearly three months to initiate the Annex raid. In addition, Van Houve was sent away to a work camp after his arrest. Had he turned in eight Jews that day, he most likely would have been released.

As for Richard and Ruth Weisz, they may well

have known that Van Hoeve was delivering food to the Annex. However, as with Van Hoeve, if they gave up that information upon their arrest, the SD would not have waited so long to act. Still, the fact that they arrived at Westerbork as penal cases and after a short period of time had their status changed continued to give the Cold Case Team pause. Had the Weiszes given up something of value—i.e., a list of Jews in hiding? But again, the timing was off; the Weiszes' status was upgraded in Westerbork sometime in June 1944, well before the Annex was raided on August 4. The Nazis were not in the habit of rewarding informants before confirming that the information they gave was accurate.

With all of the other scenarios eliminated, only one was still viable: the Van den Bergh scenario, the only theory ever bolstered by a piece of physical evidence identifying the name of the betrayer. All of the theories proposed by the helpers, researchers, and authors were grounded in assumptions as to the identity of the betrayer, based on either their suspicious activity or their past actions. The piece of evidence that the Cold Case Team recovered, although not the original note, was an actual copy made by Otto Frank. Although that alone did not prove that the allegation in the note was true, it did provide inherent credibility since Otto clearly took it seriously.

Of course, the Cold Case Team had to consider that the note was sent anonymously by someone with a vendetta against Van den Bergh. But why send the note to Otto? If there was no list of addresses handed over by Van den Bergh, how and why would the sender have settled on the Annex address as opposed to other possible addresses in Amsterdam?

The wording of the note—"Your hideout in Amsterdam was reported at the time to the Jüdische Auswanderung"—would seem to suggest that the betrayer didn't have the names of the *onderduikers* in the Annex but only knew that there were some. The probability that the sender directed the note to a random address, which just happened to be the site of the betrayal of Jews and also Otto Frank's address, is minuscule.

The Cold Case Team also considered the possibility that whoever sent the note might have sent similar ones to other addresses on the list. If so, they have never been discovered—possibly because most of the Jews who were betrayed at those addresses did not survive the camps, besides which, most had been hiding at addresses other than their own homes or offices. Otto was the exception. He was hiding in his own building—and he survived the war.

If the letter had arrived ten years later—say in the mid-1950s—it could be argued that someone was just trying to use Otto's fame to cast a negative light on Van den Bergh. But at the time the note was received in 1945, the diary was not yet published and Otto Frank was just one of 5,500 Jews returning to the Netherlands. In a sea of Dutch people coming back from the labor camps, hundreds of thousands of people coming out of hiding, and the returning Jews struggling to put their lives back together, he was an unknown figure.

In other words, if the accusation in the note was false, the sender would have to have been someone who:

1. *Had a specific vendetta against Arnold van den Bergh yet inexplicably did not want to notify the postwar authorities, who were aggressively pursuing and locking up collaborators and betrayers within days of the liberation*

2. *Knew that Otto had been betrayed while in hiding—and had survived the camps*

3. *Knew that Otto had returned to his wartime address*

4. *Was aware that lists of Jews in hiding were passed by members of the Jewish Council to the SD*

The odds of the sender knowing all of that are exceedingly slim. It can be assumed that the author of the anonymous note is now dead, but there is always the possibility that he or she informed family members who passed the story down. Vince believes that after the Van den Bergh theory is made public, the team may hear from them.

Through the Arrest Tracking Project, by which the arrests of all Jews in the Netherlands between 1943 and 1944 were analyzed, the Cold Case Team discovered that the raid on the Annex was somewhat different from other raids, specifically in that a German officer led the team. This was very unusual and suggests that it was not the Dutch desk officer, Sergeant Abraham Kaper, at the Zentralstelle who called in Silberbauer. Kaper would not have called a German officer to accompany Dutch policemen. The call must have come from higher up, which in fact Silberbauer always claimed when he said that SS Lieutenant Julius Dettmann at Euterpestraat took the call and then ordered him to organize the raid. Furthermore, if an ordinary Dutch civilian was intent on betraying Jews, he or she would have called the JA; Kaper's number was listed in the phone directory. Dettmann was too senior an officer to receive a random call. His number was not listed in the phone book, he did not operate V-persons, and he did not speak Dutch. If he received the call, it almost certainly came from within the German organization, either from another German department or from someone he knew. Among the suspects the Cold Case Team examined, only Van den Bergh had connections with high-ranking German officials, was in contact with important individuals such as Tietje, and would have been known to the German intelligence services.

For Vince, what made the Van den Bergh scenario convincing is that, unlike any of the other suspects, Van den Bergh met all of the criteria of the law enforcement axiom:

Knowledge: *It's almost certain that the Jewish Council had lists of addresses of Jews in hiding. Through his key position on the Jewish Council, Van den Bergh would have had access to those lists. He may also have had access to the lists of addresses collected by the Contact Committee at Camp Westerbork.*[3] *Prinsengracht 263 could easily have been on a list in 1943 or 1944, placed there by a member of the resistance who'd been turned or by an informant and available for purchase if the money was sufficient.*

Motive: *Van den Bergh's motive was to safeguard himself and his family from capture and deportation* *by making himself useful to the Nazi occupiers, some of whom were "friends" or business acquaintances. The fact that the note states that the list contained addresses and not names makes it more plausible that Van den Bergh used it to guard his own family. Addresses are less personal.*

Opportunity: *At a time when anyone could have had a motive for betrayal, Van den Bergh possessed something that most other Jews did not: freedom to move about and access to the SD. He was in regular contact with highly placed Nazis. He could have passed on the information he had at any time.*

Even though the Van den Bergh theory was clearly the most likely, Vince said he had played the devil's advocate with all of the key points over and over. Time and again, Van den Bergh emerged as the most likely perpetrator. In fact, it was the only theory that explained Otto's behavior and the statements he and Miep had made over the years. But before officially concluding anything, Vince wanted to conduct one more test: he wanted to present all of the evidence in the form of a closing argument to Pieter in a manner similar to the way prosecutors present a case at the conclusion of a trial.

Vince and Pieter often found themselves alone in the office after everyone else was gone. "I was sitting at my desk, and Pieter was sitting in Brendan's chair with the pictures of the SD IV B4 Dutch detectives over his shoulder," Vince recalled. "I began by reminding him of Melissa Müller's statement that 'this is not so much a case unsolved as a secret well kept.'" Then he listed Otto's actions as they related to the Van den Bergh theory.

The fact that Otto survived the horror of the concentration camps demonstrated his profound will to live. Obviously, he was sustained by his determination to be reunited with his wife and daughters. But his return to Amsterdam was overshadowed by his uncertainty about their fate. To those who encountered Otto at the time, he seemed to be a man purged by fire, walking through Amsterdam as though in a strange dream, searching for news of his children. Finding out that he was his family's sole survivor must have sent him to a very dark place. Vince hypothesized that Otto's grief had eventually turned into a mission to find the people responsible for the Annex raid, although his motive was not vengeance; he was seeking accountability and justice. There is evidence of his saying this, both in a letter he sent to his mother in November 1945 and later in the CBS documentary *Who Killed Anne Frank?*, which aired on December 13, 1964.

But, Vince asked, was it also possible that his search for justice was influenced by the anonymous note he'd received naming Van den Bergh as the betrayer? The note must have occasioned endless questions. Why would Van den Bergh, a fellow Jew, pass on his address to the SD? How did he get the Annex address? What did he receive in return for providing the addresses? Otto must have asked himself if he should go to the authorities with the allegation. He certainly conducted his own investigation. He, Kugler, and Kleiman went to the Bureau of National Security as early as November 1945 to review photos of the Dutch detectives who'd worked for IV B4. Then he, Kugler, and Kleiman went to Amstelveenseweg prison to confront the two men they'd identified as having participated in the raid. Otto even returned with his friend Ab Cauvern to question Detective Gringhuis, and that time he pointedly asked about Van den Bergh. He also made numerous visits to the Dutch collaboration authorities between 1945 and 1948, although some of the visits probably dealt with the inquiries concerning Tonny Ahlers and Job Jansen.

At the time, it must have been a tough decision for Otto not to inform Kugler or Kleiman about the anonymous note, for they, too, were victims of the betrayal and ended up in internment camps. Perhaps Otto thought that if he did tell them, they would immediately contact the collaboration authorities, which he was not prepared to do.

Otto was closer to Miep than to any of the other helpers. Vince concluded that it would have made sense for him to inform her of the note's contents, and he probably did so sometime after the 1947–48 investigation and well before the Schnabel book came out in 1958. Reading Miep's statements to investigators in 1947, it's clear that she still believed Van Maaren was the culprit, but when she was interviewed later by Schnabel, she was much more circumspect. By that time, she and Otto knew about Van den Bergh.

Otto was making inquiries about Van den Bergh between late 1945 and 1949. He would have known that, during that time, Van den Bergh was being targeted by the Jewish Honor Court for his membership on the board of the Jewish Council. This poses a question: Why didn't Otto present the contents of the note to the court, since it was Jews judging the actions of Jews, something quite different from the collaboration investigations? Perhaps as he followed the court's proceedings, Otto was waiting for others to come forward with similar anonymous notes as the tipster had referred to Van den Bergh's list of addresses. Since that did not happen, Otto may have felt uncertain about how to proceed.

After the Jewish Honor Court's verdict, which was only mildly punitive to Van den Bergh, Otto might again have considered the consequences of revealing the existence of the note. And if he learned that Van den Bergh was suffering from cancer and would soon leave Amsterdam for treatment in London, would he likely have pursued the case?

In the years following Van den Bergh's death, the astonishing success of Anne's diary, play, and movie dominated Otto's life. By staying busy and focusing on other things, it was probably easier to assign the uncertainty concerning the betrayer of the Annex to the recesses of his mind. The world knew the story of the Annex only up until Anne's last entry, made on August 1, 1944, and so far, there was no public curiosity regarding the betrayer. But that changed in the mid-1950s, when Otto was convinced by the German publisher of the diary to collaborate with Ernst Schnabel on a book that would tell the full story of the Annex before, during, and after the raid.

Such a book might help dispel the rumors that Anne's diary was fake. By agreeing to collaborate on the book, Otto and the helpers hoped to prove to the world that Anne Frank was real, the diary was real, and so were the people whom Anne wrote about. But Schnabel's book also provided information about the raid and clues as to who might have caused it, thus unintentionally opening a Pandora's box. Otto had asked Miep to disguise the name of the SD officer Silberbauer. Why? The only reasonable explanation is that he feared that Silberbauer might know who made the anonymous phone call and might point to Van den Bergh—and by now Otto did not want his name revealed.

Sometime just prior to or immediately after Schnabel's book was published, Otto decided to take a bold but very risky step about the anonymous note he'd kept secret all these years. He knew that Schnabel's book contained information that would cause the news media, along with readers, to question him or the others about the raid. Clearly, he decided not to destroy the note. Instead, he found someone to whom to entrust it. In case he were ever confronted about its existence, he could truthfully respond that he no longer had it. One might have expected him to choose Kleiman, but he gave the note to his friend, the notary Jakob van Hasselt, who also happened to be a friend and business contact of Van den Bergh.

Looking at it from multiple perspectives, Vince and the Cold Case Team speculated that, without irrefutable proof that Van den Bergh was the betrayer, Otto chose never to publicly mention the name or the note. But by cooperating with Schnabel to prove the validity of the diary, he actually created the possibility that Van den Bergh's name might surface if the SD officer were located. So he went out of his way to make it harder for even someone as committed as Simon Wiesenthal to find Silberbauer.

Otto had been involved in several well-publicized civil suits to disprove claims that Anne's diary was fake, but when Wiesenthal tried to do the same thing, Otto chose not to help. At first, the Cold Case Team was puzzled by that contradiction, but it later came to make sense. Otto knew he could defend the diary without exposing the true name of the SD officer, but he wouldn't be able to control Wiesenthal, who already had a dogged reputation as a Nazi hunter, if he were to find it. And although it did take him six years, Wiesenthal eventually did locate Silberbauer, at which point the world press descended on Otto and the helpers. Only then did Otto admit he had known the arresting officer's name, but he said that Wiesenthal had never contacted him for the information. He also implied that the SD officer would not remember much after so long a time.[4]

It wasn't until the State Department of Criminal Investigation initiated its inquiry into the raid on the Annex in late 1963 that Otto decided to inform Detective Van Helden about the anonymous note and hand over the copy he'd made. Van Helden interviewed Otto over a period of two days at the beginning of December 1963, but surprisingly, there is no mention of the note in the interview report. However, in Van Helden's forty-page summary report produced at the conclusion of the investigation in the fall of 1964, there are several paragraphs in which he described Otto informing him about the anonymous note. Based on Van Helden's handwritten comments on the *Abschrift* copy, he had received it on December 16, 1963, approximately two weeks after Otto's interview. It would seem that Van Helden was convinced by Otto's claim that he didn't know Van den Bergh, because the issue was dropped and the *Abschrift* copy of the note that Otto had provided him never made it into the official case file.

The Cold Case Team reviewed Otto's correspondence during the period of the investigation and found a small but perhaps significant clue: the day before Otto's scheduled interview with Van Helden on December 1, he wrote a letter to Miep expressing his doubt about any conviction of Willem van Maaren, since there was no "written evidence" that he was the betrayer.[5] It's an odd statement and possibly a veiled reference to the anonymous note—"written evidence"—that explicitly pointed to Van den Bergh.

Having survived the curiosity of the world press, Otto instructed the remaining helpers, Miep, Bep, and Kugler, that he would be the sole spokesperson of the Annex story. Kugler, who was now living in Canada, defied that instruction when he agreed to collaborate on a book with a writer named Eda Shapiro, a book she intended to call "The Man Who Hid Anne Frank." Kugler did not inform Otto about it, and when Otto found out, he was furious. After learning that the book did not have Otto's support, the publisher canceled the book's publication.[6]

After Otto's death, Miep became the spokesperson and protector of the Annex legacy. Although she was skilled at keeping the secret, she was not so adept at hiding the fact that she had one. In her many press interviews, speeches, and private conversations, she let clues regarding the betrayer leak out. And all the clues pointed to Arnold van den Bergh. The betrayer was someone Otto knew. He knew Van den Bergh. The betrayer had been Jewish. Van den Bergh was Jewish. The betrayer died before 1960. Van den Bergh died in 1950. Otto did not wish to punish the family and children of the man who betrayed his family. Van den Bergh was the father of three children who survived the war and outlived Otto Frank.

Vince remembered the question that John Goldsmith, the president of the Anne Frank Fonds in Basel, posed to him back in 2018: "You know that Otto lied to Wiesenthal about knowing the identity of Silberbauer. Why do you think he did this?" At the time, Vince didn't completely understand what Goldsmith was telling him, but now it made sense. Otto didn't want to reveal Van den Bergh's complicity. What's more, he went to great lengths to conceal it.

Both Otto Frank and Arnold van den Bergh made choices. From the perspective of survival, Otto Frank made the wrong choice—although at the time, of course, he thought he was protecting his family and four other people by finding them a hiding place. From the perspective of survival, Van den Bergh made the right choice. He saved his family by giving up addresses, including Prinsengracht 263, to the SD. But he, perhaps, paid a price, too. He died of throat cancer, which was strangely apt: he lost the ability to speak.

Vince is careful to say that there was no "aha" moment to end the investigation; the emergence of Van den Bergh as the betrayer was just that: a slow coming together of evidence and motive, a jigsaw puzzle piece that suddenly, undeniably fit. And as confident as the team is about its conclusion, there was no joy in the discovery. Vince would later say that he was overcome by "a weight of great sadness" that has stayed with him. As the team separated, going back to their jobs, families, and home countries, each of them grappled individually with their shared experience. By the time the investigation ended in 2021, they knew they'd lived through something powerful and important. They came to refer to the people in the case as if they were people they'd actually known. Vince admitted to dreaming about the Franks and wondering aloud how he himself would have behaved under the circumstances.

Just as complex were the team's feelings about sharing their findings with the world. Everyone knew how powerful—and upsetting—their conclusions would be; they're braced for the world's reaction. The fact that a respected Dutch Jew had likely passed addresses to the SD, that someone not all that dissimilar from Otto Frank himself had been Otto's betrayer . . . it is shocking. But they could not remain silent. As Rabbi Sebbag had told Thijs at the beginning of the investigation, the most important thing, the only real loyalty any of us should have, is to the truth.

Arnold van den Bergh was a person put into a devil's dilemma by circumstances for which he was not to blame, and, under pressure, he may have failed to understand fully the consequences of his actions. He did not turn over information out of wickedness or for self-enrichment, as so many others had. Like Otto Frank's, his goal was simple: to save his family. That he succeeded while Otto failed is a terrible fact of history.

By the summer of 1944, it was well known that extermination awaited people at the end of the transports. Could one imagine that for one's children? Living in a state of constant dread of arrest and deportation, how does a person maintain moral equilibrium? A few can; most don't. One can never be sure how one might act unless and until one finds oneself in the midst of such horror.

Arnold van den Bergh's choices proved to be deadly. But he was not ultimately responsible for the deaths of the residents of Prinsengracht 263. That responsibility rests forever with the Nazi occupiers who terrorized and decimated a society, turning neighbor against neighbor. It is they who were culpable in the deaths of Anne Frank, Edith Frank, Margot Frank, Hermann van Pels, Auguste van Pels, Peter van Pels, and Fritz Pfeffer. And millions of others, in hiding or not.

And this can never be understood or forgiven.

Epilogue
The Shadow City

Otto Frank died on August 19, 1980, at the age of ninety-one. On his return from Auschwitz, he'd tried to rebuild his Opekta business, but neither pectin nor spices were available after the war. By the late 1940s, his time was entirely consumed by his daughter's diary. After he moved to Switzerland in 1952, Johannes Kleiman assumed control of the firm.

Otto and his wife, Fritzi, were committed to answering all letters they received about the diary, and with the increasing international attention, the letters soon numbered in the thousands. Otto often traveled to Amsterdam to preside over the Anne Frank Foundation, established in 1957, and to direct the restoration of Prinsengracht 263, which opened as Anne Frank House in 1960.

On January 24, 1963, Otto and Fritzi set up the Anne Frank Fonds, a charitable foundation with offices in Basel, where they continued to reside. The copyright to Anne's diary and all royalties from the book, the play, the film, and any radio and television presentations would devolve to the Anne Frank Fonds. To his relatives he left bequests and portions of the royalties, up to a certain amount, during their lifetimes. The rest went to the Fonds. However, wanting to ensure that the diaries would never be sold—who knew what would become of the Anne Frank Foundation in fifty years?—Otto willed the physical diaries to the Netherlands Institute for War Documentation (NIOD), knowing that the Dutch government would never sell them and they would be safe.[1]

Otto and Fritzi lived on the outskirts of Basel but often spent the summer months in Beckenried, on Lake Lucerne. Fritzi spoke about her years with Otto as "among the happiest of my whole life. . . . He had an innate sense of what it meant to be family."[2] Otto was close to Fritzi's daughter, Eva, and Eva's husband and three children. He and Fritzi spent three months of every year living with them in London.

There were many trips: to the United States and to Germany for events related to the diary. And many awards. On May 12, 1979, Otto celebrated his ninetieth birthday in London, and then, on June 12, he traveled to Amsterdam for the Anne Frank Fiftieth Birthday Tribute in the Westerkerk on Prinsengracht, after which he escorted the queen to the Anne Frank House for a private tour.

But age was catching up with him, and in his last year he suffered from lung cancer, though he would insist he was not sick, just tired. One of the last people to visit him before his death was Joseph Spronz, a friend and fellow survivor whom Otto had met in Auschwitz. Spronz's wife described the visit:

> *When we arrived, Otto was in bed, but he heard us and got up, holding out his arms. He looked into my husband's eyes, and they embraced. Otto murmured against my husband's shoulder, "My dear friend Joseph." He was so weak. The hospital staff arrived to collect him a few minutes later. We followed, and my husband was allowed into Otto's room. They spoke of Auschwitz.*[3]

Otto died that night.

Among the helpers, Miep Gies was always the closest to Otto. He lived with her and her husband for seven years after his return from the east. He always said he associated Amsterdam with friendship unto death, and by that he meant Miep Gies. Miep said that people often asked her what it was like to outlive almost everyone whose history she'd shared. She would respond that it was "strange." "Why me?" she would ask. Why was she spared the concentration camp when Kugler and Kleiman were caught hiding Jews and it was clear that she'd been doing so, too?

After Otto moved to Basel, she and Jan visited him every year. When the film of her book *Anne Frank Remembered* was nominated for an Academy Award for Best Documentary in 1996, Miep went with the director, Jon Blair, to Hollywood. She became in effect the spokesperson for Anne's diary after Otto's death, saying:

> *The message to take from Anne's story is to stop prejudice and discrimination right at its beginning. Prejudice starts when we speak about THE Jews, THE Arabs, THE Asians, THE Mexicans, THE Blacks, THE Whites. This leads to the feeling that all members of each such group think and act the same.*[4]

Miep died in 2010 at the age of one hundred.

After the publication of Anne's diary in 1947, Johannes Kleiman regularly took journalists and visitors on guided tours of the secret Annex. Even after Otto moved to Switzerland, Kleiman held power of attorney for him and functioned almost as Otto's private secretary, particularly in his dealings with publishers of Anne's diary. He was deeply involved in the restoration of the Anne Frank House and in 1957 became a member of the board of the Anne Frank Foundation, although he didn't live to see the opening of the museum. He died of a stroke in his office on January 30, 1959. He was sixty-three years old.

Victor Kugler's wife, who had been ill for a long time, died in 1952. Three years later, he married again and moved to Toronto, where his second wife's family lived. He died in Toronto in 1989 at the age of eighty-one. The book about him with the unfortunate title *The Man Who Hid Anne Frank* (it is clear that he was not the only helper) was published in 2008 after both his and Otto's deaths.

Bep Voskuijl married in 1946 and had four children. She never lost contact with Otto, visiting him every week when he was still in Amsterdam and three times a year after he moved to Switzerland. She was always reticent about the war years and her role as a helper and gave few interviews. She met Queen Juliana at the Dutch premiere of the film *The Diary of Anne Frank* by George Stevens, but in a letter to Otto, she admitted that she found it all uncomfortable. She wanted to support what she called "the symbol of the idealized Anne," but it always brought back the pain of what she'd witnessed. "This great pain never leaves my heart," she said.[5]

Everyone who knew Bep remarked that the "once cheerful young woman" always struggled to maintain her balance, unable to accept the deaths of the Annex residents.[6] She died in Amsterdam of an aortic rupture in 1983 at the age of sixty-three.

At Otto's request, in 1972 the four helpers were awarded the Yad Vashem honorary title of Righteous Under the Nations, including Johannes Kleiman, who was acknowledged posthumously.

Otto Frank was determined to be a survivor and not a victim. To be a victim was to give the victory to the Nazis. But tellingly, he never watched a single performance of the play or film based on Anne's diary. According to his stepdaughter, Eva, "He couldn't bear the thought that actresses would be saying the words he once heard Anne and Margot speak, pretending to be the children that he would never see again."[7]

He despised generalizations. Proud of his German heritage, he did not accept the idea of collective guilt. He spent extra time replying to letters from German schoolchildren, wanting them to learn what had happened during the war. As Otto Frank's biographer recorded, in 1952, 88 percent of Germans "said they felt no personal responsibility for the mass exterminations."[8] It would only be the next generation who would confront what actually happened in Germany that gave license to the murderousness of Hitler and the Nazis.

Otto knew that his daughter was a symbol for the millions—both Jews and non-Jews—who had been murdered. Her diary and the secret Annex stood in his mind as both a warning from the past and a source of hope.[9] He wanted people to remember so it wouldn't happen again. He wanted them to know that fascism builds slowly and then one day it is an iron wall that looms and cannot be circumvented. He wanted them to know what can be lost and how fast it can happen.

One can imagine Otto Frank walking the streets of Amsterdam alone in June 1945. How was it possible that the place could still exist when everything he had was gone: his wife, his daughters, his home, his business? He told his mother he was walking in a strange dream and was not yet normal.

Amsterdam today is a city of memory. With eighty monuments to the war, memory is part of the fabric of the present, immediately accessible. You can take a tour of the shadow city, beginning at the Anne Frank House. The bookcase, so indelible in your mind, is as heavy and imposing as you'd imagined. The stairs up to the Annex are steep. The space is so much smaller than you'd thought. In this claustrophobic place, it is impossible not to imagine the fear of occupation.

Next you can go to the infamous Jewish Theater. It is only a facade now. The original interior has been gutted, and one wall now bears a list in bronze of more 6,700 Jewish families who were deported from that location. Each day hundreds of prisoners were crammed into the small space, awaiting transport to Westerbork and then on to one of the extermination camps. People were taken to the station by tram, by truck, or on foot, always at night so there would be few eyewitnesses.

On the second floor of the theater is an interactive map of Bergen-Belsen. When I was there, I watched an elderly man step forward and point to a list. He told the friends who surrounded him that he was number 29: "Unbekannter Jude [unknown Jew]. Hamburger? Alfred?" Fifty children were found hiding with Gentiles, and the Nazis weren't sure that they were Jews. On September 13, 1944, they were transported from Westerbork to Bergen-Belsen. Two months later, they were deported to Theresienstadt. Forty-nine of the children survived, including the man beside me. "What was it like?" his friends asked. "I was four years old. I don't remember," he replied.

Across the street from the theater you can visit the children's nursery. Walter Süskind, a German Jewish refugee who worked for the Expositur at the theater, managed to establish a relationship with Ferdinand aus der Fünten, convincing him to allow the captive children to attend day care. Süskind then connected with the resistance to find places for them to hide. Day care workers would take young children onto the street when the tram stopped in front, obstructing the view of the guards at the theater just across the way. They would then walk away with the children, using the tram for camouflage. The workers also smuggled children out in backpacks and laundry baskets. The gardens of the Pedagogical School two doors down were connected with the day care center, and children were also smuggled out through the fence. The teachers and students at the school were aware of what was happening, but no one spoke of it. At least six hundred children were saved. Walter Süskind was eventually deported and died in Central Europe on February 29, 1945. Today the school is the National Holocaust Museum.[10]

Up the street and around the corner is the beautiful Artis Zoo. At night, during the occupation, dozens of people—Jews, members of the resistance, and those escaping forced labor—would hide there. They "hid in the hayloft above the wild animals, in the aviaries with the ibises, or in the night dens of the polar bears."[11] The manager of the zoo kept their secret. When a *Razzia* was under way, the keeper of the monkeys would put down a plank over the moat surrounding the monkey house to let men and women cross and then remove the plank to keep them safe.

One woman, Duifje van der Brink, lived in the zoo for a couple of years, spending her nights in the wolf house. During the day she sat on a bench near the monkey house and chatted with people, including Germans. No one knew she was Jewish. Over time an estimated two hundred to three hundred people managed to hide in the zoo. You can't help thinking: the animals provided shelter while many humans did not.

Across the avenue from the zoo is the Resistance Museum, filled with the paraphernalia of the underground: presses for printing newspapers, pamphlets, fake ID and food stamps; examples of grotesque anti-Semitic NSB propaganda; weapons for clandestine attacks.

On the walls of the Resistance Museum are murals of NSB parades. Individual figures explain their motives for joining the Nazis:

> *"What attracted me was the energy, the singing, and the sense of belonging."*

"I saw only one choice: National Socialism or the chaos of Communism."

"We couldn't make a living from the shop and the NSB claimed things would get better for the middle class."

"With Germany in power, membership of the NSB offered opportunities for starting a career."

"There was enormous poverty and division in our country. The NSB was opposed to such a pretense of democracy."

"Leadership was something we could build a national community on. With too many choices nothing gets decided and there's always that self-interest hiding round the corner."

Fascism counts on people's credulity, on their craving to believe, on their fear that there is nothing in which to believe.

You might drop by Wilhelmina Catharina School, the only school from which Jewish children were not expelled. Of the 175 children at the school, 71 were Jewish. The Germans did not want Jews and Gentiles in the same classroom, but to expel the Jews would have meant closing the school. Instead, the school authorities built a wall splitting the school in two. The front side was for Gentile children, the back for Jewish children, who came to be called "Backsiders." Eventually the wall was taken down. The children in the front were overjoyed to see the horrible wall gone, but when they crossed over, none of their Jewish friends were left on the other side of the wall; all had been deported. A plaque on the building memorializes them.[12]

If you walk to the old Jewish Quarter, you will see the famous statue of the dockworker. On February 25, 1941, the rolling strike to protest the mass arrest of young Jewish men began, first with workers at the Municipal Cleaning Service and Public Works, then railway workers and tram workers, and finally the dockworkers in the harbor. Shops closed. Citizens accompanied the marchers, smashing the windows of trams still running. The resistance paper asked, "Am I my brother's keeper?" The answer was "Yes." The strike lasted two days before the Germans, armed with guns, violently put down the protest.

You can go sit on Lotty's bench, which you'll find in the upscale Apollolaan district of the city. It is in the exact spot where Lotty and her friend Beppie slept after their return from Auschwitz. When the Germans evacuated the camp, they pulled out the women and sent them on a death march to Beendorf concentration camp, more than four hundred miles away. When the Allies eventually freed Beendorf, those few such as Lotty and Beppie who survived were exchanged for German POWs. When the women finally arrived in Amsterdam on August 26, there was hardly any shelter for Holocaust survivors. They were thrown a horse blanket and left to fend for themselves. "Come," said Lotty to Beppie. "Let's go posh."[13] They slept on a bench in a park in the fancy Apollolaan.

The Dutch government refused to give special preference to returning Jews. The logic was that "the Nazis had treated the Jews differently from the rest of the population and treating the Jews differently now again would no doubt remind everyone of Nazi ideology."[14] The Dutch were simply following the policy set by the Allied authorities, who claimed that to differentiate Jews from other displaced persons would be unfair to non-Jews and would "constitute religious discrimination."[15] In September 2017, Lotty, age ninety-six, was finally recognized for the horrors she had endured and honored with her own bench.

The bronze bust of Geertruida "Truus" Wijsmuller-Meijer, inaugurated in 1965, is now on the Bachplein in south Amsterdam. Truus was a Dutch resistance fighter.

In 1938, the British government agreed to let Jewish children under the age of seventeen enter the United Kingdom for a temporary stay. The Dutch Children's Committee in Amsterdam asked Wijsmuller-Meijer, who was known to be imperturbable and fearless, to go to Vienna to meet Adolf Eichmann, the one in charge of the forced "emigration" of Jews. Apparently, Eichmann found her unbelievable: *"so rein-arisch und dann so verrückt!"* (so purely Aryan and then so crazy!).[16] He promised that he would give her ten thousand Jewish children if she could collect six hundred children in six days after their meeting and get them onto a ship to England. She succeeded. On December 10, six hundred Jewish children left Vienna by train. Until the outbreak of war, she organized *Kindertransporten* (children's transports). Several times a week, she traveled to Germany and Nazi-occupied territories to pick up children. By the time war was declared on September 1, 1939, her organization had saved ten thousand Jewish children. The Germans called her *die verrückte Frau Wijsmuller* (that crazy woman Wijsmuller) because she had helped Jews for free.

Since 1995, the German artist Gunter Demnig has been creating commemorative "stumbling stones." In Amsterdam there are several hundred stones placed in front of the last known formal home addresses of Jews, Roma, Sinti, and others murdered by the Nazis. The stones are inlaid with bronze plaques. As you stumble over them, you stumble over the past; it is part of the fabric of the present. You remember.

Afterword

In the course of this investigation, I was asked many times if I thought we would be able to answer its central question definitively. I couldn't promise, of course, but I did say that we would make a real attempt to discover the most likely cause of the raid on the secret Annex. The process took us nearly five years of scouring the globe, looking for reports that had been lost or misfiled and witnesses who had never been consulted. In the end, our talented, dedicated team of investigators, researchers, and volunteers met our goal: to figure out what happened at Prinsengracht 263. As is common in many cold case investigations, it turned out that a dismissed piece of evidence ended up being the key to solving the nearly eighty-year-old mystery.

As powerful as that discovery is, it is not the only

accomplishment of our investigation. Through the years, we came upon a great deal of information that adds to the understanding of the time period as well as insights into the SD, the V-persons, and the collaborators. We also located and analyzed nearly one thousand *Kopgeld* receipts that shed new light on the SD's payment incentive program to hunt Jews and other Nazi nondesirables. And we cast such a large net with our investigative research that we determined, or at least clarified, what happened in a number of other betrayal cases. I hope that our results might provide some closure to the descendants of those who were captured.

My generation, the so-called baby boomers, are the sons and daughters of the servicemen and -women who fought in World War II. We are the last generation with a true connection to that time. I remember many of the war stories my father and uncles used to tell me—not stories read in books but true first-person accounts. Most baby boomers in law enforcement have already retired or are reaching retirement age. While someone with first-person knowledge is still alive, while records are still available, while relatives of witnesses can come forward, the stories must be told.

I believe that once this book is published and people become familiar with our discoveries, anyone possessing relevant information will contact us and fill in the missing pieces of the puzzle of what happened on August 4, 1944. I truly believe that investigating the past and our interpretation of it is not a finite exercise. For that reason, we have donated our research database to the Dutch state so that others can gain insight into this important period in history.

For me, it has been an honor and a privilege to play some small part in reminding the world that the victims of the Annex and other Jews who were betrayed have not been forgotten.

—Vince Pankoke

THE COLD CASE TEAM

Thijs Bayens	Project director (company CEO)
Luc Gerrits	Project finances (company CFO)
Pieter van Twisk	Head of research (company COO)
Vince Pankoke	Lead case agent (retired special agent of the FBI)
Monique Koemans	Criminologist, historian, and author
Brendan Rook	War crimes investigator
Joachim Bayens	Translator
Veerle de Boer	Researcher
Circe de Bruin	Public historian
Amber Dekker	Military historian
Rory Dekker	Translator
Matthijs de Die le Clercq	Researcher
Nienke Filius	Forensic scientist
Anna Foulidis	Public historian
Marius Helf	Data scientist

Anna Helfrich	Historian
Jean Hellwig	Project manager
Soeliah Hellwig	Gender researcher
Robbert van Hintum	Data scientist
Christine Hoste	Public historian
Nina Kaiser	Documentalist
Linda Leestemaker	Archaeologist, journalist
Bram van der Meer	Investigative psychologist
Lilian Oskam	Criminologist
Welmoed Pluim	Criminologist
Marin Rappard	Heritage researcher
Isis de Ruiter	Documentalist
Cerianne Slagmolen	Historian
Patricia Spronk	Gender researcher
Rinsophie Vellinga	External researcher
Machteld van Voskuilen	Social historian

CONSULTANTS TO THE TEAM

Gerard Aalders	Historian and author
Frans Alkemade	Expert in Bayesian analysis at Alkemade Forensic Reasoning (AFR)
Hubert Berkhout	Archivist
Gertjan Broek	Historian at the Anne Frank House
Roger Depue	Behavioral scientist/profiler (retired from the FBI Behavioral Science Unit)
Wil Fagel	Forensic handwriting examiner
Corien Glaudemans	Historian and researcher at the Haags Gemeentearchief
Bernhard Haas	Forensic document examiner
Eric Heijselaar	Archivist at Stadsarchief Amsterdam
Peter Kroesen	Archivist at Stadsarchief Amsterdam
Carina van Leeuwen	Forensic cold case detective
Guus Meershoek	Historian
Quentin Plant	Data scientist

Sierk Plantinga	Archivist
Leo Simais	Police adviser
Eric Slot	Historian, author, and journalist
Hans Smit	Police adviser
Erik Somers	Historian at NIOD
Gerrold van der Stroom	Historian
Sytze van der Zee	Journalist and author

Acknowledgments

From idea to conclusion, the investigation into what led to the raid on the Annex took well over five years and was aided by two hundred people. While we focused our attention in the book on the leaders and other senior members of the team, there are many more without whom this research would not have been possible. First and foremost, we wish to thank the day-to-day research team that consisted of our regular researchers, Christine Hoste, Circe de Bruin, and Anna Foulidis. They in turn were supported by a team of freelancers, volunteers, and interns: Joachim Bayens, Veerle de Boer, José Boon, Amber Dekker, Rory Dekker, Matthijs de Die le Clercq, Nienke Filius, Anna Helfrich, Soeliah Hellwig, Gülden Ilmaz, Nina Kaiser, Eline Kemps, Linda Leestemaker, Patrick Minks, Lilian Oskam, Welmoed Pluim, Marin Rappard, Anita Rosmolen, Isis de Ruiter, Dorna Saadati, Cerianne Slagmolen, Babette Smits van Warsberghe, Patricia Spronk, Logan Taylor-Black, Mattie Timmer, Maudy Tjho, Rinsophie Vellinga, Marlinde Venema, Machteld van Voskuilen, and Mary Beth Warner.

We are also deeply indebted to many specialists who endorsed our investigation and who assisted us frequently in their areas of expertise. We called them our subject matter experts, or SMEs. They are Roger Depue (retired FBI behavioral science specialist); Bram van der Meer (investigative psychologist and offender-profiling expert); Frans Alkemade (forensic statistician); Bernhard Haas (forensic document examiner); Wil Fagel (former NFI handwriting expert); Carina van Leeuwen (head of police cold case team Amsterdam); Menachem Sebbag (chief rabbi at the Dutch Ministry of Defense); Leo Simais (cold case team, Dutch National Police), and Hans Smit (Dutch National Police). We wish to thank the archivists who aided us: Peter Kroesen and Eric Heijselaar (archivists, SAA), Hubert Berkhout (archivist, NIOD), and Sierk Plantinga (retired archivist, NA). As laymen in the field of digital storage and AI, we also owe gratitude to our digital consultant Quentin Plant. Last, we thank the following authors and historians who were so important to us: Gerard Aalders (historian), David Barnouw (historian), Gertjan Broek (researcher, AFF), Corien Glaudemans (researcher, HGA), Ad van Liempt (journalist and author), Guus Meershoek (historian), Erik Somers (historian), Gerrold van der Stroom (historian), and Sytze van der Zee (journalist and author). (Though we studied and cited and much appreciated their work and in some cases consulted with or interviewed them, these authors and researchers should not be assumed to be supporters of the outcome of our investigation. Indeed, they may not have been informed of our final findings.)

And then there are all those people who provided personal assistance in a different way and on a less frequent basis. These could be witnesses, authors to whom we spoke, archivists who helped us navigate vast public and private records, family researchers and historians, and people representing important institutes.

In alphabetical order, we would like to thank Guido Abuys (Camp Westerbork), Jelmar Ahlers (relative of Tonny Ahlers), Edith Albersheim-Chutkow (Holocaust survivor), Svetlana Amosova (Jewish Museum and Tolerance Center, Moscow), Floriane Azoulay (Arolsen Archives), Freek Baars (Spaarnestad Photo), Francis van den Berg (Historisch Centrum Overijssel), Albert Beuse (Groningen Archives), Rene Bienert (Simon Wiesenthal Center), Gerrit and Sien Blommers (neighborhood experts), Mirjam Bolle (Holocaust survivor and former secretary of the Jewish Council), Petra Boomgaart (historian), Eric Bremer (relative of Jetje Bremer), Monique Brinks (historian), Jeroen de Bruyn and Joop van Wijk (coauthors), Peter Buijs (Jewish Historical Museum), Cornelis Cappon (University of Amsterdam), Greg Celerse (World War II researcher), Marcelle Cinq-Mars (Library and Archives Canada), Sara-Joelle Clark and Ron Coleman (United States Holocaust Memorial Museum), Alexander Comber (Library and Archives Canada), Ryan Cooper (pen pal of Otto Frank), Jopie Davidse (World War II resident of Amsterdam), Peter Douwes (relative of Cor Suijk), Jan Erik Dubbelman (friend of Cor Suijk), Rebecca Erbelding (United States Holocaust Memorial Museum), Zeno Geradts (professor of forensic data analysis, University of Amsterdam), Joop Goudsmit (Dutch Holocaust survivor), Koos Groen (journalist and author), Louis de Groot (Dutch Holocaust survivor), Katja Happe (historian), Ron van Hasselt (author), Hubertine Heijermans (relative of Hubert Selles), René van Heijningen (historian, NIOD Institute for War, Holocaust and Genocide Studies), Maarten van Helden (son of Detective Arend van Helden) and his wife, Els, Stephan van Hoeve (son of greengrocer Hendrik van Hoeve), Jan Hopman (journalist and author), Fleur van Houwen (linguistic expert, Free University of Amsterdam), Ann Huitzing (historian), Abraham Kaper (grandson of Abraham Kaper), J. van der Kar (notary), Christine Kausch (historian), Nancy Kawalek (professor, University of Chicago), Edwin Klijn (researcher, NIOD Institute for War, Holocaust and Genocide Studies), Teun Koetsier and Elbert Roest (coauthors), Bas Kortholt (historian), Hans Krol (historian, Noord-Hollands Archief), Gerlof Langerijs (history researcher), Carol Ann Lee (author), Richard Lester (author), Jacqueline van Maarsen (friend of Anne Frank and author), Myriam Maater–van Hulst (Holocaust survivor), Eva Moraal (historian), Claudia Morawetz (daughter of the composer Oskar Morawetz), Melissa Müller (author), Sylvia Naylor (National Archives at College Park), John Neiman (friend of Miep and Jan Gies), Jean Nieuwenhuijse (Centraal Bureau voor Genealogie, Den Haag), Albert Oosthoek (historian, NA), Jan Out (Dutch National Police Archivist), Albert Penners (physiotherapist and informer), Joost Rethmeier (historian), Jan Rijnders (historian), Sally Rosen (investigator), Regina Salle (witness), Eva Schloss (Holocaust survivor and stepdaughter of Otto Frank), Kyra Schuster (United States Holocaust Memorial Museum), Raymund Schütz (historian), Derek Selles (grandson of Hubert Selles), Eda Shapiro and Rick Kardonne (coauthors), Eric Slot (historian), Dineke Stam (former researcher, Anne Frank House), Jol van Soest (family historian), Michel Theeboom (Dutch National Police/ Jewish Police Network), Paul Theelen (family historian), Stephan Tyas (historian), Jacob Nathan Velleman (psychiatrist), Rian Verhoeven (historian), Gerrit van der Vorst (historian), Hugo Voskuijl (relative of Bep Voskuijl), Jan Watterman (historian), Rene Wessels (relative of former Prinsengracht 263 owner), Joop van Wijk (son of Bep Voskuijl), Cara Wilson-Granat (pen friend of Otto Frank), Rolf Wolfswinkel (historian and professor, New York University), Elliot Wrenn (United States Holocaust Memorial Museum), Kees Jan van der Zijden (notary), Giora Zwilling (Arolsen Archives), and many, many others.

We also want to thank all the people who helped us develop our own digital investigational infrastructure and artificial intelligence, principally Xomnia, whose managing director, Ollie Dapper, from the start fully supported our project and whose data scientists Robbert van Hintum and Marius Helf were responsible for the data store that functioned as the foundation of the later AI program. This program was run on Microsoft Azure software, which was made available for us by Microsoft, thanks to Brian Marble and Jordan Passon. The software was further customized by a team from

Plain Concepts: Ingrid Babel, Manuel Rodrigo Cabello Malagón, Marta de Carlos López, Alejandro Hidalgo, Carlos Landeras Martinez, Olga Martí Rodrigues, Francisco Pelaez Aller, Fleurette Poiesz, Sara San Luis Rodríguez, and Daniela Solis. And finally, we are grateful to the people from the Branded Entertainment Network—Hannah Butters, Erin Larnder, Abigail Mieszczak, and Loriel Weiss—who provided much of the hardware needed to run the software, as well as Paul Oranje and Anton Raves, who provided all ICT support for the project.

The archives played a crucial role in our investigation. They are mentioned all through the book and in many of the sources and footnotes, but we would still like highlight some of them. First of all, the people at the Anne Frank Stichting were very helpful, especially Teresien da Silva, Maatje Mostart, and Annemarie Bekker. We also owe gratitude to the Jewish Historical Museum in Amsterdam and especially its director, Emile Schrijver. At the Amsterdam City Archives we received great support from its director, Bert de Vries, and program manager, Benno van Tilburg.

And finally, the two institutes where, without doubt, our researchers spent most of their time, the NIOD Institute for War, Holocaust and Genocide Studies in Amsterdam and the National Archives in The Hague.

Of the first we would like to mention its director, Frank van Vree, who immediately sympathized with our project, and of the latter we would especially like to thank its former director, Collections and Public, Irene Gerrits, and service manager, Fenna Flietstra. We are grateful also to the many archive employees of both institutions who patiently continued to provide us with all requested files.

Ultimately, the investigation is key, but as with most things in life, it required adequate funding. From the start it was clear that this would be an expensive endeavor, and it took us quite some time to raise the necessary funds. From the moment we went public with our idea, it became clear that we were touching on a very sensitive topic. Afraid of the outcome, many potential sponsors did not want to take the risk of being involved. We were adamant that the investigation would be absolutely objective, and there were some parties who showed interest in a sponsorship, but we ultimately declined their support because we suspected that they might have interests that conflicted with the independence and objectivity we required. We reached out to the public and received many small private donations, for which we are extremely grateful. Jaap Rosen Jacobson and Oshri Even-Zohar came to our rescue in our darkest hour of need.

We also received a generous grant from the City of Amsterdam, thanks particularly to city councilors Simone Kukenheim and Touria Meliani, who fully understood that during the war the city of Amsterdam lost 10 percent of its citizens, an atrocity that should never be forgotten and that left a permanent scar on the city. We are also deeply indebted to Ger Baron, Tijs Roelofs, and Tamas Erkelens of the City of Amsterdam for their advice and support. And, of course, we received publisher advances for this book.

Then there are, of course, the people who made this publication possible. First, author Rosemary Sullivan, who, notwithstanding the great distance between Canada and the Netherlands as well as the severe covid-19 restrictions, managed to capture the essence of this project in a poignant way and produce this wonderful book. With so many actors scattered over multiple countries and continents, over so much time, and with so much information to sift through, we can only appreciate, admire, and respect her work.

We are deeply grateful to our HarperCollins editor, Sara Nelson, who, with her never-ending enthusiasm and confidence, made this an unforgettable journey for us all. We are also very grateful to our publisher, Jonathan Burnham, who along with Sara believed in this project from the beginning and on whose advice and support we could always count. Our gratitude also extends to our Dutch publishers, managing director Tanja Hendriks and publisher Laurens Ubbink of Ambo|Anthos, who gave us valuable input during the writing process. Our gratitude also extends to our literary agents, Marianne Schönbach and Diana Gvozden from the Marianne Schönbach Literary Agency in Amsterdam.

International projects of this size also need legal counsel. For legal advice we initially turned to Job Hengeveld of Hengeveld Advocaten and Philip van Wijnen. Eventually we were supported by the international law firm Bird & Bird and would especially like to thank Jeroen van der Lee, Jochem Apon, and Olaf Trojan. All of them did excellent work for us. We would also like to thank independent adviser Martin Senftleben of the University of Amsterdam for his excellent advice.

We owe great gratitude to several external advisers who guided us on our long and arduous journey: Edward Asscher, Boris Dittrich, Harry Dolman, Nelleke Geel, Dries van Ingen, Willem van der Knaap, Margreet Nanning, Kate Pankoke, Bert Wiggers, and many others. And then there are the esteemed members of our advisory board, who guided us through some of the more sensitive matters we encountered; we would like to express our gratitude to Roger van Boxtel, Job Cohen (chairman), and Michiel Westermann. Their advice was invaluable, but they should bear no responsibility with regard to our conclusions.

Finally, a project of this magnitude is not possible without people who tirelessly take care of business and logistics. Two people in particular helped make this project happen: our project manager, Jean Hellwig, and our executive assistant, Wieke van der Kley. We also owe much gratitude to our production manager, Mardou Jacobs, and our financial controller, Ali Banyahia; our two wonderful interns, Jason Akkerman and Daniel Osterwald; and Stan Schram, who found our office.

Amsterdam, December 4, 2020
Thijs Bayens
Pieter van Twisk
Luc Gerrits

It's been a privilege to work on this project, and for that I thank Thijs Bayens, Pieter van Twisk, and Vince Pankoke. Thijs provided inspiration, Pieter provided precision, and Vince provided knowledge and moral support. They made my initial stay in Amsterdam immensely fruitful and, after COVID 19 attacked the world, patiently answered my Zoom calls and my thousands of emails. I would like to thank Brendan Rook for his professionalism, which helped sharpen my own angle of vision, and Monique Koemans for her warmth and expertise as she invited me to join her research sessions. Jean Hellwig, the project manager, was most generous with his time in solving all the logistical problems that came up. I would also like to thank the young researchers I worked with, including Circe de Bruin, Christine Hoste, Anna Foulidis, Linda Leestemaker, and Wieke van der Kley, all of whom facilitated my various visits to the archives, including the NIOD Institute for War, Holocaust and Genocide Studies and the Amsterdam City Archives; to museums such as the National Holocaust Museum and the Resistance Museum; and especially road trips to the Memorial Center Camp Westerbork and The Hague. I would like to thank the Amsterdam Writers' Residency of the Nederlands Letterenfonds for providing me with a wonderful apartment in the heart of Amsterdam in which to pursue my work.

I would like to acknowledge my sister Colleen Sullivan, who read my manuscript in its early drafts and offered vital encouragement; Karen Mulhallen, whose support and advice through the long process of writing were invaluable; Plum Johnson, who listened to my deliberations; and Mary Germaine, who was always there in a computer emergency.

I would like to thank my Canadian editor, Iris Tupholme, with whom I first worked in 1987 and who has shepherded my books through the difficult process of writing. As always, here, too, she has been wonderfully supportive, wise, and a joy to work with. She has always known how to encourage me to move beyond my own expectations. I owe her a lifetime debt.

It's been a privilege to work with Sara Nelson. She is a great editor, always and immediately there; exacting and brilliant in her editorial comments; a perfectionist who encourages and demands the highest standards. Her patience is legion. All writers should be so lucky to have such an editor. I would especially like to thank Jonathan Burnham, president and publisher of the Harper division, who initially suggested me as the writer for this project, launching me on a deeply moving journey. He generously read the manuscript and offered crucial suggestions. And finally, I would like to thank my agent, Jackie Kaiser, who, like Iris, has always been there for me, providing support and advice whenever I need them. She is wise and impassioned and cares deeply about writers and writing. I am fortunate that she is my agent.

I dedicate this book to my sisters, Patricia, Sharon, and Colleen; to my brother, Terry; and to my husband and lifetime companion, Juan Opitz. With love and gratitude.

Toronto, April 1, 2021
Rosemary Sullivan

Archives and Institutes

Anne Frank Stichting (Anne Frank Foundation), Amsterdam, Netherlands

Arolsen Archives (formerly International Tracing Service), Bad Arolsen, Germany

Bundesarchiv Berlin (Federal Archives Berlin), Berlin, Germany

Deutsches Literaturarchiv Marbach (German Literature Archive Marbach), Marbach, Germany

Gedenkstätte und Museum Sachsenhausen (Memorial and Museum Sachsenhausen), Oranienburg, Germany

Groninger Archieven (Groningen Archives), Groningen, Netherlands

Haags Gemeentearchief (Hague City Archives), Den Haag, Netherlands

Herinneringscentrum Kamp Westerbork (Memorial Center Camp Westerbork), Hooghalen, Netherlands

Historisch Centrum Overijssel (Historical Center Overijssel), Zwolle, Netherlands

Jewish Cultural Quarter, Amsterdam, Netherlands

Library and Archives Canada, Ottawa, Canada

Nationaal Archief (National Archives), Den Haag, Netherlands

The National Archives at College Park, MD

Nationaal Monument Oranjehotel, Scheveningen, Netherlands

Nederlands Dagboekarchief (National Diary Archives), Amsterdam, Netherlands

NIOD Institute for War, Holocaust and Genocide Studies, Amsterdam, Netherlands

Noord-Hollands Archief (North Holland Archives), Haarlem, Netherlands

Österreichisches Staatsarchiv (Austrian State Archives), Vienna, Austria

Pickford Center for Motion Picture Study, Los Angeles

Russian State Military Archive, Moscow, Russia

Simon Wiesenthal Center, Vienna, Austria

Stadsarchief Amsterdam (Amsterdam City Archives), Amsterdam, Netherlands

Streekarchief Gooi en Vechtstreek (Regional Archives of Gooi and Vechtstreek), Hilversum, Netherlands

United States Holocaust Memorial Museum, Washington, DC

USC Shoah Foundation—The Institute for Visual History and Education, Los Angeles

Verzetsmuseum (Resistance Museum), Amsterdam, Netherlands

The Wiener Holocaust Library, London, UK

Wiener Stadt- und Landesarchiv (City and Provincial Archives of Vienna), Vienna, Austria.

Yad Vashem Archives, Jerusalem, Israel

Glossary

Abteilung Hausraterfassung (Household Inventory Agency): The department that dealt with the confiscation of Jewish household goods, which were subsequently transported to Germany. This department fell under the Zentralstelle für Jüdische Auswanderung and also worked closely with the Einsatzstab Reichsleiter Rosenberg (ER) and the Lippmann-Rosenthal bank. The Henneicke Column worked for this department.

Abwehr: German military intelligence.

Amersfoort camp: A German police concentration and transit camp in the Netherlands south of the city of Amersfoort. It was operational from August 1941 to April 1945. During that period 37,000 people were incarcerated there, of whom around 20,000 were deported to camps in the east. Around 670 people died in the camp.

Anne Frank Fonds (AFF): A foundation established in Basel, Switzerland, in 1963 by Otto Frank. It represents the Frank family, distributes Anne's diary, and manages copyrights.

Anne Frank Stichting (AFS) (Anne Frank Foundation): The Amsterdam-based foundation established in 1957 by Otto Frank. Originally established to save the Anne Frank House and Annex from demolition, the foundation is also entrusted with the management of property and the propagating of Anne's story and her ideals. The AFS organizes exhibitions and information about Anne Frank all over the world and is also committed to fighting anti-Semitism and racism.

Arbeitseinsatz: Forced labor for workers from the occupied territories during World War II to replace the labor of the German men who served as soldiers. In the Netherlands, *Arbeitseinsatz* was mandatory from January 1942. Men who would not respond to their call-up had to go into hiding.

Arrest Tracking Project: An investigative initiative by the Cold Case Team to research all arrests of Jews in 1943 and 1944 to determine the modi operandi of the Jew hunters: who worked with whom, what methods they used, how they obtained information, and so on.

Auschwitz (Auschwitz-Birkenau) concentration camp: The largest concentration and death camp in the Third Reich. It consisted of almost forty subcamps, of which Birkenau was the largest. It was established in 1942 near the south Polish city of Oświęcim. During the war almost 1 million people, predominantly Jews, were exterminated there.

Bergen-Belsen camp: One of the larger prisoner of war and concentration camps, near Celle in the north of Germany, where more than seventy thousand people died during the Second World War. This is the camp where Anne and Margot died in early 1945.

Besluit Buitengewone Rechtspleging (Special Justice Act): A special law drawn up by the Dutch government in exile in London at the end of 1943; it regulated the organization and prosecution of people who had collaborated with the Germans or were considered war criminals.

Bureau Joodse Zaken (BJA) (Bureau of Jewish Affairs): Originally a department of the Amsterdam police charged with detecting violations of Jewish measures imposed by the Germans in the occupied Netherlands. After the Netherlands was declared "Jew free" in 1943, the officers of this unit were assigned to department IV B4 of the Sicherheitsdienst (SD) and predominantly hunted Jews in hiding.

Bureau Nationale Veiligheid (BNV) (Bureau of National Security): A provisional postwar Dutch intelligence and security service (founded in 1945). It later became the Binnenlandse Veiligheidsdienst (BVD), or Internal Security Service, and is now known as the Algemene Inlichtingen- en Veiligheidsdienst (AIVD), or General Intelligence and Security Service.

Centraal Archief van de Bijzondere Rechtspleging (CABR) (Central Archives of Extraordinary Justice): The special archive of all cases that were brought to justice after the war under the Special Justice Act of 1943 by the exiled Dutch government in London. It is kept for the most part at the Nationaal Archief (National Archives) in The Hague.

Colonne Henneicke (Henneicke Column): A group of over fifty Dutch Nazi collaborators, led by the (partly) German Wim Henneicke. They were active as bounty hunters in the period between March and October 1943. The group is estimated to have been responsible for the deportation of more than eight thousand Jews. The group worked for the Abteilung Hausraterfassung.

Comité voor Joodsche Vluchtelingen (CJV) (Committee for Jewish Refugees): An aid organization set up in the Netherlands to accommodate the growing number of Jewish refugees from Germany; active between

1933 and 1941. The CJV mediated in matters concerning emergency relief, education, emigration, exit visas, and residence permits.

Dachau concentration camp: The first concentration camp in Nazi Germany, established in 1933 in the vicinity of Munich. Almost fifty thousand people died in Dachau.

Dolle Dinsdag (Mad Tuesday): September 5, 1944. After major Allied advances, the rumor spread that the Netherlands would be liberated at any moment. The Dutch started to celebrate openly, and Germans and collaborators fled on a large scale. Ultimately, the Allied advance was limited to the southern part of the Netherlands, and the Germans held out for another eight months.

Einsatzstab (Operation Staff) Reichsleiter Rosenberg (ER): A Nazi looting organization named after Alfred Rosenberg that systematically stole artwork and cultural goods from the German-occupied countries and took them to Germany.

Euterpestraat: The name commonly used for the Amsterdam Sicherheitsdienst (SD) headquarters located at Euterpestraat 99, Amsterdam, opposite the Zentralstelle building at Adama van Scheltema Square, which also housed the IV B4 Jew-hunting unit.

Expositur: The office of the Jewish Council, responsible for liaising with the German authorities.

Februaristaking (February Strike): A labor strike on February 25 and 26, 1941, that started in Amsterdam and spread to the rest of the Netherlands. The strike was the only massive and open protest against the persecution of the Jews in occupied Europe. The strike was triggered by the first raids in Amsterdam, in which hundreds of Jewish men were arrested.

Geheime Staatspolizei (Gestapo): The secret political police in Nazi Germany. The Gestapo fell under the SS.

Grüne Polizei (Green Police): The Ordnungspolizei, police units that carried out the day-to-day policing tasks in Germany and occupied countries. Due to the green color of their uniforms, they were nicknamed Grüne Polizei. SD officers were often mistakenly called Grüne Polizei.

Hollandsche Schouwburg (Dutch Theater): A theater on Plantage Parklaan in Amsterdam. It was situated in the Jewish Quarter established by the Germans during the occupation of the Netherlands. In 1942, it became a gathering place from which Jews were deported via Camp Westerbork and Camp Vught to extermination camps. It is now a memorial site.

De IJzeren Garde (Iron Guard): A small fascist splinter party that had broken away from the somewhat larger Nationaal-Socialistiche Nederlandsche Arbeiderspartij (NSNAP). The movement was strongly anti-Semitic and pro-Nazi.

***Het Joodsche Weekblad* (The Jewish Weekly):** A weekly magazine published by the Jewish Council that appeared in the Netherlands during the Second World War. The weekly was the only permitted Jewish publication. It appeared every Friday from April 1941 to September 1943 and was used to proclaim the anti-Jewish measures imposed by the Germans. Since it was distributed only to Jews, the measures could be hidden from non-Jews, and thus it was a means of further isolating the Jews from Dutch society.

Joodse Coördinatie Commissie (JCC) (Jewish Coordination Commission): A Jewish organization founded immediately after the German occupation to provide support to the Jewish community. The committee offered advice, organized cultural activities, and provided financial assistance. The JCC refused to negotiate directly with the Germans since it felt that only the Dutch government could do so. After the Jewish Council was established, the JCC was disbanded by the Germans.

Joodse Ereraad (Jewish Honor Council): An organization that called to account Jews thought to have collaborated with the Germans. Established at the beginning of 1946, it continued until 1950. The council had no legal authority, but it published its verdicts and could call for people's expulsion from the Jewish community.

Joodse Raad/Judenraete (JR) (Jewish Council): A Jewish organization established on German orders in February 1941 to manage and control the Jewish community. It started in Amsterdam but soon gained influence over the rest of the Netherlands.

Jordaan: An old neighborhood in the center of Amsterdam where Otto's business/annex was located. It was a typical working-class neighborhood with many craftsmen and small businesses, with housing in poor condition and many people unemployed. But it was known for its distinct culture.

Kopgeld: The name of the bounty that was paid to Jew hunters and police officers for Jews they arrested. The amount varied from 7.50 guilders at the start of the war to as much as 40 guilders at the end.

Landelijke Knokploegen (KP, LKP): An armed resistance group founded by the Landelijke Organisatie voor Hulp aan Onderduikers (LO). People in hiding urgently needed all kinds of documents, such as identity cards and coupon cards, and the KP seized those items by robbery or violence.

Landelijke Organisatie voor Hulp aan Onderduikers (LO) (National Organization for Aid to People in Hiding): A Dutch resistance movement that from 1942 until the end of the war was active in helping people who needed to go into hiding.

Lippmann-Rosenthal bank/LIRO bank: A formerly Jewish bank that was confiscated and turned into a Nazi bank that registered Jewish property and subsequently robbed Jews. The stolen assets were used, among other things, to finance the Holocaust.

Mapping Project: An investigative initiative by the Cold Case Team in which all registered addresses of NSB members, SD informants, and V-people living in Amsterdam were identified. Xomnia used this data for the interactive digital maps.

Mauthausen concentration camp: A concentration camp near Linz, Austria. The camp was established in 1938. Almost one hundred thousand people died in the camp. It was well known in the Netherlands even during the war, since most of the Jews who were arrested in February 1941 were sent there and died within a couple of months. The name "Mauthausen" became synonymous with "death."

Mischling: A legal term used in Nazi Germany to denote persons who were deemed not fully Jewish. *Mischlinge* were classified into various categories depending on the number of their Jewish ancestors.

Mittelbau (Mittelbau-Dora) concentration camp: A concentration camp and labor camp in central Germany that became operational in August 1943 and consisted of many dozens of subcamps. Primarily a labor camp where prisoners produced V1 and V2 rockets, it was also a site where twenty thousand people died.

Nationaal-Socialistische Beweging (NSB) (National Socialist Movement): The Dutch National Socialist movement, which was led by Anton Mussert and existed from 1931 to 1945. Before the war it had some thirty thousand members; during the occupation it grew to around one hundred thousand members at its peak in 1943. In the beginning it was not anti-Semitic and even had Jewish members, which changed in 1938. At the end of 1941, all political parties except the NSB were dissolved.

Nationalsozialistische Deutsche Arbeiterpartei (NSDAP) (National Socialist German Workers' Party): The formal political party of the National Socialist movement in Germany, established in 1920. Adolf Hitler was the head of the party.

Nationalsozialistisches Kraftfahrkorps (NSKK) (National Socialist Motor Corps): A military unit that with the help of motorized transport supplied the various fronts. During the war the corps was filled with people from the occupied territories.

Nederlandse Beheersinstituut (NBI) (Netherlands Administrative Institute): The institute established in August 1945 that was charged with tracing, managing, and possibly liquidating traitors' assets, enemy assets, and the assets of persons who had disappeared during the war.

Neuengamme concentration camp: A concentration camp near Hamburg, Germany. It was established in 1938 and run by the SS. Around forty-three thousand people are estimated to have been murdered there.

Nürnberger Gesetze (Nuremberg Laws): A collection of anti-Jewish racial laws introduced in Germany in 1935. The laws were intended to legislate the deprivation of the rights of Jews. During the occupation of the Netherlands, the population was also subject to measures based on these laws.

Opekta/Nederlandsche Opekta Maatschappij: A subsidiary of the German company Opekta GmbH of Cologne, founded in 1933. The company was managed by Otto Frank for twenty years. During the war the company was renamed Gies & Co. The company sold pectin products that were used in the production of jam.

Oranjehotel: The nickname of the police prison in Scheveningen during the war. More than twenty-five thousand people were imprisoned there, accused of various crimes including resistance, derogatory language toward Germans, and economic crimes, such as theft and war profiteering. Jews, Jehovah's Witnesses, Roma, and Sinti were also imprisoned there.

Ordedienst (OD): One of the biggest resistance groups in the Netherlands prior to the LO. It was founded in 1940 with the aim of filling the power vacuum that the Germans would leave behind after their departure. During the war, the OD was involved in sabotage and providing intelligence to the Allies.

Het Parool (The Password or The Motto): One of the most famous resistance newspapers in the Netherlands. What started as a short newsletter developed into a real newspaper in February 1941. During the war, about ninety people working for the newspaper were arrested and murdered. *Het Parool* still exists and is a Social Democratic newspaper in the Amsterdam region.

Pectacon: Otto Frank's company, established in June 1938 to sell ground meat, herbs, and spices. Hermann van Pels worked for Pectacon.

Persoonsbewijs (PB): An identity card that, from April 1941, all Dutch citizens aged fifteen and older were required to carry. It was introduced by order of the Germans and turned out to be a great help in the persecution of Jews and resistance fighters. The identity card of Jews was printed with a large black *J*. People with a *Sperre* had a *Sperre* stamp on their identity cards.

Politieke Opsporingsdienst (POD) (Political Investigation Service): A police branch dedicated to tracing and arresting people suspected of collaboration and war crimes. The POD was started in February 1945 and fell under the military authority that was in power directly after the war.

Politieke Recherche Afdeling (PRA) (Political Investigation Department): The new name of the POD from March 1946 after the military authority handed over power to the civil administration and political order was restored. It was under the Ministry of Justice.

Pulsen (pulses): The nickname for the emptying of houses of Jews in Amsterdam who were deported, after the Abraham Puls moving company, which would come within a few days to empty the homes. Abraham Puls was a Dutch NSB member.

Radio Oranje (Radio Orange): The name of a fifteen-minute radio program that was broadcast every evening at

20:15 by BBC European Service. It was organized by the Dutch government in exile in London. The first broadcast took place on July 28, 1940. Many people in the Netherlands had access to an illegal radio set and would secretly listen to the program.

Ravensbrück concentration camp: A concentration camp predominantly for women, about fifty miles north of Berlin. From its opening in 1939 until liberation, approximately thirty thousand people died there.

Razzia (pl. Razzias): A large-scale Nazi hunt for a certain group of people (Jews, resistance fighters, people who were dodging mandatory labor duty). *Razzias* were held throughout the Third Reich.

Referat IV B4 (section): The section within the Sicherheidsdienst (SD) charged with Jewish affairs. Under Adolf Eichmann, it was the organization responsible for the deportation of Jews to the extermination camps. It was referred to colloquially as the Jew-hunting unit.

Reichskommissar für die besetzten niederländischen Gebiete: Civilian Reich Commissioner for the Netherlands Arthur Seyss-Inquart.

Residents Project: An investigative initiative by the Cold Case Team in which all homes surrounding the Annex were researched to determine who lived where and what could be discovered about their history, political orientation, criminal records, and other information.

Rijksinstituut voor Oorlogsdocumentatie (RIOD): Netherlands State Institute for War Documentation; now called the NIOD Institute for War, Holocaust and Genocide Studies.

Sachsenhausen concentration camp: A concentration camp situated twenty-five miles north of Berlin. It was a relatively large camp that, from its start in 1936 until liberation, housed over two hundred thousand prisoners, of whom approximately fifty thousand died. The conditions in Sachsenhausen were barbaric, and prisoners were shot or hanged on a daily basis.

Schutzstaffel (SS): Originally a paramilitary organization, founded in 1925, that acted as Adolf Hitler's personal bodyguard. The group grew into what the Nazis saw as an elite unit, led by Heinrich Himmler, and was divided into the regular SS and the Waffen-SS. It was the most powerful organization in the Nazi state and was predominantly responsible for the execution of the Holocaust.

Sicherheitsdienst (SD) (Security Service): The intelligence service of the German state, which also provided support to the Gestapo and cooperated with the Administration of the Interior. It was under the SS and was led by Reinhard Heydrich. The SD was tasked with observing and prosecuting political opponents of the Third Reich, including the Jews.

Sicherheitspolizei (SiPo): The German security police.

Signalementenblad: A magazine published beginning in October 1943 by the Ordedienst (OD) resistance movement. It contained the names, descriptions, and photos of more than seventy traitors and collaborators. It was printed for resistance workers so that they could identify hostiles.

Sobibor concentration camp: An extermination camp in eastern Poland. The camp operated from April 1942 to November 1943. At least 170,000 people, mostly Jews, were deported to Sobibor. Hardly anyone who was deported to Sobibor survived. An estimated 34,000 Dutch Jews were murdered there.

Sperre (pl. Sperres): A temporary exemption from deportation that was issued by the Jewish Council after approval by the Zentralstelle. There were many grounds on which to qualify for a *Sperre*, including being indispensable to the war industry and working for the Jewish Council. Many of the *Sperres* needed to be purchased or had a processing fee associated with them (such as the 120,000 *Sperre*). The funds would ultimately go to the German war effort.

Staatsbedrijf der Posterijen, Telegrafie en Telefonie (PTT): The Dutch state-owned company responsible for the post, telegraph, telephone, and radiotelephone. Privatized in 1998, it is now known as KPN.

Stadsarchief Amsterdam: Amsterdam City Archives (ACA).

Statements Project: An investigative initiative of the Cold Case Team to collect all statements made by witnesses over the years in print, audio, or video format with regard to the raid. These were placed onto a timeline to identify contradictions or corroborations.

Stichting Toezicht Politieke Delinquenten (STPD) (Political Deliquents Supervision Foundation): An organization founded in September 1945 out of concern about the possible social disruptions caused by the presence of so many political delinquents. Its aim was to assist in their return to society. People suspected of collaboration could be excluded from prosecution if they were placed under the supervision of the STPD.

Theresienstadt concentration camp: A concentration camp and ghetto approximately forty-five miles north of Prague established by the Schutzstaffel (SS) in 1941. It served three purposes: a way station to the extermination camps, a "retirement settlement" for elderly and prominent Jews, and a camp used to mislead the public about the horrors of the Holocaust.

United States Holocaust Memorial Museum (USHMM): A museum located in Washington, DC.

Utrechts Kindercomité (Utrecht Children's Committee): A Dutch resistance group from Utrecht that was engaged in the hiding of several hundred Jewish children.

Verzuiling (pillarization): The division of a society into groups, or "pillars," on a philosophical, religious, or socioeconomic basis. These groups voluntarily separated from one another. For example, Protestants would go to Protestant shops, Protestant sports clubs, and Protestant schools, listen to Protestant radio, read Protestant newspapers, and vote for Protestant political parties. Since the members of the various pillars seldom mixed, there was little solidarity between them.

Vertrouwens-Mann, Vertrouwens-Frau (V-Man, V-Woman): Terms used for civilians working undercover for the Sicherheitsdienst (SD). They were used for gathering information on Jews in hiding, downed pilots, and members of the resistance. Those informants were ideologically motivated, acted for profit, or were coerced.

Vught concentration camp: A concentration camp near the city of Den Bosch in the south of the Netherlands.

The camp was completed in 1942 and was under command of the SS. It was designed to relieve the pressure on the Amersfoort and Westerbork camps and to serve as a labor camp for surrounding industries. In October 1944, it was liberated by the Allies. During the war it held around thirty thousand prisoners, of whom almost eight hundred died.

Waffen-SS: The military fighting branch of the SS under Heinrich Himmler. Founded in 1934 under the name SS-Verfügungstruppe, it was renamed Waffen-SS in 1940. It was considered an elite fighting force, and its members were known for their fanatical ideological zeal.

Wannsee Conference: A meeting of fifteen senior Nazi officials (among others Reinhardt Heydrich and Adolf Eichmann) held on January 20, 1942, at Villa Marlier on the Wannsee near Berlin. The main subject of the meeting was the large-scale destruction of European Jewry.

Weerbaarheidsafdeling (WA) (Resilicnce Department): The uniformed militia of the Dutch Nationaal-Socialistische Beweging (NSB).

Wehrmacht: The German Army.

Westerbork camp: A refugee camp in the northeast of the Netherlands built by the Dutch government in 1938. During the war, the camp was transformed into a transit camp from which 102,000 Jews and more than 200 Roma were deported by train to concentration and extermination camps in the east. After liberation the camp was used to imprison suspected war criminals and collaborators.

Wirtschaftsprüfstelle (WSP) (Economic Inspection Agency): The agency by which the German occupier kept records of all Jewish property. From October 1940, Jewish companies were obliged to register with the WSP, which was part of the Generalkommission für Finanzen und Wirtschaft (General Commission for Finance and Economy). From March 1941, Jewish companies could be taken over by Aryan deputies and eventually liquidated. This was done by the trust company known as Omnia-Treuhandgesellschaft.

Zentralstelle für Jüdische Auswanderung (Central Agency for Jewish Emigration): The organization founded on the orders of Sicherheitsdienst (SD) leader Reinhard Heydrich that aimed to expel Jews from society, first by emigration and later by forced deportation to concentration and extermination camps. The Zentralstelle's Amsterdam office was located on Adama van Scheltemaplein opposite the SD headquarters. Both buildings were bombed on November 26, 1944, by twenty-four RAF Hawker Typhoon bombers.

Notes

Preface

1 Femke Halsema, speech at the May 4, 2019, National Remembrance Day commemoration on Dam Square, Amsterdam, translated by the Cold Case Team.

Chapter 1: The Raid and the Green Policeman

1 French television interview, 1960s, cited in Carol Ann Lee, *The Hidden Life of Otto Frank* (New York: Harper Perennial, 2003), 130.

2 Menno Metselaar et al., eds., *Anne Frank House: A Museum with a Story* (Amsterdam: Anne Frank Stichting, 2001), 176.

3 Ernst Schnabel, *The Footsteps of Anne Frank*, translated by Richard and Clara Winston (Harpenden,

UK: Southbank Publishing, 2014), 133. One in four prisoners in Theresienstadt died.

4 Jeroen de Bruyn and Joop van Wijk, *Anne Frank: The Untold Story: The Hidden Truth About Eli Vossen, the Youngest Helper of the Secret Annex*, trans. Tess Stoop (Laag-Soeren, Netherlands: Bep Voskuijl Productions, 2018), 112.

5 Schnabel, *The Footsteps of Anne Frank*, 139.

6 Jules Huf, "Listen, We Are Not Interested in Politics: Interview with Karl Silberbauer," translated by Joachim Bayens and Rory Dekker, *De Groene Amsterdammer*, May 14, 1986 (first published in *Kurier* on November 22, 1963).

Chapter 2: *The Diary of Anne Frank*

1 Anne Frank, diary entry, October 29, 1943, in *The Diary of a Young Girl: The Definitive Edition*, edited by Otto H. Frank and Mirjam Pressler (New York: Doubleday, 1995), 139.

2 Anne Frank, diary entry, April 11, 1944, in ibid., 262.

3 Elie Wiesel, *Night*, translated by Marion Wiesel (New York: Farrar, Straus and Giroux, 2006), ix.

4 Ian Thomson, *Primo Levi* (New York: Vintage, 2003), 244.

5 Frank, diary entry, July 15, 1944, in *The Diary of a Young Girl*, 333.

6 Cynthia Ozick, "Who Owns Anne Frank?," *New Yorker*, September 28, 1997, https://www.newyorker.com/magazine/1997/10/06/who-owns-anne-frank.

7 Frank, diary entry, May 3, 1944, in *The Diary of a Young Girl*, 281.

8 Walter C. Langer, *Psychological Analysis of Adolf Hitler's Life and Legend* (Washington, DC: Office of Strategic Services, 1943), 219 (secret document approved for release in 1999). See also Henry A. Murray, *Analysis of the Personality of Adolph Hitler: With Predictions of His Future Behavior and Suggestions for Dealing with Him Now and After Germany's Surrender* (Cambridge, MA: Harvard Psychological Clinic, 1943), https://ia601305.us.archive.org/22/items/AnalysisThePersonalityofAdolphHitler/AnalysisofThePersonalityofAdolphHitler.pdf.

Chapter 3: The Cold Case Team

1 "Twisk, Pieter van," Systeemkaarten voor verzetsbetrokkenen (OVCG) (index cards for those involved in the resistance), no. 2183, Groninger Archieven, https://www.groningerarchieven.nl

/archieven?mivast=5&mizig=210&miadt=5&micode =2183&milang=nl&mizk_alle=van%20Twisk &miview=inv2.

Chapter 4: The Stakeholders

1 Cold Case Team (hereafter CCT), interview with Jan van Kooten, March 4, 2016.

2 The committee is called Nationaal Comité 4 en 5 mei.

3 Gerrit Bolkestein, broadcast on Radio Oranje, March 28, 1944.

Chapter 5: "Let's See What the Man Can Do!"

1 Otto Frank, letter to Leni Frank, May 19, 1917, quoted in Carol Ann Lee, *The Hidden Life of Otto Frank* (New York: Harper Perennial, 2003), 18.

2 Adolf Hitler, *Mein Kampf*, translated by Ralph Manheim (New York: Mariner Books, 1998) (originally published 1926).

3 R. Peter Straus, interview with Otto Frank, *Moment*, December 1977, quoted in Lee, *The Hidden Life of Otto Frank*, 37–38.

4 Ernst Schnabel, *The Footsteps of Anne Frank*, translated by Richard and Clara Winston (Harpenden, UK: Southbank Publishing, 2014), 24.

5 Bob Moore, *Victims and Survivors: The Nazi Persecution of the Jews in the Netherlands 1940–1945* (London: Arnold, 1997), 2.

6 Pim Griffioen and Ron Zeller, "The Netherlands: The Greatest Number of Jewish Victims in Western Europe," Anne Frank House, https://www.annefrank.org/en/anne-frank/go-in-depth/netherlands-greatest-number-jewish-victims-western-europe/.

7 Moore, *Victims and Survivors*, 72–73.

8 Ibid., 257–58.

9 Ibid., 182–84.

Chapter 6: An Interlude of Safety

1 Melissa Müller, *Anne Frank: The Biography*, translated by Rita and Robert Kimber (New York: Picador, 2013), 94.

2 Eda Shapiro and Rick Kardonne, *Victor Kugler: The Man Who Hid Anne Frank* (Jerusalem: Gefen Publishing House, 2008), 29.

3 Miep Gies with Alison Leslie Gold, *Anne Frank Remembered: The Story of the Woman Who Helped to Hide the Frank Family* (New York: Simon & Schuster, 2009), 30.

4 Ibid., 23.

5 Carol Ann Lee, *The Hidden Life of Otto Frank* (New York: Harper Perennial, 2003), 52.

6 Harry Paape (then director of NIOD), interviews with Jan and Miep Gies, February 18 and 27 and December 12 and 18, 1985, NIOD.

7 Gies, *Anne Frank Remembered*, 11.

8 Lee, *The Hidden Life of Otto Frank*, 52.

9 Müller, *Anne Frank: The Biography*, 92.

10 Milly Stanfield, interviewed in Carl Fussman, "The Woman Who Would Have Saved Anne Frank," *Newsday*, March 16, 1995. Includes her version of Otto Frank's reply.

Chapter 7: The Onslaught

1 Bob Moore, *Victims and Survivors: The Nazi Persecution of the Jews in the Netherlands 1940–1945* (London: Arnold, 1997), 63.

2 Miep Gies with Alison Leslie Gold, *Anne Frank Remembered: The Story of the Woman Who Helped to Hide the Frank Family* (New York: Simon & Schuster, 2009), 61.

3 "Thorbeckeplein," Joodsamsterdam, https://www.joodsamsterdam.nl/thorbeckeplein/.

4 Arthur Seyss-Inquart, speech to NSNAP, Concertgebouw, Amsterdam, March 12, 1941. See

Gerben Post, *Lotty's Bench, The Persecution of the Jews of Amsterdam Remembered*, translated by Tom Leighton (Volendam, Netherlands: LM Publishers, 2018), 44.

5 Ibid.

6 Moore, *Victims and Survivors*, 70.

7 Ibid., 69–73.

8 Ad van Liempt, *Hitler's Bounty Hunters: The Betrayal of the Jews*, translated by S. J. Leinbach (New York: Berg, 2005), 10.

9 Moore, *Victims and Survivors*, 71–73.

10 Melissa Müller, *Anne Frank: The Biography*, translated by Rita and Robert Kimber (New York: Picador USA, 2013), 144–46.

11 Ibid., 160.

12 Breckinridge Long, memorandum to colleagues in State Department, June 26, 1940, quoted in ibid., 147.

13 Müller, *Anne Frank: The Biography*, 152–53.

14 Ibid., 163.

Chapter 8: Prinsengracht 263

1 Gerben Post, *Lotty's Bench: The Persecution of the Jews of Amsterdam Remembered*, translated by Tom Leighton (Volendam, Netherlands: LM

Publishers, 2018), 50. See also Bob Moore, *Victims and Survivors: The Nazi Persecution of the Jews in the Netherlands 1940–1945* (London: Arnold, 1997), 105.

2 Gerard Aalders, *Nazi Looting: The Plunder of Dutch Jewry During the Second World War*, translated by Arnold Pomerans with Erica Pomerans (Oxford: Berg, 2004), 49, 129.

3 Reinhard Rürup, *Topography of Terror: Gestapo, SS, and Reichssicherheitshauptamt on the "Prinz -Albrecht-Terrain": A Documentation* (Berlin: Verlag Willlmuth Arenhovel, 1989), 152–53.

4 Etty Hillesum, *An Interrupted Life: The Diaries, 1941–1943, and Letters from Westerbork* (New York: Picador USA, 1996), 150.

Chapter 9: The Hiding

1 Ernst Schnabel, *The Footsteps of Anne Frank*, translated by Richard and Clara Winston (Harpenden, UK: Southbank Publishing, 2014), 84–85.

2 Melissa Müller, *Anne Frank: The Biography*, translated by Rita and Robert Kimber (New York: Picador USA, 2013), 193.

3 Jeroen de Bruyn and Joop van Wijk, *Anne Frank: The Untold Story: The Hidden Truth About Eli Vossen, the Youngest Helper of the Secret Annex* (Laag-Soeren, Netherlands: Bep Voskuijl Productions, 2018), 43.

4 Ibid., 38.

5 Miep Gies, quoted in Dienke Hondius, "A New Perspective on Helpers of Jews During the Holocaust: The Case of Miep and Jan Gies," in *Anne Frank in Historical Perspective: A Teaching Guide for Secondary Schools*, edited by Alex Grobman and Joel Fishman (Los Angeles: Martyrs Memorial and Museum of the Holocaust, 1995), https://files.eric.ed.gov/fulltext/ED391710.pdf, 38.

6 Miep Gies with Alison Leslie Gold, *Anne Frank Remembered: The Story of the Woman Who Helped to Hide the Frank Family* (New York: Simon & Schuster, 2009), 88.

7 Müller, *Anne Frank: The Biography*, 194.

8 Gies, *Anne Frank Remembered*, 94.

9 Ibid., 119.

10 Ibid., 133.

11 Müller, *Anne Frank: The Biography*, 195.

12 Gies, *Anne Frank Remembered*, 117.

13 Ibid., 98.

Chapter 10: You Were Asked. You Said Yes.

1 Miep Gies with Alison Leslie Gold, *Anne Frank Remembered: The Story of the Woman Who Helped to Hide the Frank Family* (New York: Simon & Schuster, 2009), 126.

2 Alex Grobman and Joel Fishman, eds., *Anne Frank in Historical Perspective: A Teaching Guide for Secondary Schools* (Los Angeles: Martyrs Memorial and Museum of the Holocaust, 1995), 38.

3 Ibid., 40.

4 Ernst Schnabel, *The Footsteps of Anne Frank*, translated by Richard and Clara Winston (Harpenden, UK: Southbank Publishing, 2014), 124.

5 Grobman and Fishman, *Anne Frank in Historical Perspective*, 40–41.

6 Ibid., 41.

7 Ibid., 42.

8 Schnabel, *The Footsteps of Anne Frank*, 126.

9 Gies, *Anne Frank Remembered*, 103, 117.

10 Schnabel, *The Footsteps of Anne Frank*, 102–03.

11 Harry Rasky, "The Man Who Hid Anne Frank," CBC documentary, 1980. See also Gies, *Anne Frank Remembered*, 111.

12 Grobman and Fishman, *Anne Frank in Historical Perspective*, 39.

13 Gies, *Anne Frank Remembered*, 109.

14 Jeroen de Bruyn and Joop van Wijk, *Anne Frank: The Untold Story: The Hidden Truth About Eli Vossen, the Youngest Helper of the Secret Annex* (Laag-Soeren, Netherlands: Bep Voskuijl Productions, 2018), 56–57.

15 Ibid., 76.

16 Gies, *Anne Frank Remembered*, 129.

Chapter 11: A Harrowing Incident

1 Ernst Schnabel, *The Footsteps of Anne Frank*, translated by Richard and Clara Winston (Harpenden, UK: Southbank Publishing, 2014), 146.

2 Jeroen de Bruyn and Joop van Wijk, *Anne Frank: The Untold Story: The Hidden Truth About Eli Vossen, the Youngest Helper of the Secret Annex* (Laag-Soeren, Netherlands: Bep Voskuijl Productions, 2018), 63.

3 Miep Gies with Alison Leslie Gold, *Anne Frank Remembered: The Story of the Woman Who Helped to Hide the Frank Family* (New York: Simon & Schuster, 2009), 102.

4 Melissa Müller, *Anne Frank: The Biography*, translated by Rita and Robert Kimber (New York: Picador USA, 2013), 277.

5 Ibid., 278.

6 Anne Frank, diary entry, April 11, 1944, in *The Diary of a Young Girl: The Definitive Edition*, edited by Otto H. Frank and Mirjam Pressler (New York: Doubleday, 1995), 260.

7 Carol Ann Lee, *The Hidden Life of Otto Frank* (New York: Harper Perennial, 2003), 121.

Chapter 12: Anatomy of a Raid

1 Ernst Schnabel, *The Footsteps of Anne Frank*, translated by Richard and Clara Winston (Harpenden, UK: Southbank Publishing, 2014), 128.

2 Miep Gies with Alison Leslie Gold, *Anne Frank Remembered: The Story of the Woman Who Helped to Hide the Frank Family* (New York: Simon & Schuster, 2009), 193.

3 Dr. Josef Wiesinger, interview with Karl Silberbauer, August 21, 1963, Austrian Archive, Ministry of the Interior.

4 Jules Huf, "Erstes interview mit Häscher Anne Frank" ["The First Interview of the Capturer of Anne Frank"], *Kurier*, November 22, 1963 (reprint in *De Groene Amsterdammer*, May 14, 1986).

5 Interviews with Karl Silberbauer, Austrian Archives,

Ministry of the Interior, November 25, 1963, and March 2, 1964.

6 Arend J. van Helden, State Department of Criminal Investigation, Amsterdam, interview with Otto Frank, December 2–3, 1963, NIOD, Doc. 1 Van Maaren.

7 Arend J. van Helden, State Department of Criminal Investigation, Amsterdam, interview with Willem van Maaren, October 6, 1964, NIOD, Doc. 1 Van Maaren.

8 Ibid.

9 Schnabel, *The Footsteps of Anne Frank*, 128.

10 Notarized statement to A. J. Dragt, Anne Frank, NIOD inventory no. 4, 212c.

11 Gies, *Anne Frank Remembered*, 193.

12 Schnabel, *The Footsteps of Anne Frank*, 129.

13 Evelyn Wolf, audio interview with Victor Kugler, 1972, Anne Frank Stichting (hereafter AFS).

14 Schnabel, *The Footsteps of Anne Frank*, 129.

15 Ernst Schnabel, original notes for *The Footsteps of Anne Frank*, 1957, German Literature Archive Marbach.

16 Eda Shapiro and Rick Kardonne, *Victor Kugler: The Man Who Hid Anne Frank* (Jerusalem: Gefen Publishing House, 2008), 53.

17 "I Hid Anne Frank from the Nazis," interview with Victor Kugler, *Pittsburgh Press*, August 2, 1958.

18 Arend J. van Helden, State Department of Criminal Investigation, Amsterdam, interview with Otto Frank, December 2–3, 1963, NIOD, Doc. 1 Van Maaren.

19 Ibid.

20 Schnabel, *The Footsteps of Anne Frank*, 134.

21 Interview with Bep Voskuijl, "Wie pleegde het verraad van het achterhuis" [Who Betrayed the Secret Annex], *Panorama*, December 13,1963.

22 Elisabeth (Bep) Voskuijl, audio interview with Oskar Morawetz, October 1978, Library and Archives Canada, Ottawa, Canada.

23 Arend J. van Helden, State Department of Criminal Investigation, Amsterdam, interview with Jan Gies, December 23, 1963, NIOD, Doc. 1 Van Maaren.

24 Gies, *Anne Frank Remembered,* 194–95.

25 Ibid., 195.

26 Ibid., 196–97.

27 Ibid., 197.

28 Schnabel, *The Footsteps of Anne Frank*, 138.

29 Arend J. van Helden, State Department of Criminal Investigation, Amsterdam, interview with Jan Gies, December 23, 1963, NIOD, Doc. 1 Van Maaren.

30 Schnabel, *The Footsteps of Anne Frank*, 140.

31 Arend J. van Helden, State Department of Criminal Investigation, Amsterdam, interview with Otto Frank, December 2–3, 1963, NIOD, Doc. 1 Van Maaren.

32 Schnabel, *The Footsteps of Anne Frank*, 143.

Chapter 13: Camp Westerbork

1 Miep Gies with Alison Leslie Gold, *Anne Frank Remembered: The Story of the Woman Who Helped to Hide the Frank Family* (New York: Simon & Schuster, 2009), 198.

2 Ernst Schnabel, *The Footsteps of Anne Frank*, translated by Richard and Clara Winston (Harpenden, UK: Southbank Publishing, 2014), 187.

3 Jeroen de Bruyn, telephone interview with Diny Voskuijl, September 2, 2012.

4 Jeroen de Bruyn and Joop van Wijk, *Anne Frank: The Untold Story: The Hidden Truth About Eli Vossen, the Youngest Helper of the Secret Annex* (Laag-Soeren, Netherlands: Bep Voskuijl Productions, 2018), 113.

5 Ibid., 115–16.

6 Janny Brandes-Brilleslijper, cited in Willy Lindwer, *The Last Seven Months of Anne Frank: The Stories of Six Women Who Knew Anne Frank*, translated

by Alison Meersschaert (New York: Pan Macmillan, 2004), 52.

7 Schnabel, *The Footsteps of Anne Frank*, 145.

8 Ibid., 151.

9 Ibid., 163.

10 Ad van Liempt, "Van Riet schetst genuanceerd beeld van Joodse Ordedienst," *Volkskrant*, November 19, 2016, https://www.volkskrant.nl/cultuur-media/van-riet-schetst-genuanceerd-beeld-van-joodse-ordedienst~b382e88b/.

11 Schnabel, *The Footsteps of Anne Frank*, 155–56.

12 Carol Ann Lee, *The Hidden Life of Otto Frank* (New York: Harper Perennial, 2003), 138.

Chapter 14: The Return

1 Carol Ann Lee, *The Hidden Life of Otto Frank* (New York: Harper Perennial, 2003), 157.

2 Ibid., 164.

3 Ernst Schnabel, *The Footsteps of Anne Frank*, translated by Richard and Clara Winston (Harpenden, UK: Southbank Publishing, 2014), 163–64.

4 Ibid., 161.

5 Miep Gies with Alison Leslie Gold, *Anne Frank Remembered: The Story of the Woman Who Helped*

to Hide the Frank Family (New York: Simon & Schuster, 2009), 231.

6 Eda Shapiro and Rick Kardonne, *Victor Kugler: The Man Who Hid Anne Frank* (Jerusalem: Gefen Publishing House, 2008), 77.

7 Lee, *The Hidden Life of Otto Frank*, 177, 179.

8 Willy Lindwer, *The Last Seven Months of Anne Frank: The Stories of Six Women Who Knew Anne Frank*, translated by Alison Meersschaert (New York: Pan Macmillan, 2004), 83–84.

9 Lee, *The Hidden Life of Otto Frank*, 195.

10 Jeroen de Bruyn and Joop van Wijk, *Anne Frank: The Untold Story: The Hidden Truth About Eli Vossen, the Youngest Helper of the Secret Annex* (Laag-Soeren, Netherlands: Bep Voskuijl Productions, 2018), 130. The eyewitness was Rachel van Amerongen-Frankfoorder. This has not been corroborated by other witnesses.

11 Otto Frank, letter to his mother, December 12, 1945, in Melissa Müller, *Anne Frank: The Biography*, translated by Rita and Robert Kimber (New York: Picador USA, 2013), 354.

12 Lindwer, *The Last Seven Months of Anne Frank*, 33.

13 Müller, *Anne Frank: The Biography*, 299.

14 Lindwer, *The Last Seven Months of Anne Frank*, 32.

15 Lee, *The Hidden Life of Otto Frank*, 196.
16 Lindwer, *The Last Seven Months of Anne Frank*, 27.
17 Ibid., 28–29.
18 Schnabel, *The Footsteps of Anne Frank*, 182. She is identified as Renate LA.

Chapter 15: The Collaborators

1 Bob Moore, *Victims and Survivors: The Nazi Persecution of the Jews in the Netherlands 1940–1945* (London: Arnold, 1997), 230.
2 Ibid., 229.
3 Carol Ann Lee, *The Hidden Life of Otto Frank* (New York: Harper Perennial, 2003), 173, 212.
4 Bart van Es, *Cut Out Girl: A Story of War and Family, Lost and Found* (London: Fig Tree, 2019), 190.
5 Miep Gies with Alison Leslie Gold, *Anne Frank Remembered: The Story of the Woman Who Helped to Hide the Frank Family* (New York: Simon & Schuster, 2009), 228.
6 Ad van Liempt, *Hitler's Bounty Hunters: The Betrayal of the Jews*, translated by S. J. Leinbach (New York: Berg, 2005), 30.
7 Ibid., 78.

8 Ibid., 33.
9 Ibid., 63.

Chapter 16: They Aren't Coming Back

1 Miep Gies with Alison Leslie Gold, *Anne Frank Remembered: The Story of the Woman Who Helped to Hide the Frank Family* (New York: Simon & Schuster, 2009), 234.
2 Ibid., 242.
3 Ibid., 240.
4 Carol Ann Lee, *The Hidden Life of Otto Frank* (New York: Harper Perennial, 2003), 86.
5 Otto Frank, "Anne Frank Would Have Been Fifty This Year," *Life*, March 1979.
6 Eva Schloss with Karen Bartlett, *After Auschwitz: A Story of Heartbreak and Survival by the Stepsister of Anne Frank* (London: Hodder & Stoughton, 2013), 173.
7 Arthur Unger, interviews with Otto Frank, New York, 1977, AFS.
8 Schloss, *After Auschwitz*, 225.
9 Otto Frank, letter to Meyer Levin, July 8, 1952, cited in Lee, *The Hidden Life of Otto Frank*, 238.
10 Lee, *The Hidden Life of Otto Frank*, 251.

11 Lothar Schmidt, letter to Otto Frank, June 1959, quoted in David de Jongh, *Otto Frank. Vander van Anne* [Otto Frank. Father of Anne], documentary, 2010. Also in Jeroen de Bruyn and Joop van Wijk, *Anne Frank: The Untold Story: The Hidden Truth About Eli Vossen, the Youngest Helper of the Secret Annex* (Laag-Soeren, Netherlands: Bep Voskuijl Productions, 2018), 205.

12 Interview with Father John Neiman, April 2001, quoted in Lee, *The Hidden Life of Otto Frank*, 272–74.

13 Lee, *The Hidden Life of Otto Frank*, 272.

Chapter 18: The Documents Men

1 Jessie Kratz, "The Return of Captured Records from World War II," Pieces of History, August 24, 2016, US National Archives, https://prologue.blogs.archives.gov/2016/08/24/the-return-of-captured-records-from-world-war-ii/.

Chapter 20: The First Betrayal

1 Gijsbert Willem van Renen, Office of the Amsterdam Police Force, investigation of Josephus Marinus Jansen, June 2, 1948, Netherlands National Archives, The Hague (hereafter NI-HaNa) file no. 8082.

2 Otto Frank, letter to the Bureau of National Security (Bureau Nationale Veiligheid; BNV), August 21, 1945, denouncing Job Jansen. Other versions have Ahlers asking for money, but this is Otto's official declaration to the BNV. Otto claimed that Ahlers had said he was a courier between the NSB and SD and handed him the letter. He had not asked for money. Otto had offered him money, obviously understanding that that was what was required. Otto wrote to the BNV to help a man who he believed had saved his life, and certainly it was easy to slip past the issue of who had asked for and who had offered money.

3 Job Jansen, protocol report, June 2, 1948, Centraal Archief van de Bijzondere Rechtspleging (hereafter CABR), NI-HaNa.

4 Otto Frank, letter to POD, August 21, 1945, no. 23834, NI-HaNa.

5 Vince Pankoke, interview with Eric Bremer, April 23, 2017, Amsterdam.

6 Job Jansen, CABR, NI-HaNa, translated by Joachim Bayens and Rory Dekker.

7 Van Renen, investigation of Josephus Marinus Jansen, June 2, 1948.

8 Job Jansen, CABR, NI-HaNa.

9 Canton judge, Amsterdam, Special Court, judgment of Josephus Marinus Jansen, March 21, 1949.

Chapter 21: The Blackmailer

1 Ernst Schnabel, *The Footsteps of Anne Frank*, translated by Richard and Clara Winston (Harpenden, UK: Southbank Publishing, 2014), 77.

2 Ibid., 78.

3 Amsterdam Stadsarchief, RC (resident card) for Prinsengracht 253, address for mother of A. (Tonny) Ahlers.

4 Carol Ann Lee, *The Hidden Life of Otto Frank* (New York: Harper Perennial, 2003), 125.

5 Sytze van der Zee, *Vogelvrij: De jacht op de joodse onderduiker* (Amsterdam: De Bezige Bij, 2010), 21.

6 Otto Frank, letter to BNV, August 21, 1945, Tonny Ahlers, CABR, NI-HaNa.

7 Tonny Ahlers, CABR, NI-HaNa.

8 Amsterdam Stadsarchief, AC (personal card) for A. (Tonny) Ahlers, registered at Leger Des Heils; – Military status Ahlers_ongeschikt (Not suitable) _ parents divorced; Ad to Vereeniging Nora for neglected children.

9 NI-HaNa, CABR, Anton (Tonny) Ahlers; *Telegraaf* article vandalizing 04-03-1939.

10 Joseph van Poppel, CABR, NI-HaNa.

11 Copy of *De Telegraaf* newspaper article with photo of Ahlers, February 18, 1941, Anton (Tonny) Ahlers, CABR, NI-HaNa.

12 Tonny Ahlers, CABR, NI-HaNa.

13 Tonny Ahlers, social welfare file notes, Stadsarchief Amsterdam.

14 *De Waarheid* (The Truth), December 1945. File 22, NIOD.

15 Otto Frank, letter about Tonny Ahlers, no 19450830, July 20, 1945, Tonny Ahlers, CABR, file 18, NIOD.

16 Schnabel, *The Footsteps of Anne Frank*, 77.

17 Gertjan Broek, "An Investigative Report on the Betrayal and Arrest of the Inhabitants of the Secret Annex," Anne Frank House, December 2016, https://www.annefrank.org/en/downloads/filer_public/4a/c6/4ac6677d-f8ae-4c79-b024-91ffe694e216/an_investigative_report_on_the_betrayal_and_arrest.pdf, 17.

18 Lee, *The Hidden Life of Otto Frank*, 315–16.

19 David Barnouw and Gerrold van der Stroom, "Who Betrayed Anne Frank?," NIOD, https://www.niod.nl/sites/niod.nl.

Chapter 22: The Neighborhood

1 See maps at https://www.google.com/maps/d/viewer?mid=1BfecsUvhYhQqXVDX6NgQpohdMV4&ll=52.37625107530956%2C4.860590119128467&z=12) (SD informant and V-person map). Tracking database produced for the CCT by computer scientists at Xomnia, Amsterdam, Netherlands.

2 Jeroen de Bruyn and Joop van Wijk, *Anne Frank: The Untold Story: The Hidden Truth About Eli Vossen, the Youngest Helper of the Secret Annex* (Laag-Soeren, Netherlands: Bep Voskuijl Productions, 2018), 98.

Chapter 23: The Nanny

1 Nouschka van der Meijden, "Amerikaans Coldcaseteam onderzoekt verraad Anne Frank," *Het Parool*, September 30, 2017, https://www.parool.nl/nieuws/amerikaans-coldcaseteam-onderzoekt-verraad-anne-frank~b543dae7/.

2 Stichting Toezicht Politieke Delinquenten (Foundation for the Supervision of Political Offenders) (hereafter STPD), Jacobus Van Kampen, file no. 21103, 85111, CABR, NI-HaNa.

3 Amsterdam police incident reports, March 8, 1944, Stadsarchief Amsterdam.

Chapter 24: Another Theory

1 Gerard Kremer, speech at his book presentation, Westerkerk church, Amsterdam, May 25, 2018, attended by CCT members.

2 *De achtertuin van het achterhuis* [The Backyard of the Annex] was published in English in 2020 under the title *Anne Frank Betrayed: The Mystery Unraveled After 75 Years.*

3 Miep Gies with Alison Leslie Gold, *Anne Frank Remembered: The Story of the Woman Who Helped to Hide the Frank Family* (New York: Simon & Schuster, 2009), 121.

4 Jeroen de Bruyn and Joop van Wijk, *Anne Frank: The Untold Story: The Hidden Truth About Eli Vossen, the Youngest Helper of the Secret Annex* (Laag-Soeren, Netherlands: Bep Voskuijl Productions, 2018), 52–53.

Chapter 25: The "Jew Hunters"

1 Ad van Liempt, *Hitler's Bounty Hunters: The Betrayal of the Jews*, translated by S. J. Leinbach (New York: Berg, 2005), 46–57.
2 Eva Schloss with Karen Bartlett, *After Auschwitz: A Story of Heartbreak and Survival by the Stepsister of Anne Frank* (London: Hodder & Stoughton, 2013), 94–96.
3 Eduard Moesbergen, 248-0575A, NIOD, Doc. 1. Copy of CABR file at NI-HaNa.
4 Eduard Moesbergen, 248-1163A, NIOD, Doc. 1. Copy of CABR file at NI-HaNa.

Chapter 26: The V-Frau

1 Ans van Dijk, CABR, NI-HaNa.
2 Bob Moore, *Victims & Survivors: The Nazi Persecution of the Jews in the Netherlands 1940–1945* (London: Arnold, 1997), 209.
3 Ans van Dijk, CABR, NI-HaNa.
4 Koos Groen, *Een prooi wordt jager: De Zaak van de joodse verraadster Ans van Dijk* (Meppel, Netherlands: Just Publishers, 2016), 90.
5 Samuel Clowes Huneke, "The Duplicity of Tolerance:

Lesbian Experiences in Nazi Berlin," *Journal of Contemporary History* 54 (1): 30–59.

6 Statement by Mies de Regt, November 11, 1945, translated by Circe de Bruin, Ans van Dijk, CABR, NI-HaNa.

7 Groen, *Een prooi wordt jager*, 123.

8 Willy Lindwer, *The Last Seven Months of Anne Frank: The Stories of Six Women Who Knew Anne Frank*, translated by Alison Meersschaert (New York: Pan Macmillan, 2004), 169–70.

9 Case of Andries Posno, who entrusted Van Dijk with information about his family and helpers, Ans van Dijk, CABR, NI-HaNa.

10 CCT, interview with Louis de Groot, Washington, DC, May 30, 2018.

11 Sytze van der Zee, *Vogelvrij: De jacht op de joodse onderduiker* (Amsterdam: De Bezige Bij, 2010), 361.

12 Statement by Mies de Regt, November 11, 1945, translated by Circe de Bruin, Ans van Dijk, CABR, NI-HaNa.

Chapter 27: No Substantial Proof, Part I

1 Johannes Kleiman, letter to Politieke Opsporingsdienst (hereafter POD), February 1945, file no. 23892, CABR, NI-HaNa. It must have been misdated, as it was not possible to write to the POD for investigation in February 1945.

2 Otto Frank, letter to Alice Frank-Stern, November 11, 1945, reg. code Otto Frank Archive-72, AFS.

3 Johannes Kleiman, letter to Politieke Recherche Afdeling (hereafter PRA), July 16, 1947, NI-HaNa, CABR W. Van Maaren.

4 Ibid.

5 Ibid.

6 Interview with Willem van Maaren, PRA investigation report, February 2, 1948, Willem van Maaren, CABR, NI-HaNa.

7 Ibid.

8 PRA, investigation report, 1948, dossier 61196, Willem van Maaren, CABR, NI-HaNa.

9 Dossier 6634, session of August 13, 1949, translated by Joachim Bayens and Rory Dekker, Cantonal Court, Amsterdam, Willem van Maaren, CABR, NI-HaNa.

Chapter 28: "Just Go to Your Jews!"

1 Ernst Schnabel, *The Footsteps of Anne Frank*, translated by Richard and Clara Winston (Harpenden, UK: Southbank Publishing, 2014), 103.

2 Vince Pankoke, interview with Joop van Wijk, Proditione Office, Herengracht, December 7, 2018.

3 Police file, November 1, 1941, Stadsarchief Amsterdam.

4 Jeroen de Bruyn and Joop van Wijk, *Anne Frank: The Untold Story: The Hidden Truth About Eli Vossen, the Youngest Helper of the Secret Annex* (Laag-Soeren, Netherlands: Bep Voskuijl Productions, 2018), 99.

5 Teresien da Silva, AFS, interview with Diny Voskuijl, November 14, 2011, AFS.

6 Nelly Voskuijl, application for German visa, cert. no. 19612, December 18, 1942, Stadsarchief Amsterdam. See also Gertjan Broek, "An Investigative Report on the Betrayal and Arrest of the Inhabitants of the Secret Annex," Anne Frank House, December 2016, https://www.annefrank.org/en/downloads/filer_public/4a/c6/4ac6677d-f8ae-4c79-b024-91ffe694e216/an_investigative_report_on_the_betrayal_and_arrest.pdf, 19.

7 Teresien da Silva, interview with Diny Voskuijl, November 14, 2011, AFS.

8 Jeroen de Bruyn and Joop van Wijk, interview with Bertus Hulsman, February 20, 2014, Amsterdam. See De Bruyn and Van Wijk, *Anne Frank: The Untold Story*, 102.

9 CCT, interview with Joop van Wijk, December 7, 2018.

10 Anne Frank, diary entry, May 6, 1944, in *The Diary of Anne Frank: The Revised Critical Edition*, edited by David Barnouw and Gerrold van der Stroom, translated by Arnold J. Pomerans, B. M. Mooyaart-Doubleday, and Susan Massotty (New York: Doubleday, 2003), 655.

11 Anne Frank, diary entry, May 11, 1944, ibid., 668.

12 Anne Frank, diary entry, May 19, 1944, ibid., 674.

13 Jeroen de Bruyn and Joop van Wijk, *Bep Voskuijl, het zwijgen voorbij: En biografie van de jongste helpster van het Achterhuis* (Amsterdam: Prometheus Bert Bakker, 2018), 192. Rhijja Jansen, "Dat Nelly fout was, daar werd nooit over gesproken," *Volkskrant*, April 26, 2018.

14 Bruyn and Wijk, *Anne Frank: The Untold Story*, 102; Jeroen de Bruyn and Joop van Wijk, interview with Bertus Hulsman, February 20, 2014, Amsterdam.

15 Dineke Stam, interview with Bertus Hulsman, AFS, tape 1, time: 25:30, AFS.

16 Ibid., tape 2, time: 19:15.

17 Ibid., tape 2, time: 10:51

18 Vince Pankoke, interview with Melissa Müller, Munich, February 17, 2019.

19 CCT, interview with Gerlof Langerijs, March 28, 2019.

20 Joop van Wijk, interview and email exchange with Hugo Voskuijl.

21 Inventory 13, 15, 17, 22, Interneringsarchieven (Internment Archives), 1945–50, Groningen Archives.

22 Nelly Voskuijl, AC card, Groningen Archives. Unpublished research by Ben Wegman shows that Nelly lived not only at Grote Rozenstraat 14, Steentilstraat 47, and Gedempte Zuiderdiep 25a but also at Noorderstationsstraat 20 for two months. Wegman's research and a Delpher search show that Diny's memories about Nelly's work and the Voet family are correct: she is registered as an in-house clerk for widow A. Hendriks at Grote Rozengracht 14 from October 26, 1945, until May 23, 1947, when she moved to Noorderstationsstraat 20a. At number 20 Noorderstationsstraat the son of the Voet family lived with his wife and young baby. After two months, on July 28, 1947, Nelly moved to Gedempte Zuiderdiep 25a, the house with the café of the head of the Voet family, Gozen Theo Voet. Nelly was registered as

an in-house maid. This information, together with the vague remarks of Joop van Wijk that the "family Voet" was friends with Nelly, confirms that Nelly Voskuijl was not in prison between October 26, 1945, and April 8, 1953, when she moved back to Amsterdam.

23 Bruyn and Wijk, *Anne Frank: The Untold Story*, 233.

24 CCT, interview with Joop van Wijk, December 7, 2018.

25 To answer this question, CCT conducted extensive interviews, as well as document searches. They spoke with Melissa Müller and conducted two interviews with Joop van Wijk and one with Jeroen de Bruyn; Bertus Hulsman was interviewed by a researcher at AFS, Dineke Stam. Diny Voskuijl could not be interviewed because of poor health, but they closely reviewed the interview she had given to the *Volkskrant* newspaper in 2018. They also interviewed Hugo Voskuijl, an amateur genealogist who had done extensive research into his family.

Chapter 29: Probing Memory

1 Evelyn Wolf, audio interview with Victor Kugler, 1972, AFS.

2 Ernst Schnabel, original notes for *The Footsteps*

of Anne Frank, 1957, German Literature Archive Marbach.

3 "A Tragedy Revealed," *Life*, August 18, 1958, 78–90.

4 Ernst Schnabel, *The Footsteps of Anne Frank*, translated by Richard and Clara Winston (Harpenden, UK: Southbank Publishing, 2014), 129.

5 Ibid.

6 Arend J. van Helden, State Department of Criminal Investigation, Amsterdam, interview with Otto Frank, December 2–3, 1963, NIOD, Doc. 1 Van Maaren.

7 Jan Rijnders, *Report: Telefoonnet Amsterdam 1940–1945*, March 25, 2019. Report for Cold Case Team, not publicly available.

8 Gertjan Broek, "An Investigative Report on the Betrayal and Arrest of the Inhabitants of the Secret Annex," Anne Frank House, December 2016, https://www.annefrank.org/en/downloads/filer_public/4a/c6/4ac6677d-f8ae-4c79-b024-91ffe694e216/an_investigative_report_on_the_betrayal_and_arrest.pdf, 8. Broek concluded that this remark has been misread because it depends on Silberbauer's statement being correct.

Chapter 30: "The Man Who Arrested Frank Family Discovered in Vienna"

1 Simon Wiesenthal, *The Murderers Among Us: The Simon Wiesenthal Memoirs*, edited by Joseph Wechsberg (New York: Bantam Books, 1968), 171–72.

2 Ibid., 174.

3 Ibid., 177.

4 Harry Paape (then director of NIOD), interview with Miep Gies, February 18 and 27, 1985, NIOD.

5 Wiesenthal, *The Murderers Among Us*, 175. Assuming that Kugler had misspelled it, Wiesenthal changed Silvernagl to Silbernagel, which was a common name in Austria.

6 Ibid., 178. In a CBS documentary, *Who Killed Anne Frank?*, the director of RIOD (now NIOD), Loe de Long, claimed it was he who had given the phone directory with Silberbauer's name to Wiesenthal.

7 Tony Paterson, "Nazi Who Arrested Anne Frank Became a Spy for West Germany," *Independent*, April 11, 2011.

8 "Der Mann, der Anne Frank verhaftete" [The Man Who Betrayed Anne Frank], *Volksstimme*, November 11, 1963.

9 Simon Wiesenthal, letter to Dr. Wiesinger, Austrian Ministry of the Interior, November 15, 1963, AFS.

10 "Nieuw onderzoek naar het verraad van familie Frank" [New Investigation into the Betrayal of the Frank Family], *Het Vrije Volk*, November 27, 1962. See also "Frank wist wie hem weghaald" [Frank Knew Who Took Him Away], translated by the Cold Case Team, *De Telegraaf*, November 22, 1963.

11 "SS'er die gezin Frank arresteerde, gevonden" [SS'er Who Arrested Frank Family Found], Volkskrant, November 21, 1963.

12 Carol Ann Lee, *The Hidden Life of Otto Frank* (New York: Harper Perennial, 2003), 278.

13 Miep Gies with Alison Leslie Gold, *Anne Frank Remembered: The Story of the Woman Who Helped to Hide the Frank Family* (New York: Simon & Schuster, 2009), 196.

14 Eda Shapiro and Rick Kardonne, *Victor Kugler: The Man Who Hid Anne Frank* (Jerusalem: Gefen Publishing House, 2008), 54.

15 Detective Scherer, State Department of Criminal Investigation, Amsterdam, interview with Miep Gies, May 3, 1963, NIOD, Doc. 1 Van Maaren.

16 *De Groene Amsterdammer* republished the full article in 1986. See Jules Huf, "Listen, We Are Not

Interested in Politics," *De Groene Amsterdammer*, May 14, 1986.

17 Wiesenthal, *The Murderers Among Us*, 180.

18 Karl Josef Silberbauer, signed statement, November 25, 1963, translated by Joachim Bayens, Austrian Department of the Interior, Austrian State Archives, VieNI-HaNa.

19 Jeroen de Bruyn and Joop van Wijk, *Anne Frank: The Untold Story: The Hidden Truth About Eli Vossen, the Youngest Helper of the Secret Annex* (Laag-Soeren, Netherlands: Bep Voskuijl Productions, 2018), 191.

20 Huf, "Listen, We Are Not Interested in Politics."

Chapter 31: What Miep Knew

1 Miep Gies, Wallenberg Lecture, University of Michigan, October 11, 1994.

2 Drake Baer, "The Real Reason Keeping Secrets Is So Hard, According to a Psychologist," The Cut, June 1, 2016, https://www.thecut.com/2016/06/real-reason-keeping-secrets-is-hard.html.

3 Quoted in Carol Ann Lee, *The Hidden Life of Otto Frank* (New York: Harper Perennial, 2003), 322–23.

4 Vince Pankoke, interview with Father John Neiman, February 19, 2019.

5 Jeroen de Bruyn and Joop van Wijk, *Anne Frank: The Untold Story: The Hidden Truth About Eli Vossen, the Youngest Helper of the Secret Annex* (Laag-Soeren, Netherlands: Bep Voskuijl Productions, 2018), 169.

6 Miep and Jan Gies, cited in Hieke Jippes, "Voices from the Front House," *NRC Handelsblad*, March 14, 1981. See also De Bruyn and Van Wijk, *Anne Frank: The Untold Story*, 169.

Chapter 32: No Substantial Proof, Part II

1 Arend J. van Helden, State Department of Criminal Investigation, Amsterdam, interview with Willem Grootendorst, January 7, 1964; Arend J. van Helden, interview with Gezinus Gringhuis, December 23, 1963, NIOD, Doc. 1 Van Maaren.

2 Arend J. van Helden, State Department of Criminal Investigation, Amsterdam, summary report, December 3, 1964, NIOD, Doc. 1 Van Maaren.

3 Arend J. van Helden, State Department of Criminal Investigation, Amsterdam, interview with Willem van Maaren, October 6, 1964, NIOD, Doc. 1 Van Maaren.

4 Arend J. van Helden, State Department of Criminal Investigation, final report to prosecutor, November 6, 1964.

5 Carol Ann Lee, *The Hidden Life of Otto Frank* (New York: Harper Perennial, 2003), 123.

6 Umberto Bacchi perpetuated the rumor of the female caller in "Anne Frank: Book Identifies Betrayer as Helper's Sister and Gestapo Informer Nelly Voskuijl," *International Business Times*, April 9, 2015, but did not substantiate it. See also: Interview with Jan Erik Dubbelman, head of educational projects, Anne Frank House (AFH), Amsterdam, July 8, 2019.

7 Simon Wiesenthal, *The Murderers Among Us: The Simon Wiesenthal Memoirs*, edited by Joseph Wechsberg (New York: Bantam Books, 1968), 182.

8 Detective Meeboer, interview with Lammert Hartog, March 20, 1948, PRA.

9 Detective Meeboer, interview with J. Kleiman, January 12, 1948, PRA.

10 Vince Pankoke, interview with Melissa Müller, Munich, February 14, 2019.

Chapter 33: The Greengrocer

1 Ernst Schnabel, *The Footsteps of Anne Frank*, translated by Richard and Clara Winston (Harpenden, UK: Southbank Publishing, 2014), 95–96.

2 Anecdote reported by E. Schnabel during visit to Hendrik van Hoeve in 1957; Monique Koemans and Christine Hoste, interview with Stef van Hoeve, February 27, 2019.

3 Hendrik van Hoeve, memoirs, AFS; Christine Hoste and Monique Koemans, interviews with Stef van Hoeve, February 27, and July 10, 2019.

4 Johannes Gerard Koning, CABR, NI-HaNa. A detailed account of the early-morning raid appears in the file along with the names of the IV B4 Dutch detectives who participated.

5 Anne Frank, diary entry, May 25, 1944, in Anne Frank, *The Diary of Anne Frank: The Revised Critical Edition*, edited by David Barnouw and Gerrold van der Stroom, translated by Arnold J. Pomerans, B. M. Mooyaart-Doubleday, and Susan Massotty (New York: Doubleday, 2003), 681.

6 The German name of the camp was Konzentrationslager Herzogenbusch; see Hendrik van Hoeve, memoirs, AFS, and Christine Hoste and Monique Koemans, interviews with Stef van Hoeve, February 27 and July 10, 2019.

7 Research by Gerrit van der Vorst, Buun, 2014, 133. His brother, by contrast, was the opposite. Alfred Meiler had acted as a double spy for the Germans in

World War I and had been sent to the United States on an espionage mission.

8 "Max Meiler," Joods Monument, https://www.joodsmonument.nl/nl/page/402501/max-meiler.

9 Hendrik van Hoeve, memoirs, AFS.

10 Ibid.

11 Inventory number/obtained during call, Dutch Red Cross Archive.

12 Monique Koemans and Pieter van Twisk, interview with Guido Abuys, curator, Herinneringscentrum Kamp Westerbork, October 10, 2018.

13 Ibid.

14 Hendrik van Hoeve, memoirs, AFS.

15 Bob Moore, *Victims and Survivors: The Nazi Persecution of the Jews in the Netherlands 1940–1945* (London: Arnold, 1997), 133.

16 Ruth and Richard Weisz, entry cards, Herinneringscentrum Kamp Westerbork.

17 Ad van Liempt, *Hitler's Bounty Hunters: The Betrayal of the Jews*, translated by S. J. Leinbach (New York: Berg, 2005), 129.

18 F. Pleij and P. Schaap, CABR, NI-HaNa.

19 Testimony of Gerrit Mozer, POD Groningen, P. Schaap, CABR, NI-HaNa.

20 F. Pleij and P. Schaap, CABR, NI-HaNa.

21 File 91980, F. Pleij, CABR, NI-HaNa. After the war

she was charged with illegal trade in food coupons. The amounts in question would sometimes be as high as 4,000 guilders per month.

22 Sytze van der Zee, *Vogelvrij: De jacht op de joodse onderduiker* (Amsterdam: De Bezige Bij, 2010).

23 Richard Weisz, Joodse Raad card (entered Westerbork on May 26, 1944); Leopold de Jong, arrest record (June) and entry card (entered Westerbork in July); both Herinneringscentrum Kamp Westerbork.

24 Transport lists to Kamp Westerbork, Dutch Red Cross Archive.

25 Anne Frank, diary entry, April 11, 1944, in *The Diary of a Young Girl: The Definitive Edition*, edited by Otto H. Frank and Mirjam Pressler (New York: Doubleday, 1995), 257.

26 Police report/charge sheet (proces verbaal) against P. Schaap, POD Groningen, no. 67, SI-M-33/45, August 14, 1945, NIOD Doc. 2. Translation: Joachim Bayens and Rory Dekker.

27 Hendrik van Hoeve, memoirs, AFS; CCT interview with Stef van Hoeve, February 27 and July 10, 2019.

28 Statement by Johannes Gerard Koning, July 6, 1948, CABR, NI-HaNa.

29 *The Diary of Anne Frank* (1959), directed by George Stephens.

30 Door Willem (By Willem), "De groenteman van de familie Frank leeft nog," [Anne Frank's Greengrocer Is Still Alive], translated by the Cold Case Team, *Het Parool*, February 26, 1972.

Chapter 34: The Jewish Council

1 Bob Moore, *Victims and Survivors: The Nazi Persecution of the Jews in the Netherlands, 1940–1945* (London: Arnold, 1997), 75.

2 Ibid., 95–96.

3 Ibid., 96. Moore cited the memoir of Gertrud van Tijn–Cohn, the head of the Department of Emigration and Displaced Persons of the Jewish Council.

4 Ibid., 132. Philip Mechanicus wrote about this in Mechanicus, *In dépôt: Dagboek uit Westerbork* (Laren, Netherlands: Uitgeverij Verbum, 2008), 213.

5 Willy Lindwer, *The Last Seven Months of Anne Frank: The Stories of Six Women Who Knew Anne Frank*, translated by Alison Meersschaert (New York: Pan Macmillan, 2004), 24.

6 Moore, *Victims and Survivors*, 131–32.

7 Ibid., 119–23.

8 Ido de Haan, "*Jurys d'honneur*: The Stakes and

Limits of Purges Among Jews in France After Liberation," in *Jewish Honor Courts: Revenge, Retribution, and Reconciliation in Europe and Israel after the Holocaust*, edited by Laura Jockusch and Gabriel N. Finder (Detroit: Wayne State University Press, 2015), 124.

Chapter 35: A Second Look

1 Translated by Joachim Bayens and Rory Dekker.

2 See Carol Ann Lee, *The Hidden Life of Otto Frank* (New York: Harper Perennial, 2003), 219; and David Barnouw and Gerrold van der Stroom, "Who Betrayed Anne Frank?," NIOD, https://www.niod.nl/sites/niod.nl/files/WhobetrayedAnneFrank.pdf. These authors mentioned the note but dismissed it.

3 Mirjam Bolle, *Ik zal je beschrijven hoe een dag er hier uitziet* [Let Me Tell You What a Day Here Is Like], translated by Jeannette K. Ringold (Amsterdam: Contact, 2003), 41.

Chapter 36: The Dutch Notary

1 Jewish Council meeting minutes, Joodsche Raad voor Amsterdam NIOD, file 182-1.3.

2 Raymund Schütz, letter to Vince Pankoke, October 1, 2020.

3 Hans Tietje, file no. 248-1699, NIOD Doc. I. The CCT located a document with the names of people Tietje claimed to have helped. The five Van den Berghs (spelled Berg) were on the list, along with his Jewish Council colleague A. Soep.

4 Hans Tietje, File no. 248-1699, NIOD Doc. 2.

5 Raymund Schütz, *Kille mist: Het nederlands notariaat en de erfenis van de oorlog* (Amsterdam: Boom, 2016), 163.

6 See "Nuremberg Race Law Teaching Chart for Explaining Blood Purity Laws," United States Holocaust Memorial Museum, https://collections.ushmm.org/search/catalog/irn11299.

7 A. van den Bergh, Calmeyer Archive, Centrum voor Familiegeschiedenis (Central Bureau for Genealogy) (hereafter CBG), NI-HaNa.

8 Ibid.

9 Ibid.

10 J.W.A. Schepers, letter to Lippmann, Rosenthal & Co. (hereafter LIRO), October 15, 1943, CBG file, NI-HaNa; LIRO, letter to Calmeyer Office, The Hague, November 29, 1943.

11 Inventory no. 22356, J.W.A. Schepers, CABR,

NI-HaNa. The attorneys were Jacob van Proosdij and A. N. Kotting.

12 Kadaster (land registry) Records, Noord-Hollands Archief, Haarlem.

13 CCT, interview with Regina Sophia Salle, October 14, 2019.

14 Amsterdam Stadsarchief, Personal Card (PC), Arnold van den Bergh.

15 Calmeyer, letter re: A. van den Bergh, January 22, 1944, CBG, NI-HaNa.

16 NI-HaNa, CABR 554, Eduard Moesbergen.

17 Ibid., PRA investigative file no. 60678.

18 Ibid.

Chapter 37: Experts at Work

1 W. Fagel, report on handwriting comparison for the CCT, August 2, 2019.

2 Anne Frank, *The Diary of Anne Frank: The Revised Critical Edition*, edited by David Barnouw and Gerrold van der Stroom, translated by Arnold J. Pomerans, B. M. Mooyaart-Doubleday, and Susan Massotty (New York: Doubleday, 2003).

3 B. Haas, report on typeface examination for the CCT, August 21, 2019.

Chapter 38: A Note Between Friends

1 *Algemeen Handelsblad,* September 20, 1940. (General Trade Magazine—lists sales transactions and notaries present.)

2 CCT, interview with Ron van Hasselt, nephew of Jakob van Hasselt, August 12, 2019.

3 Ibid.

4 "Jakob van Hasselt," Joods Monument, https://www.joodsmonument.nl/en/page/201758/karla-hinderika-van-hasselt; https://www.joodsmonument.nl/en/page/201760/els-van-hasselt.

5 Arend J. van Helden, State Department of Criminal Investigation, Amsterdam, summary report, November 3, 1964, 18–19; NIOD, Doc. 1 Van Maaren.

6 Johannes Kleiman, letter to Otto Frank, translated by the Cold Case Team, March 31, 1958, AFS.

7 The source of this confrontation between Otto and Gringhuis is Carol Ann Lee, *The Hidden Life of Otto Frank* (New York: Harper Perennial, 2003), 219. Lee mentioned the conversation, as did David Barnouw and Gerrold van der Stroom in their investigation, "Who Betrayed Anne Frank?" Though they were confident in the assertion and suggested that the conversation would be in the Silberbauer Doc. 1 file, a thorough search could not locate the source of the information.

However, all three attest to its authenticity. We assume that the file was lost, removed, or misfiled.

Chapter 39: The Typist

1 CCT, interview with Fleur van der Houwen, September 26, 2019.

2 See photo at Hanneloes Pen, "'Moffenmeid' tante Thea was niet alleen fout," *Het Parool*, July 8, 2016, https://www.parool.nl/nieuws/moffenmeid-tante-thea-was-niet-alleen-fout~baf4ccfc/.

3 Jos Smeets, Tommy van Es, and Guus Meershoek, eds., *In de frontlinie: Tien politiemannen en de duitse bezetting* [On the Front Line: Ten Police Officers and the German Occupation] (Amsterdam: Boom, 2014), 155.

4 See Jan Hopman, *Zwijgen over de Euterpestraat: Op het hoofdkwartier van de Sicherheitsdienst in Amsterdam gingen in 1944 verraad en verzet hand in hand* [In 1944, Betrayal and Resistance Went Hand in Hand at the Headquarters of the Security Service in Amsterdam] (Zoetermeer, Netherlands: Free Musketeers, 2012), 50.

5 Jan Hopman, *De wedergeboorte van een moffenmeid: Een verzwegen familiegeschiedenis* (Meppel, Netherlands: Just Publishers, 2016).

6 "Hoogensteijn, Cornelia Wilhelmina Theresia (1918–1956)," DVN, http://resources.huygens.knaw.nl/vrouwenlexicon/lemmata/data/Hoogensteijn.

Chapter 40: The Granddaughter

1 Thijs Bayens, interview with Esther Kizio, February 15, 2018; Vince Pankoke and Brendan Rook, interview with Esther Kizio, February 23, 2019.

2 Thijs Bayens, interview with Esther Kizio, Amsterdam, February 15, 2018.

3 Thijs Bayens, interview with Esther Kizio, February 15, 2018.

4 J.W.A. Schepers, nos. 86395 and 22356, CABR, NI-HaNa.

5 Interview with Arnold van den Bergh, POD, July 12, 1945, inventory no. 22356, J.W.A. Schepers, CABR, NI-HaNa.

6 Vince Pankoke and Brendan Rook, interview with Esther Kizio, February 23, 2019.

Chapter 41: The Goudstikker Affair

1 Kenneth D. Alford, *Hermann Goering and the Nazi Art Collection: The Looting of Europe's Art*

Treasures and Their Dispersal After World War II (Jefferson, NC: McFarland, 2012).

2 NARA, Office of Strategic Services, Art Looting Investigation, Consolidated Investigation Report no. 2, September 15, 1945, The Goering Collection, NARA microfilm publication M1782.

3 "Interrogations: Miedl Case (Alois Miedl), Page 35," Fold3, https://www.fold3.com/document/270014387/.

4 Alois Miedl, NIOD, Doc. 2, file no. 248-1699.

5 Anne Frank, October 29, 1943, diary entry in *The Diary of a Young Girl: The Definitive Edition*, edited by Otto H. Frank and Mirjam Pressler (New York: Doubleday, 1995), 139. Entry 29 October 1943. In 1952, after a seven-year battle, Goudstikker's wife, Désirée, recovered a part of the collection from the Dutch government. Over five decades later, a further two hundred paintings were returned to Goudstikker's heirs. Report of Restitutie Commissie (Restitutions Committee), 2005.

6 L2731, re August 30, 1946, interrogation of Hermann Göring, Gerard Aalders Archive. Gerard Aalders, author and former NIOD researcher, has his own private archive at his home in Amsterdam.

7 Edo von Saher, *N.V. Kunsthandel J. Goudstikker. 'Overzicht van de gebeurtenissen in de periode van*

31 December 1939 tot April 1952 [Art Dealer J. Goudstikker: Overview of the Events in the Period from December 31, 1939, to April 1952]. Report of Restitutie Commissie (Restitutions Committee), 2005, 5.

8 Vince Pankoke and Brendan Rook, interview with Esther Kizio, February 23, 2019; Provenance Wanted Project Report, 2000, 52.

9 Emilie Goudstikker, Jewish Council Card, Arolsen Archive, Bad Arolsen, Germany.

10 Amsterdam Stadsarchief PC, resident card, Oranje Nassaulaan 60.

11 J. C. Berlips, memo to Dutch resistance, April 4, 1945, Alois Miedl, NIOD, Doc. 2, file no. 20200610.

12 Henriette von Schirach, *Der Preis der Herrlichkeit,* translated by CCT Director of Research Pieter Van Twisk (Munich: Herbig, 2003).

Chapter 42: A Bombshell

1 See, e.g., *Algemeen Handelsblad*, September 20, 1940. There are many advertisements making it clear VD, Spier, and Van Hasselt worked together. https://www.delpher.nl/nl/kranten/results?coll=ddd&query=Bergh&cql%5B0%5D=%28date+_gte_+%2220

-09-1940%22%29&cql%5B1%5D=%28date +_lte_+%2221-09-1940%22%29&redirect=true.

2 "Work of the Contact-Afdeling (Contact Division) at Westerbork," deposition, Screen Writers Guild, no. 50943, 11. See also NIOD, Doc. 1, file no. 248-0294, no. 20, 56.

3 Officer J. Schoenmaker, Assen, the Netherlands, Process Verbal (police report), No. 414, 6–7, Bureau oorlogsmisdrijven 58 (Office of War Crimes 58), June 4, 1948. The report is 117 pages long.

4 Detective Marinus van Buren, police report, March 16, 1948, NIOD, Doc. 1, 248-0040.

5 Albert Konrad Gemmeker, testimony, folder 2 (31), September 15, 1947; Willy Lages, testimony, folders 2a and 2b, CABR, inventory no. 107491, t/m (to and including) VIII Box 1; both NI-HaNa.

6 Ernst Philip Henn, testimony, September 15, 1947, inventory no. 107491, t/m (to and including) VIII, CABR, NI-HaNa.

7 Sytze van der Zee, *Vogelvrij: De jacht op de joodse onderduiker* (Amsterdam: De Bezige Bij, 2010), 361; NIOD Doc. 1, R. Pollak, Signalcentenblad lists, 384–90.

8 POD interview with Arnold van den Bergh, July 12, 1945, NI-HaNa, CABR-Scheppers.

9 Vince Pankoke and Brendan Rook, interview with Esther Kizio, February 26, 2019.

10 Only David Cohen, one of the two chairmen of the Jewish Council, actually appeared for trial. See Ido de Haan, "*Jurys d'honneur*: The Stakes and Limits of Purges Among Jews in France After Liberation," in *Jewish Honor Courts: Revenge, Retribution, and Reconciliation in Europe and Israel After the Holocaust*, edited by Laura Jockusch and Gabriel N. Finder (Detroit: Wayne State University Press, 2015), 124.

11 Ibid., 122.

12 Philip Staal, *Settling the Account*, translated by Scott Rollins (Bloomington, IN: iUniverse, 2015), 213.

13 Otto Frank's conversation with Friso Endt, city desk editor of *Het Parool*, which occurred sometime between 1947 and 1949, as reported to the Cold Case Team by Sytze van der Zee, who spoke to Endt in the early 1960s.

14 Verdict published in *Nieuw Israëlietisch Weekblad* [New Israelite Weekly], May 21, 1948.

15 Vince Pankoke and Brendan Rook, interview with Esther Kizio, February 26, 2019.

16 *Nieuw Israëlietisch Weekblad* [New Israelite Weekly], November 3, 1950. Report regarding the funeral of Arnold van den Bergh.

Chapter 43: A Secret Well Kept

1 Koos Groen, *Een prooi wordt jager: De Zaak van de joodse verraadster Ans van Dijk* (Meppel, Netherlands: Just Publishers, 2016), 142. See also Ans van Dijk, CABR, NI-HaNa, and Sytze van der Zee, *Vogelvrij: De jacht op de joodse onderduiker* (Amsterdam: De Bezige Bij, 2010), 361.

2 Jeroen de Bruyn and Joop van Wijk, *Anne Frank: The Untold Story: The Hidden Truth About Eli Vossen, the Youngest Helper of the Secret Annex* (Laag-Soeren, Netherlands: Bep Voskuijl Productions, 2018), 241.

3 The Contact Committee, an arm of the Jewish Council in Westerbork, was in charge of processing exemptions from deportation and keeping lists. In the spring of 1944, the commander of Westerbork, Albert Gemmeker, ordered the members of the Contact Committee to contact Jews in hiding in Amsterdam and elsewhere and offer them the possibility of buying their freedom with money and valuable jewelry. See Officer J. Schoenmaker, Assen, the Netherlands, Process Verbal (police report), No. 414, 6–7, Bureau oorlogsmisdrijven 58 (Office of War Crimes 58), June 4, 1948. The report is 117 pages long.

4 On November 20, 1963, Otto spoke with the *Het Vrije Volk* newspaper and provided this statement. It appeared in *Het Vrije Volk* on November 22, 1963, under the title "De Oostenrijkse politieagent die Anne Frank arresteerde, bekent en legt uit: Ik heb zojuist orders uitgevoerd" [The Austrian Police Officer Who Arrested Anne Frank Confesses and Explains: I Just Executed Orders].

5 Otto Frank, letter to Miep Gies, December 1, 1963, AFS.

6 Eda Shapiro and Rick Kardonne, *Victor Kugler: The Man Who Hid Anne Frank* (Jerusalem: Gefen Publishing House, 2004), was eventually published through the efforts of Eda Shapiro's late husband, Irving Naftolin, and her coauthor, Rick Kardonne.

Epilogue: The Shadow City

1 Carol Ann Lee, *The Hidden Life of Otto Frank* (New York: Harper Perennial, 2003), 314.

2 Ibid., 294.

3 Ibid., 292.

4 This was Miep's response to a student's question. Scholastic published her replies to students' questions on its website. See "Interview Transcript: Miep

Gies," Scholastic, http://teacher.scholastic.com/frank/tscripts/miep.htm.

5 Jeroen de Bruyn and Joop van Wijk, *Anne Frank: The Untold Story: The Hidden Truth About Eli Vossen, the Youngest Helper of the Secret Annex* (Laag-Soeren, Netherlands: Bep Voskuijl Productions, 2018), 169. See also Wikipedia, s.v. "Bep Voskuijl," https://en.wikipedia.org/wiki/Bep_Voskuijl.

6 Melissa Müller, *Anne Frank: The Biography*, translated by Rita and Robert Kimber (New York: Picador USA, 2013), 395.

7 Eva Schloss with Karen Bartlett, *After Auschwitz: A Story of Heartbreak and Survival by the Stepsister of Anne Frank* (London: Hodder & Stoughton, 2013), 270.

8 Lee, *The Hidden Life of Otto Frank*, 227.

9 Ibid., 274.

10 Gerben Post, *Lotty's Bench: The Persecution of the Jews of Amsterdam Remembered*, translated by Tom Leighton (Volendam, Netherlands: LM Publishers, 2018), 150. See also Bob Moore, *Victims and Survivors: The Nazi Persecution of the Jews in the Netherlands 1940–1945* (London: Arnold, 1997), 185–86.

11 Post, *Lotty's Bench*, 113–14.

12 Ibid., 67.

13 Ibid., 202.

14 Ibid., 195.

15 David Nasaw, *The Last Million: Europe's Displaced Persons from World War to Cold War* (New York: Penguin, 2020).

16 Wikipedia, s.v. "Geertruida Wijsmuller-Meijer," https://en.wikipedia.org/wiki/Geertruida_Wijsmuller-Meijer.

Bibliography

Aalders, Gerard. *Nazi Looting: The Plunder of Dutch Jewry During the Second World War.* Translated by Arnold Pomerans with Erica Pomerans. Oxford: Berg, 2004.

Aalders, Gerard, and Coen Hilbrink. *De Affaire Sanders: Spionage en intriges in herrijzend Nederland.* The Hague: SDU Uitgivers, 1996.

Aerde, Rogier van. *Het grote gebod: Gedenkboek van het verzet in LO en LKP.* 2 vols. Kampen: Kok, 1989.

Alford, Kenneth D. *Hermann Goering and the Nazi Art Collection: The Looting of Europe's Art Treasures and Their Dispersal After World War II.* Jefferson, NC: McFarland, 2012.

Barnouw, David, and Gerrold van der Stroom. "Who Betrayed Anne Frank?" NIOD. https://www.niod.nl/sites/niod.nl/files/WhobetrayedAnneFrank.pdf.

Bauman, Zygmunt. *Modernity and the Holocaust.* Cambridge: Polity Press, 1991.

Becker, Tamara, An Huitzing, Annemie Wolff, and Rudi Boon. *Op de foto in oorlogstijd: Studio Wolff, 1943.* Eindhoven, Netherlands: Lecturis, 2017.

Boer, Joh Franc Maria den, S. Duparc, and Arthur de Bussy. *Kroniek van Amsterdam over de jaren 1940–1945.* Amsterdam: De Bussy, 1948.

Bolle, Mirjam. *Letters Never Sent: Amsterdam, Westerbork, Bergen-Belsen.* Translated by Laura Vroomen. Jerusalem: Yad Vashem Publications, 2014.

Boomgaard, Petra van den. *Voor de Nazi's geen Jood: Hoe ruim 2500 Joden door ontduiking van rassenvoorschriften aan de deportaties zijn ontkomen.* Hilversum, Netherlands: Uitgiverij Verbum, 2019.

Boterman, Frits. *Duitse daders: De jodenvervolging en nazificatie van Nederland (1940–1945).* Amsterdam: Uitgiverij de Arbeiderspers, 2015.

Brinks, Monique. *Het Scholtenhuis, 1940–1945.* Vol. 1: *Daden.* Bedum, Netherlands: Profiel, 2009.

Broek, Gertjan. "An Investigative Report on the Betrayal and Arrest of the Inhabitants of the Secret Annex." Anne Frank House, December 2016. https://www.annefrank.org/en/downloads/filer_public/4a

/c6/4ac6677d-f8ae-4c79-b024-91ffe694e216/an_investigative_report_on_the_betrayal_and_arrest.pdf.

Brongers, E. H. *De slag om de Residentie 1940.* Baam, Netherlands: Hollandia, 1968.

Browning, Christopher. *Ordinary Men: Reserve Police Battalion 101 and the Final Solution in Poland.* New York: HarperCollins, 2017.

Bruïne, Gabi de, et al. *Een rwandees kaartenhuis: Een wirwar van wankelende verklaringen.* Den Haag: Boom Criminologie, 2017.

Bruyn, Jeroen de, and Joop van Wijk. *Anne Frank: The Untold Story: The Hidden Truth About Eli Vossen, the Youngest Helper of the Secret Annex.* Translated by Tess Stoop. Laag-Soeren, Netherlands: Bep Voskuijl Productions, 2018.

Burrin, Philippe. *Het ontstaan van een volkerenmoord: Hitler en de Joden.* Amsterdam: Van Gennep, 1991.

Callahan, Debbie J. *Lest We Forget: Lessons from Survivors of the Holocaust.* Ocala, FL: Bruske Books, 2014.

Cohen, Jaap. *Anne Frank House* (museum catalogue). Amsterdam: Anne Frank Stichting, 2018.

Cohen, Mischa. *De Nazi-leerling: Se schuldige jeugd van Dick Woudenberg.* Amsterdam: Uitgiverij Atlas Contact, 2017.

Croes, Marnix, and Peter Tammes. *"Gif laten wij niet Voortbestaan": Een onderzoek naar de overlevingskansen van joden in de Nederlandse gemeenten, 1940–1945.* Amsterdam: Aksant, 2004.

Diederichs, Monika. *Wie geschoren wordt moet stil zitten: Nederlandse meisjes en vrouwen die in de periode 1940–1945 omgang hadden met duitse militairen.* Soesterberg, Netherlands: Uitgiverij Aspekt, 2015.

Engels, M. J. Adriani. *Nacht over Nederland: Journalistiek reportage van vijf bezettingsjaren: 1940–1945.* Utrecht: Ons Vrije Nederland, 1946.

Enzer, Hyman A., and Sandra Solotaroff-Enzer, eds. *Anne Frank: Reflections on Her Life and Legacy.* Champaign: University of Illinois Press, 2000.

Es, Bart van. *Cut Out Girl: A Story of War and Family, Lost and Found.* London: Fig Tree, 2019.

Faber, Sjoerd, and Gretha Donker. *Bijzonder gewoon: Het Centraal Archief Bijzondere Rechtspleging (1944–2010) en de "lichte gevallen."* Zwolle, Netherlands: Uitgeverij Waanders, 2010.

Föllmer, Moritz. *Culture in the Third Reich.* New York: Oxford University Press, 2020.

Frank, Anne. *The Diary of a Young Girl: The Definitive Edition.* Edited by Otto H. Frank and Mirjam Pressler. New York: Doubleday, 1995.

Gieling, Wilco. *Seyss-Inquart*. Soesterberg, Netherlands: Aspekt, 2011.

Gies, Miep, with Alison Leslie Gold. *Anne Frank Remembered: The Story of the Woman Who Helped to Hide the Frank Family*. New York: Simon & Schuster, 2009.

Goldhagen, Daniel Jonah. *Hitlers gewillige beulen*. Antwerp: Standaard Uitgeverij, 1996.

Griffioen, Pim, and Ron Zeller. *Jodenvervolging in Nederland, Frankrijk en België, 1940–1945*. Amsterdam: Boom, 2015.

Grobman, Alex, and Joel Fishman, eds. *Anne Frank in Historical Perspective: A Teaching Guide for Secondary Schools*. Los Angeles: Martyrs Memorial and Museum of the Holocaust, 1995. https://files.eric.ed.gov/fulltext/ED391710.pdf.

Groen, Koos. *Fout en niet goed: De vervolging van collaboratie en varraad na WO2*. Hilversum, Netherlands: Just Publishers, 2009.

———. *Landverraders, wat deden we met ze? Een dokumentaire over de bestraffing en berechting van NSBers en kollaborateurs en de zuivering van pers, radio, kunst, bedrijfsleven na de Tweede Wereldoorlog*. Baarn, Netherlands: In den Toren, 1974.

———. *Een Prooi wordt jager: De Zaak van de joodse*

verraadster Ans van Dijk. Meppel, Netherlands: Just Publishers, 2016.

Hagen, Louis E. *Ik vocht om Arnhem: Dagboek van een zweefvliegtuig-piloot.* Nijmegen, Netherlands: De Koepel, 1947.

Happe, Katja. *Veel valse hoop: De jodenvervolging in 1940–1945 Nederland.* Amsterdam: Uitgiverij Atlas Contact, 2018.

Hasselt, Ron van. *De oorlog van mijn vader: Een halve familiegeschiedenis.* Bedum, Netherlands: Profiel, 2012.

Hausner, Gideon. *Justice in Jerusalem.* New York: Harper & Row, 1966.

Heijden, Chris van der. *Grijs verleden: Nederland en de Tweede Wereldoorlog.* Amsterdam: Uitgiverij Contact, 2008.

———. *Joodse NSB'ers: De vergeten geschiedenis van Villa Bouchima in Doetichem.* Utrecht: Begijnekade 18 Uitgivers, 2006.

Herzberg, Abel J. *Amor fati: Zeven opstellen over Bergen-Belsen.* Amsterdam: E. Querido Uitgiverij, 1987.

———. *Kroniek der jodenvervolging, 1940–1945.* Amsterdam: E. Querido Uitgiverij, 1985.

Hillesum, Etty. *An Interrupted Life: The Diaries, 1941–1943, and Letters from Westerbork.* New York: Picador USA, 1996.

Hoffer, Eric. *The True Believer: Thoughts on the Nature of Mass Movements.* New York: Harper Perennial Modern Classics, 2002.

Hofman, Jaap. *De collaborateur.* Soesterberg, Netherlands: Aspekt, 2011.

Hollander, Pieter den. *Roofkunst: De zaak Goudstikker.* Amsterdam: Meulenhoff, 2007.

Hopman, Jan. *Zwijgen over de Euterpestraat: Op het hoofdkwartier van de Sicherheitsdienst in Amsterdam gingen in 1944 verraad en verzet hand in hand.* Zoetermeer, Netherlands: Free Musketeers, 2012.

———. *De wedergeboorte van een moffenmeid: Een verzwegen familiegeschiedenis.* Meppel, Netherlands: Just Publishers, 2016.

Huizing, Bert, and Koen Aartsma. *De Zwarte Politie, 1940/1945.* Weesp, Netherlands: De Haan, 1986.

Iperen, Roxane van. *'t Hooge Nest.* Amsterdam: Lebowski Publishers, 2018.

Jansen, Ronald Wilfred. *Anne Frank: Silent Witnesses: Reminders of a Jewish Girl's Life.* Zwaag, Netherlands: Pumbo, 2014.

Jong, Loe de. *Het Koninkrijk der Nederlanden in de Tweede Wereldoorlog.* 26 vols. The Hague: SDU Uitgevers, 1969–91.

Jong, Louis de. *The Netherlands and Nazi Germany.* Cambridge, MA: Harvard University Press, 1990.

———. *Tussentijds: Historische studies.* Amsterdam: E. Querido Uitgiverij, 1977.

Kempner, Robert M. W. *Twee uit Honderdduizend: Anne Frank en Edith Stein: Onthullingen over de nazimisdaden in Nederland voor heet gerechthof te München.* Bilthoven: Uitgeverij H. Nelissen, 1969.

Knoop, Hans. *De Joodsche Rood: Het drama van Abraham Asscher en David Cohen.* Amsterdam: Elsevier, 1983.

Koetsier, Teun, and Elbert Roest. *Schieten op de maan: Gezag en verzet in Laren NH in WO II.* Laren, Netherlands: Uitgeverij van Wijland, 2016.

Kremer, Gerard. *De achtertuin van het achterhuis.* Ede, Netherlands: De Lantaarn, 2018.

———. *Anne Frank Betrayed: The Mystery Unraveled After 75 Years.* Ede, Netherlands: De Lantaarn, 2020.

Künzel, Geraldien von Frijtag Drabbe. *Het geval Calmeyer.* Amsterdam: Mets & Schilt, 2008.

Lans, Jos van der, and Herman Vuijsje. *Het Anne Frank Huis: Een biografie.* Amsterdam: Boom, 2010.

Lee, Carol Ann. *The Hidden Life of Otto Frank.* New York: Harper Perennial, 2003.

Lester, Richard. *Flight of the Blue Heron.* Morgan Hill, CA: Bookstand, 2009.

Levi, Primo. *Surviving Auschwitz.* Translated by Stuart Woolf. New York: Simon & Schuster, 1996.

Liempt, Ad van. *Gemmeker: Commandant van kamp Westerbork.* Amsterdam: Uitgiverij Balans, 2019.

———. *Hitler's Bounty Hunters: The Betrayal of the Jews.* Translated by S. J. Leinbach. New York: Berg, 2005.

———. *De jacht op het verzet: Het meedogenloze optreden van Sicherheitsdienst en nederlandse politie tijdens de Tweede Wereldoorlog.* Amsterdam: Uitgiverij Balans, 2013.

———. *Jodenjacht: De onthutsende rol van de nederlandse politie in de Tweede Wereldoorlog.* Amsterdam: Uitgiverij Balans, 2013.

Lifton, Robert J. *Nazi-dokters: De psychologie van de rassenmoord in het Derde Rijk.* Utrecht: Bruna, 1987.

Lindwer, Willy. *The Last Seven Months of Anne Frank: The Stories of Six Women Who Knew Anne Frank.* Translated by Alison Meersschaert. New York: Pan Macmillan, 2004.

———. *Wolf en Ryfka: Kroniek van een joodse familie.* Amsterdam: Prometheus, 2019.

Lipstadt, Deborah E. *Denying the Holocaust: The Growing Assault on Truth and Memory.* New York: Penguin, 1994.

Luijters, Guus, Raymond Schütz, and Marten Jongman. *De deportaties uit Nederland, 1940–1945: Portretten uit de archieven.* Amsterdam: Nieuw Amsterdam, 2017.

Maarsen, Jacqueline van. *Inheriting Anne Frank.* Translated by Brian Doyle. London: Arcadia Books, 2009.

———. *My Friend Anne Frank.* Translated by Debra F. Onkenhout. New York: Vantage, 1996.

Mardo, Esther (pseudonym of Herman Nicolaas van der Voort). *Vrouwenkamp.* Rotterdam: De Vrije Pers, 1962.

Mechanicus, Philip. *In dépôt: Dagboek uit Westerbork.* Laren, Netherlands: Uitgeverij Verbum, 2008.

Meershoek, Guus. *Dienaren van het gezag: De amsterdamse politie tijdens de bezetting.* Amsterdam: Van Gennep, 1999.

Meeuwenoord, Marieke. *Het hele is hier een wereld op zichzelf: De geschiedenis van kamp Vught.* Amsterdam: De Bezige Bij, 2014.

Meihuizen, Joggli. *Richard Fiebig en de uitbuiting van de nederlandse industrie.* Amsterdam: Boom, 2018.

Metselaar, Menno. *Anne Frank: Dreaming, Thinking, Writing.* Amsterdam: Anne Frank House, 2016.

Metselaar, Menno, Ruud van der Rol, Dineke Stam, and Ronald Leopold, eds. *Anne Frank House: A Museum with a Story.* Amsterdam: Anne Frank Stichting, 2001.

Meulenbroek, Lex, and Paul Poley. *Kroongetuige DNA: Onzichtbaar spoor in spraakmakende zaken.* Amsterdam: De Bezige Bij, 2014.

Middelburg, Bart. *Jeanne de Leugenaarster: Adriana Valkenburg: Hoerenmadam, verraadster, femme fatale.* Amsterdam: Nieuw Amsterdam, 2009.

Moore, Bob. *Victims and Survivors: The Nazi Persecution of the Jews in the Netherlands, 1940–1945.* New York: St. Martin's Press, 1997.

Müller, Melissa. *Anne Frank: The Biography, Updated and Expanded.* Translated by Rita and Robert Kimber. New York: Picador, 2013.

Oudheusden, Jan van, and Erik Schumacher. *1944: Verstoorde verwachtingen.* Amsterdam: Spectrum /NIOD, 2019.

Piersma, Hinke. *Op eigen gezag: Politieverzet in oorlogstijd.* Amsterdam: E. Querido Uitgiverij, 2019.

Post, Gerben. *Lotty's Bench: The Persecution of the Jews of Amsterdam Remembered.* Translated by Tom Leighton. Volendam, Netherlands: LM Publishers, 2018.

Presser, J. *De Nacht der Girondijnen: Novelle.* Amsterdam: Meulenhoff, 2007.

———. *Ondergang: De vervolging en verdelging van het nederlandse jodendom, 1940–1945.* Soesterberg, Netherlands: Aspekt, 2013.

Riet, Frank van. *De bewakers van Westerbork.* Amsterdam: Boom Uitgevers, 2016.

Romijn, Peter, et al. *The Persecution of the Jews in the Netherlands, 1940–1945: New Perspectives.* Amsterdam: Vossiuspers UvA, 2010.

Rubin, Susan Goldman. *The Anne Frank Case: Simon Wiesenthal's Search for the Truth.* New York: Holiday House, 2009.

Schaap, Inger. *Sluipmoordenaars: De Silbertanne -moorden in Nederland, 1943–1944.* Hilversum, Netherlands: Just Publishers, 2010.

Scherrenburg, Olga, et al. *De moddermoord: Over hoe een ongeval een moord werd.* 's-Gravenhage, Netherlands: Boom Lemma, 2013.

Schirach, Henriette von. *Der Preis der Herrlichkeit.* Munich: Herbig, 2003.

Schloss, Eva, with Karen Bartlett. *After Auschwitz: A Story of Heartbreak and Survival by the Stepsister of Anne Frank.* London: Hodder & Stoughton, 2013.

———. *Eva's Story.* Grand Rapids, MI: Eerdmans, 1988.

Schnabel, Ernst. *The Footsteps of Anne Frank.* Translated by Richard and Clara Winston. Harpenden, UK: Southbank Publishing, 2014.

Schütz, Raymund. *Kille mist: Het nederlands notariaat en de erfenis van de oorlog.* Amsterdam: Boom, 2016.

Schwarzschild, Ellen. *Niet lezen als 't U blieft, nicht*

lesen bitte: Onuitwisbare herinneringen (1933–1943). Amsterdam: Privately published, 1999.

Shapiro, Eda, and Rick Kardonne. *Victor Kugler: The Man Who Hid Anne Frank.* Jerusalem: Gefen Publishing House, 2008.

Shermer, Michael, and Alex Grobman. *Denying History: Who Says the Holocaust Never Happened and Why Do They Say It?* Berkeley: University of California Press, 2009.

Sijes, B. A. *Studies over jodenvervolging.* Assen, Netherlands: Van Gorcum, 1974.

Somers, Erik. *Voorzitter van de Joodse Raad: De herinneringen van David Cohen (1941–1943).* Zutphen, Netherlands: Walburg Pers, 2010.

Somers, Erik, and René Kok. *Jewish Displaced Persons in Camp Bergen-Belsen, 1945–1950.* Zwolle, Netherlands: Waanders, 2003.

Staal, Philip. *Settling the Account.* Translated by Scott Rollins. Bloomington, IN: iUniverse, 2015.

Stigter, Bianca. *De bezette stad: Plattegrond van Amsterdam, 1940–1945.* Amsterdam: Athenaeum -Polak & Van Gennep, 2005.

Strasberg, Susan. *Bittersweet.* New York: Signet, 1980.

Tongeren, Paul van. *Jacoba van Tongeren en de onbekende verzetshelden van Groep 2000*

(1940–1945). Soesterberg, Netherlands: Uitgeverij Aspekt, 2015.

Trenker, Luis. *Het intieme dagboek van Eva Braun.* Den Haag: Confidentia, 1949.

Ullman, Leo S. *796 Days: Hiding as a Child in Occupied Amsterdam During WWII and Then Coming to America.* Margate, NJ: ComteQ Publishing, 2015.

Veen, Harm van der. *Westerbork, 1939–1945: Het verhaal van vluchtelingenkamp en durchgangslager Westerbork.* Hooghalen, Netherlands: Herinneringscentrum Kamp Westerbork, 2003.

Veld, N.K.C.A. in 't. *De joodse ereraad.* 's-Gravenhage, Netherlands: SDU Uitgeverij, 1989.

Venema, Adriaan. *Kunsthandel in Nederland, 1940–1945.* Amsterdam: De Arbeiderspers, 1986.

Verhoeven, Rian. *Anne Frank was niet alleen: Het Merwedeplein, 1933–1945.* Amsterdam: Prometheus, 2019.

Verkijk, Dick. *Radio Hilversum, 1940–1945: De omroep in oorlog.* Amsterdam: De Arbeiderspers, 1974.

Veth, D. Giltay, and A. J. van der Leeuw. *Rapport door het Rijksinstituut voor Oorlogsdocumentatie uitgebracht aan de minister van justitie inzake de activiteiten van drs. F. Weinreb, gedurende de jaren 1940–1945, in het licht van nadere gegevens bezien.*

2 vols. ‘s-Gravenhage, Netherlands: Staatsuitgeverij, 1976.

Visser, Frank. *De zaak Antonius van der Waals.* Den Haag: Forum Boekerij, 1974.

Wasserstein, Bernard. *The Ambiguity of Virtue: Gertrude van Tijn and the Fate of the Dutch Jews.* Cambridge, MA: Harvard University Press, 2014.

———. *Gertrude van Tijn en het lot van de nederlandse Joden.* Amsterdam: Nieuw Amsterdam, 2013.

Wiesel, Elie. *Night.* Translated by Marion Wiesel. New York: Farrar, Straus and Giroux, 2006.

Wiesenthal, Simon. *The Murderers Among Us: The Simon Wiesenthal Memoirs.* Edited by Joseph Wechsberg. New York: Bantam Books, 1968.

Wilson, Cara Weiss (now Cara Wilson-Granat). *Dear Cara: Letters from Otto Frank: Anne Frank's Father Shares His Wisdom.* Sandwich, MA: North Star Publications, 2001.

Wolfe, Robert. *Captured German and Related Records: A National Archives Conference.* Athens: Ohio University Press, 1968.

Zee, Nanda van der. *Om erger te voorkomen.* Soesterberg, Netherlands: Uitgeverij Aspekt, 2011.

———. *The Roommate of Anne Frank.* Translated by Cees Endlich. Soesterberg, Netherlands: Uitgeverij Aspekt, 2003.

Zee, Sytze van der. *Vogelvrij: De jacht op de joodse onderduiker.* Amsterdam: De Bezige Bij, 2010.

Ziller, Robert (pseudonym of Richard Ziegler). *Wij maken geschiedenis.* Amsterdam: Het Hollandsche Uitgevershuis, 1946.

Zwaan, J. *De zwarte kameraden: Een geïllustreerde geschiedenis van de NSB.* Weesp, Netherlands: Van Holkema en Warendorf, 1984.

About the Author

ROSEMARY SULLIVAN, the author of fifteen books, is best known for her recent biography *Stalin's Daughter.* Published in twenty-three countries, it won the Biographers International Organization Plutarch Award and was a finalist for the PEN/Jacqueline Bograd Weld Award for Biography and the National Book Critics Circle Award. Her book *Villa Air-Bel* was awarded the Canadian Society for Yad Vashem Award in Holocaust History. She is a professor emeritus at the University of Toronto and has lectured in Canada, the United States, Europe, India, and Latin America.

About the Author

ROSEMARY SULLIVAN is the author of fourteen books, including the acclaimed biography Stalin's Daughter. Published in twenty-two countries, it won the Biographers International Organization Plutarch Award and was a finalist for the PEN/Jacqueline Bograd Weld Award for Biography and the National Book Critics Circle Award. Her book Villa Air-Bel was awarded the Canadian Society for Yad Vashem Award in Holocaust History. She is a professor emerita at the University of Toronto and has lectured in Canada, the United States, Europe, India, and Latin America.